Focused Energy

Executive Development from IMD

Marchand, D.A.   Competing with Information – A Manager's Guide to Creating
                   Business Value with Information Content
                   ISBN 0-471-89969-0

Strebel, P.   Focused Energy – Mastering Bottom-Up Organization

Focused Energy

Mastering Bottom-Up Organization

Edited by

Paul Strebel

IMD, Lausanne

JOHN WILEY & SONS, LTD
Chichester • New York • Weinheim • Brisbane • Singapore • Toronto

Copyright © 2000 by John Wiley & Sons Ltd,
Baffins Lane, Chichester,
West Sussex PO19 IUD, England

National   01243 779777
International   (+44) 1243 779777
e-mail (for orders and customer service enquiries): cs-books@wiley.co.uk
Visit our Home Page on http://www.wiley.co.uk
or http://www.wiley.com

Other Wiley Editorial Offices

John Wiley & Sons, Inc., 605 Third Avenus,
New York, NY 10158-0012, USA

WILEY-VCH Verlag GmbH, Pappelallee 3,
D-69469 Weinheim, Germany

Jacaranda Wiley Ltd, 33 Park Road, Milton,
Queensland 4064, Australia

John Wiley & Sons (Asia) Pte Ltd, 2 Clementi Loop #02-01,
Jin Xing Distripark, Singapore 129809

John Wiley & Sons (Canada) Ltd, 22 Worcester Road,
Rexdale, Ontario M9W 1L1, Canada

British Library Cataloguing in Publication Data

A catalogue record for this book is available from the British Library

ISBN 0-471-89971-2

Typeset in 10/12 pt Garamond by Best-set Typesetter Ltd., Hong Kong
Printed and bound in Great Britain by Biddles Ltd, Guildford and King's Lynn
This book is printed on acid-free paper responsibly manufactured from sustainable forestry, in which at least two trees are planted for each one used for paper production.

Contents

Foreword

We live in a time that is characterized by change, a time where the only constants are confusion and uncertainty. But this is also our shared opportunity to embrace change and break through to new levels of value creation.

For an organization to reach new levels of value creation, its energy in the form of creativity, innovation, ambition and achievement needs to be nurtured and allowed to flourish. It is the inseparable link and ever increasing dependency between an organization's culture, values, attitudes and management behaviour that facilitates and develops this process.

Only in an environment that encourages and focuses personal development through setting clear targets and rewarding success can both the individual and the organization develop hand in hand.

Whether a company's success is distinguished through organizational excellence or visionary leadership, it is always worth remembering the words of Lao-tzu, "A leader is best when people barely know he exists. When his work is done, his aim fulfilled, they will all say, 'We did this ourselves.'"

In today's ever-changing business landscape, we see the need more than ever before for focused energy, for organizations that stimulate energy on the frontline, show great flexibility, and focus quickly on new breakthrough opportunities. This book addresses the issues of what a bottom-up organization is and how high economic value can be created through focusing and harnessing frontline energy.

To endeavour to be the master of change, to control change rather than being controlled by change, is a characteristic of any successful organization. By energizing its organization and focusing that energy, a company becomes an orchestrator of change and master of its future.

Jorma Ollila
Chairman and CEO
Nokia

Preface

For more than fifty years, IMD has focused on one thing – state-of-the-art executive development.

Each year, more than 7000 managers, from all continents and in all industries, visit our Lausanne campus to be educated, challenged, and inspired. They receive practical guidance on current issues, not abstract theories. They work with a team of outstanding faculty, who bring conceptual rigor and real-world experience into the classroom.

The approach we take in the classroom also characterizes the books in *Executive Development from IMD*. Each book brings together in a coherent whole the latest thinking from IMD's world class faculty. The books are clearly written, efficiently presented, and focus on the most important issues for managers.

We are delighted to be working in partnership with John Wiley & Sons to create *Executive Development from IMD*. We are confident you will find the books in this series to be informative, relevant, challenging and, as importantly, enjoyable.

Peter Lorange
IMD President and Nestlé Professor

Acknowledgements

The genesis of this book occurred during sessions on managing accelerated change in IMD's program on Orchestrating Winning Performance. The managers in those sessions argued that the biggest obstacles to faster change are a lack of energy on the frontline and/or a lack of focus at the top among proliferating change projects. When not managed, energy and focus are parts of an apparent trade-off: more frontline energy implies less focus, while more focus implies less energy.

High-energy bottom-up organizations are indeed difficult to master. Driven by globalization and the emerging e-economy, structure and design are flexible and constantly changing. There is a strong bottom-up drive with dynamic teams working in a delayered structure. People are committed and ambitious, with shared values and a commitment to personal and organizational learning. In return they are well and transparently rewarded. There is an ability to learn and to pass knowledge through the corporation.

This energy produces huge centrifugal forces, whose tendency is to pull the organization apart. There are multiple bottom-up initiatives with numerous objectives and change programmes at any one time. It is often chaotic. This can cause confusion among middle managers and on the frontline, undermining the organization and possibly resulting in gradual distintegration.

To harness the energy for value creation and counter the centrifugal forces, focusing principles are essential. The effective bottom-up organization has subtle elements of leadership in place to find direction and exploit business shifts, to orchestrate activity by managing horizontally and turning information into knowledge, and to integrate commitment into a larger whole while getting the necessary frontline initiative. In addition, although concentrated on today's value creation, the organization can also refocus around new business opportunities. What makes the bottom-up organization either a resounding success or a spectacular failure is harnessing the organizational energy with flexible focusing principles.

The practice in successful fast moving companies suggests that energy and focus are not poles in an organizational trade-off. With the right management, they are complementary: effective focus generates more frontline energy and vice versa. Hence, the concept of focused energy as the key to mastering bottom-up organization.

Until now, there has been little theory identifying the factors that are essential and sufficient for mastering bottom-up organization. Truly bottom-up organizations in larger companies are a relatively new phenomenon, so it is difficult to use case studies to generalize the exact requirements. What we do know from the examples that exist and from the experience of smaller entrepreneurial companies is that multiple factors are needed for effective bottom-up organization. This means that multiple, sometimes conflicting perspectives from different management disciplines provide a practical way of determining some of the critical ingredients. Hence this book of contributions from a range of experts on the IMD faculty. In the book, we put together a whole view on mastering bottom-up organization, a view captured by the new concept of focused energy.

Part One describes what we mean by an effective bottom-up organization, why such organization is so critical, and some of the change paths for getting there. Part Two looks at the different dimensions of a highly energized organization, in terms of the nurturing of initiative, creating networks of talent, and developing flexible resources. Assuming the energy is there, Part Three shows how to focus it subtly through the finding of direction, orchestration of activity, and integration of commitment.

It is a pleasure for me to thank my co-authors, Andy Boynton, Jean-Philippe Deschamps, Jay Galbraith, Xavier Gilbert, Jacques Horovitz, J.B. Kassarjian, Peter Killing, Peter Lorange, Donald Marchand, Piero Morosini, and Thomas Vollmann, for their unstinting co-operation in putting this book together, especially, when meeting our tight publishing deadlines. Special thanks is due to Philip Rosenzweig, formerly IMD's Co-ordinator of Research, and Claire Plimmer, Publishing Editor at Wiley, for initiating this series of books on Executive Development at IMD. Their support in critical moments was key, as was the enthusiasm of IMD's President and our co-author, Peter Lorange. We are indebted also to our text editors, Jeremy Kourdi and Des Dearlove, who helped bring these chapters to life under sometimes difficult pressure. A personal word of thanks, finally, to my wife, Elizabeth, who cheerfully accepted yet another truncated holiday in the final phases of the project.

Paul Strebel
Lausanne, Switzerland

Part One

Bottom-up Organization

These introductory chapters set the stage for the discussion of focused energy. They describe what a bottom-up organization is, why it is important, and how to get there.

1

Introducing Bottom-up Organization

This chapter describes what the authors mean by "mastering bottom-up organization": nurturing a business organization that creates high economic value starting with energetic initiatives on the frontline. Top management has to focus the centrifugal forces that bottom-up initiatives produce to get significant value creation. **Paul Strebel** outlines the organizational ingredients that generate frontline energy, and what must be done to focus the energy to create value.

CASE STUDY: ENRON

In the late 1980s, Enron Corp. was a well run, regulated natural gas pipeline company in Texas, highly structured and focused on operations. By 1998, Enron was an innovative, leading energy trader and builder of power plants around the world. Its profit rose from $94 million to $783 million and the total return on its shares over the decade was 972%. Behind the scenes Enron was transformed from a traditional, functional hierarchy into a highly energized, bottom-up organization. Enron's performance provides a vivid example of the value-creating power of effective bottom-up organization.

Enron's president, Jeffrey Skilling, uses two words to sum up the company's management philosophy: "loose" and "tight" (Salpukas, 1999). "Loose" refers to the way Enron gets energy on the frontline. "We are loose on everything related to creativity," says Skilling. Creativity comes from bright people. "We like to have smart people try new things." Enron hires a lot of bright young people from all backgrounds – not only engineers, but also hundreds of MBAs and a sprinkling of new graduates in the liberal arts. "We stick them in the organization and tell them to figure something out." It doesn't matter how people dress, or whether expense reports are filled out on time. What matters is that people take initiative. To help them network and exchange ideas, offices are open without walls. More experienced executives provide internships and mentor the newer recruits to encourage them to focus their interest and possibly start a new business initiative. And after a genuine effort, if the initiative goes belly-up, failure is acceptable: "If you try new things, some will work, some won't."

Lynda Clemmons, for example, joined the company to work as an analyst in acquisitions and mergers. She transferred to work with the natural gas and electricity traders, came into contact with managers of coal-fired electricity companies, and heard they would love some protection against weather fluctuations that create huge spikes in their costs. She set up a one-person unit within Enron Capital & Trade to develop and market a hedge for utilities against the weather. Within two years, she had sold $1 billion in weather hedges and attracted 13 people from other parts of the company to work with her. As one of her entrepreneurial colleagues put it: "When people here see an opportunity, they want to participate. We do not ask permission to spread the word. We just do it."

"Tight" refers to the way Enron manages the risks and focuses the frontline energy on real value creation. "Risk taking, anytime, is managed centrally," according to Skilling. A centralized information system monitors all the company's exposures. This results in tight control at the level of business units and individual contracts. For example, once Lynda Clemmons had her first contract, she had to fill out a daily profit-and-loss statement. "It becomes very clear very quickly if you are losing a lot of money," she observed. In addition, the performance of everyone with profit and loss responsibility is evaluated in terms of his or her contribution to value creation and rewarded accordingly. One of the company values is to strive for continually better individual performance. "We will continue to raise the bar for everyone. The great fun here will be for all of us to discover just how good we really can be," (Enron Values Statement, see References).

Overview: what is bottom-up organization?

An effective bottom-up organization is one in which the initiative for value creation comes largely from people on the frontline, that is, those running the business units, processes, projects, teams, or networks, those out in the field and on the shop floor, people like Lynda Clemmons at Enron.

- They run the processes that produce a continuing flow of efficiency improvements.
- They come up with the ideas and organize the teams that drive internal entrepreneurship.

Top management provides the overall vision and the guidelines, makes sure that the organizational infrastructure, processes and enabling systems are appropriate, and from time to time selects out particular frontline initiatives as the basis for major investment in future growth.

In a turbulent, rapidly changing environment, a bottom-up organization has several advantages over a traditional top-down organization. It adapts more quickly because decisions are taken on the frontline close to the sources of information on external change. When the choice of direction is not clear, it can use frontline initiatives to experiment. Above all, the high degree of involvement engenders high levels of energy and commitment. In Part Two of this book, we will look at the enabling conditions that produce high levels of frontline energy, thereby *energizing the organization*. At Enron, for example, these enabling conditions are the loose side of Skilling's management philosophy.

The disadvantages of a bottom-up organization are that it complicates decision-making over which direction to take and how to allocate the available resources to get there. Conflicts over leadership, which of the frontline voices should be heard, and which interests should dominate, often bedevil decision-making. Without a clear overall direction, it is difficult to allocate scarce resources. As a result of these centrifugal forces, organizational gridlock is an ever-present danger. In Part Three, we will look at how top management can avoid this, with an approach that orients and orchestrates value creation in bottom-up organizations, thereby *focusing the energy*. In the Enron example, this is the tight side of the management philosophy.

The characteristics of an effective bottom-up organization are depicted in Figure 1.1 and outlined in the sections that follow. An energized organization is built on flexible financial and technological resources that support a network of human talent. This network of people, spanning the boundaries of the organization, generates and implements bottom-up initiatives. To give these multiple initiatives focus and ensure significant value creation, top management has to provide perspective to help the organization find direction, then orchestrate the activities and integrate the commitment of everybody in support of that direction.

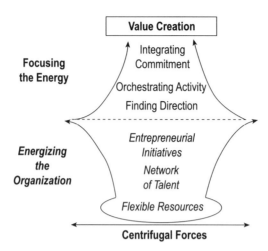

Figure 1.1: *Mastering Bottom-up Organization*

The demand for bottom-up organization

At the beginning of this new century, many industries are facing a major transition imposed by the information revolution and the related emergence of the e-economy. In addition to the increasingly apparent revolutionary impact of the Internet on distribution channels, intranets are changing the way in which people inside organizations can share information and best practice and, hence, work together. Extranets are facilitating increasing information ties between companies and their value chain partners, while new Internet start-ups are creating virtual marketplaces for business-to-business commerce.

When the forces of globalization, deregulation and privatization are added to those of the information revolution, it is no exaggeration to say that companies have to reinvent their organizations to cope with this new world. We can summarize the necessary organizational changes in three categories:

- *Need for more experimentation and innovation* – since nobody knows how these forces of change are going to play out, traditional planning and strategic analyses lose much of their value. Instead, companies have to encourage entrepreneurial initiatives on the frontline to create opportunities, test them out in the market, explore what might happen, and develop a range of options corresponding to a variety of possible futures.
- *Need for more efficiency and speed* – the low-cost infrastructure and incredible rate of change on the part of small agile start-ups in the e-economy is forcing established companies to move and change equally rapidly. The only way they can do this is by nurturing a stream of improvement initiatives on the frontline, to simplify the organization and cut out all waste of resources and time.

- *Need for more changes of focus in overall direction* – the accelerating change and pressure for a bottom-up response can easily lead to confusion, if not chaos, unless it is focused. But focus cannot come at the expense of adaptability and/or the opportunity to outpace the competition. Thus, the overall direction of the value-creating effort in the company has to change more frequently to keep up with the changing business environment. This requires a flexible organization that can reorient quickly to support a new directional focus.

Taken together these organizational needs imply an increasing demand for bottom-up organization to provide innovation, efficiency, speed and flexibility, but with a focus to deliver major value creation. In rapidly shifting industry environments, bottom-up organization is becoming a survival imperative.

It is important to note, however, that bottom-up organization is not the solution to all organizational problems. In certain environments, for cultural reasons, or due to lack of experience and training, people on the frontline may not be capable of handling a bottom-up organization. Moreover, in highly capital, or resource-intensive industries, in particular, bottom-up organization may not be technologically feasible, or may be too risky. The trend among leading companies in these industries is to centralize the upstream, capital, or resource-intensive part of the value chain, while installing a bottom-up organization downstream at the local level to exploit shifting market and customer demand.

What's in this book

In Chapter 2, Paul Strebel describes two of the more common pathways that existing large companies are taking to get to a bottom-up organization: a discontinuous one, starting with task forces followed by radical decentralization; and a continuous one, moving from task forces through broad participation to bottom-up initiatives.

Part Two of this book is about energizing the organization. It is divided into three subsections that echo what we know from the literature about encouraging innovation, the difference with this literature being that we are concerned with widespread initiative on the frontline. The first of these subsections looks at nurturing entrepreneurial initiatives. Motivating people to take entrepreneurial initiative is one of the main purposes of a bottom-up organization. In Chapter 3, Peter Lorange describes how to create a pioneering spirit, starting with the challenge this presents to top management. He then zeroes in on what it takes to nurture internal entrepreneurs and create a climate to support them. In Chapter 4, Jacques Horovitz describes five growth catalysts, organizational arrangements that provide a framework for stimulating growth initiatives. These are in contrast to numerous dysfunctional approaches to growth that destroy value.

The second subsection focuses on creating networks of talent. These networks are the source of the teams that coalesce around entrepreneurial and improvement initiatives. In Chapter 5, Andy Boynton describes how craftwork done by knowledgeable workers is at the heart of creativity on the frontline. He then outlines how to stimulate communities of practice, comprising networks of craftworkers. In Chapter 6, Tom Vollmann describes networks that cut across organizational boundaries to manage the demand/supply chain incorporating up- and downstream partners. He describes the new ways of working required to support cross-boundary networks. When they work well, these networks produce a continuing stream of improvements in the form of lower inventories and costs, and greater speed and efficiency.

The third ingredient required to energize an organization is flexible resources, so that the teams can get what they need for their initiatives. In Chapter 7, Jay Galbraith shows how to design a reconfigurable organization, in terms of structure, processes, rewards, and people management, that can rapidly reorganize around the directions in which major initiatives are being taken. In Chapter 8, Piero Morosini highlights the importance of execution and explains how to build an overall execution capability, based on the rapid sharing of competencies across internal and external boundaries.

Part Three looks at focusing the energy in a bottom-up organization. To focus the energy without destroying it, management has to adopt a more subtle approach than traditional control, or top-down alignment. Thus, the first section in Part Three is on finding direction, rather than setting it top-down. In Chapter 9, Peter Lorange explores the role of top-down vision and leadership in focusing bottom-up entrepreneurship, the balance needed between adaptation to the market and proactive strategic leaps, and how to create a climate for performance. In Chapter 10, Paul Strebel argues that to get the strategic leaps, management should treat the bottom-up initiatives as strategic options on future value creation and, based on the evolutionary and revolutionary patterns that shape an industry's life cycle, focus on those with breakthrough potential. In Chapter 11, Peter Killing describes how managers can guide the development of strategy from within, without relying on external consultants, by concentrating on people and processes, actively leading the strategy formation process, and by following a strategy formation road map. In Chapter 12, Xavier Gilbert explains how to continually adapt direction by exploiting the creative tension between divergent frontline activity and the need for convergent corporate integration. This is done through collective learning based on information openness, business road mapping, action learning, and debriefing and reflection.

The next section is on orchestrating rather than managing, activity. In Chapter 13, Don Marchand highlights the role of leadership in managing information and, thereby, orchestrating activity. He lays out seven principles of management practice for the development of an information orientation that leads to high performance. These principles require the personal commitment of top management. In Chapter 14, Jean-Philippe Deschamps describes the role of an integrated process architecture in orchestrating activity. He describes how to set up a process management infrastructure, the mechanisms needed to sustain processes over time, and how to motivate people to do so. In Chapter 15, Jay Galbraith shows how lateral co-ordination is essential to orchestrating activity in multidimensional organizations. He describes how to match different types of lateral co-ordination with strategic priorities, and how to build a lateral co-ordination capability.

The last section is on integrating the commitments associated with bottom-up initiatives into a drive for value creation. With the large scope available for initiative in bottom-up organizations, managers and employees are more self-driven, hence motivation is less of a problem than in traditional organizations. On the other hand, integrating the initiatives into a coherent whole, without smothering them, is a challenge. In Chapter 16, Paul Strebel describes how companies have begun to focus on the relationships between individuals and the organization, in order to integrate bottom-up commitments into a larger whole. He outlines the enabling processes required to support ongoing learning in individual relationships with the organization. In Chapter 17, Tom Vollmann proposes a complement to continual improvement on the frontline, in the form of breakthrough initiatives not only by managers, but also by employees. He highlights the shift in mindset involved, if this kind of energy is to be integrated and focused. Finally, in Chapter 18, J.B. Kassarjian reflects on the leadership paradox in bottom-up organizations, to encourage simultaneously both divergent energy and convergent focus. He points out the pitfalls in conventional assumptions about the roles of leaders and followers, and emphasizes the importance of leadership style and the location of talent. The way the leader defines reality is key to integrating commitments and focusing energy.

References

Enron Values Statement, **www.enron.com**.
Salpukas, A. (1999) Enron Taps into a Well of Creativity and Profit, *International Herald Tribune*, June 29, 1999: 11 and 14.

2

Pathways to Bottom-up Organization

There are two classic paths to achieving an effective bottom-up organization, and two elements – widespread participation and bottom-up initiatives – are characteristic of success. **Paul Strebel** describes the pathways to bottom-up organization and how it can be achieved in practice.

CASE STUDY: PATHWAYS TO EFFECTIVE BOTTOM-UP ORGANIZATION – NIXDORF AND IBM

Siemens Nixdorf moved to a bottom-up organization as a central part of its turn-around. With massive losses already reported and the organization in crisis, the newly-appointed CEO realized the need for top management to act quickly and decisively to reverse the situation. His approach followed a classic top-down turn-around path. First, from the top of the organization he worked with other senior managers to build a new, decentralized business driven by entrepreneurial, bottom-up initiatives. The radical reorganization that took place at Nixdorf resulted in a flexible matrix of 250 business units, each with both a geographic and business focus. Key business decisions were taken by the business unit managers. The reorganization put in place comprehensive and far-reaching measures, including training and development programmes, new reward systems and an internal venture capital fund, designed to foster innovation, flexibility and entrepreneurship. Crucially, the organization also went beyond the circle of senior managers running the business to mobilize as many employees as possible to become change agents, thereby extending the entrepreneurial momentum. While the organization encountered several difficulties - notably a focus on business unit profitability sometimes at the expense of co-operation - the results of this approach were nonetheless impressive. After steady losses the business made increasing profits, highlighted by a popular range of new products, and prospects for sustained success. (The path followed by Nixdorf is examined later in this chapter.)

*Nixdorf's approach is in contrast to **IBM Customer Services'** continuous path to an effective bottom-up organization in South America. Here, as a result of increasing globalization, the organization needed to align 1500 customer services personnel across four countries. With only limited authority, the regional vice president responsible for services started a participative process that defined the changes that were needed. This was backed up with high-profile action to show that people's aspirations for the business would be supported and could be realized. The next step was to implement measures that would gain people's commitment to action and to a clear set of objectives: a difficult and complicated process, and one that was vital in focusing the organization's energy. The final step on the path was to unlock the latent potential of individuals within the business, by opening the organization to bottom-up initiatives. (The path followed by IBM Customer Services is also examined in more detail later.)*

Whether the route was discontinuous (Nixdorf) or continuous (IBM Customer Services), the value of reaching a bottom-up organization and realizing the energy and initiatives that lay there was immense for both businesses.

Overview[1]

The demand for effective, bottom-up organizations that are flexible and can maximize opportunities and manage threats arising from change raises the question of how one

1. This chapter draws heavily on Strebel (1998).

can get to a bottom-up organization from one that is not there yet. There are two classic paths to achieving a successful bottom-up organization, one discontinuous and one continuous. These paths both involve some combination of the four basic change processes shown in Figure 2.1: top-down turnaround, task-force-driven change, widespread participation and bottom-up initiatives. Of these, *widespread participation* aimed at continual improvement and entrepreneurial *bottom-up initiatives* are characteristic of effective bottom-up organizations.

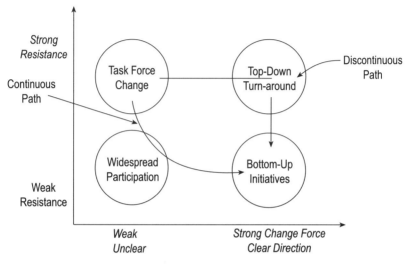

Figure 2.1: *Classic change paths*

On a discontinuous path, top management typically uses task forces to prepare the ground for a top-down turn-around. The turn-around opens the organization up, allowing management subsequently to encourage and embrace bottom-up initiatives. On a continuous path, the task forces are broadened out to stimulate widespread participation. The involvement that follows provides the basis for bottom-up initiatives. This chapter outlines the practical implications and benefits of each approach, illustrating key points with case studies. In this chapter we will:

* Explore the two paths to achieving an effective bottom-up organization, looking at the advantages and difficulties inherent in each approach.
* Outline the key steps needed for each path and use case studies to show how they can be followed successfully.

The discontinuous path

From task forces to top-down turn-around

On the discontinuous path from task forces to top-down turn-around to bottom-up initiatives, the pace of the turnaround phase is so fast that, seen in terms of an

> "The task forces need to work rapidly with top management and then roll the change out through the rest of the organization to provide the basis for bottom up initiatives"

organization's evolution, it amounts to a discontinuity, a giant step in the organization's development. Whereas task forces help shape the detail of participants' objectives and commitments, the rest of the organization is presented with the new processes and relationships as a fait accompli to be implemented. This approach makes sense when top management needs the help of task forces to clarify the detailed direction of the change, with little time for intensive solicitation of opinions.

The disadvantage of top-down change is that only the change agents can be mobilized. If the change path stops after the top-down turn-around phase, it does not lead to employee-driven initiatives. The new processes developed by the task forces require new ways of working, but top-down turnaround does not allow enough time or typically provide enough support, to foster behavioural change. In such cases, fear drives the bystanders and traditionalists who have a take-it-or-leave-it attitude and logic. They wait on the sidelines and watch how the change management deploys power to force resistors out. Under these conditions, you cannot simply ask people to take the initiative on the frontline. You have to put in extra effort to get them to buy in.

From top-down turn-around to bottom-up initiatives

The next step is to take advantage of the upheaval created by the turn-around to completely redesign the organization. This involves opening it up for bottom-up initiatives by pushing decision-making down to the frontline, thereby making room for as many change agents and converted bystanders as possible. On the economic dimension, this means converting sharply defined objectives into decentralized entrepreneurial scope for action; on the social dimension, it involves clearly building the flexibility needed for experimentation into the new rules of the game.

With this transition, you challenge the change agents to develop new business opportunities, and encourage the bystanders to follow the example of the change agents. However, it still means imposing a new organization, in the form of teams led by change agents, on the traditionalists from the old organization. From the traditionalist point of view, the change continues to look like a top-down turn-around – and resistors still have to be forced out.

Four key steps on the discontinuous path to bottom-up organization

1. Bring change agent task forces together with top management to define the scope and direction of change.
2. Force resistors out by making buy-in immediate, emphasizing the urgency of the situation.
3. Radically decentralize to offer entrepreneurial scope for change agents.

4. Use the value-creating logic embodied in the new organization to challenge as many bystanders as possible to support the change agents.

CASE STUDY: THE SIEMENS NIXDORF[2] DISCONTINUOUS PATH

Ask change agents to define direction, and force resistors out

When Gerhard Schulmayer took over, Nixdorf was in crisis with annual losses of one billion Deutschmarks. In classic turn-around fashion, Schulmayer started to replace and reconstitute the top management team with more than 10 new managers, hired from some of the most entrepreneurial and successful companies in Europe. Still in turn-around mode, Schulmayer and the top team called together 100-plus top managers from around the company to design the new Nixdorf. The new decentralized organization marked the beginning of the shift towards change driven by bottom-up initiative.

Radical reorganization to provide room for entrepreneurial change agents

The new organization design was a loose matrix of 250 business units, each with a geographic and a business line focus. The business unit managers played a central role, with full responsibility for profit and loss. The overall business system, or value chain for each business, would vary depending on whether it was a product, service, or solutions business. The business unit managers would be the real decision-makers; the geographic and business line managers sitting on the board of the business units would act only as sponsors and mentors. Nixdorf offered prospective business unit managers entrepreneurial mandates to run and develop a unit.

To facilitate the transition to entrepreneurship, all prospective managers attended the Entrepreneurship Development Program run by faculties from three leading business schools. This highly interactive, action learning program included a number of self-assessment exercises that culminated in the participants deciding whether they were ready to take up the entrepreneurial challenge of business unit leadership. In addition, the Management Development Program provided one week of training in business unit management skills to those who felt they could benefit. The training included techniques for diagnosing and optimizing business performance and managing a portfolio of businesses.

To measure performance, Nixdorf started using a standard financial management package for profit and loss accounting at the business unit level. Results went on to a balanced scorecard that included measures of customer and employee satisfaction. The company started assessing managers on both quantitative performance and qualitative behavioural factors, and aligned the new reward systems with these performance measures.

2. Based on Maletz (1997).

A critical phase in the transition from turn-around to bottom-up initiatives is to go beyond the inner circle of change agents managing the business units, to get change agents wherever they may be to come forward with their projects. Therefore, to encourage the development of new business ideas through experimentation and entrepreneurship, Schulmayer and his team launched an Innovation Initiative. Top management created an internal venture capital fund to which prospective entrepreneurs could appeal for funding outside of their business units. In addition, they had access to entrepreneurial competence throughout the company via a databank of individual expertise. This meant that someone with a product, service, or solutions idea, but no marketing or financial know-how, could get the help needed to put together a business plan.

To create a supportive environment for innovation and entrepreneurship, the Siemens Nixdorf management formed work groups in lines of business across the company to encourage the discussion of business issues and the exchange of best entrepreneurial practice. In particular, monthly Friday Forums provided opportunities for exchanging success stories and problems, and facilitating the access to expertise. In the same vein, people went on external benchmarking visits to companies known for their innovation, including several in Silicon Valley. However, the most significant support for entrepreneurial initiative came from the effort to convert hundreds of employee bystanders into change agents.

Extending the entrepreneurial effort by challenging bystanders to become change agents

The change leadership organized four events in Hannover, Germany between late 1994 and 1996, each time inviting 300 to 400 different employees who were interested in the change process. At these meetings, particular stakeholder groups shared their views about the corporate transformation and set up action teams to integrate them into the process. The theme of Hannover I was The voice of the employees. *It gave participants the opportunity to discuss the new values and informal rules needed to make Siemens Nixdorf an entrepreneurial company. 59 action teams were formed. Each agreed to produce some results within 90 days and a substantial value-creating impact inside 180 days. Hannover II focused on* The voice of the customers. *54 key clients attended a meeting of 350 employees to discuss what customers expected of the company. Some participated in the 20 action teams set up to address customer issues. Hannover III was concerned with* The voice of the partners. *40 suppliers and distributors joined several hundred employees to raise partner issues and join the related action teams. Finally, the theme of Hannover IV was* Institutionalizing the capability to change. *Some 400 employees looked at ways of taking the output from the first three events and making it part of the ongoing life of the company.*

The challenge for the action teams from the last event was how to take proposals from what were essentially offline task forces with a temporary mandate, and integrate them into the company's ongoing online activity. Among the proposals were new forms of communication based on the company's intranet to encourage cooperation across the business units. But here they ran into the limits imposed by the independent nature of bottom-up entrepreneurial activity. The communication took place, but co-operation was more difficult to implement. With each business unit and new venture responsible primarily for its own bottom line, people were happy to give lip service to co-operation and new proposals as long as it didn't cost them anything.

Yet the transformation at Siemens Nixdorf has, after all, created impressive bottom-up initiatives at the level of the business unit managers, as well as an ongoing series of one-time initiatives by employees with new venture ideas. It is important to note that these change agents had explicit mandates to initiate change based on their business unit, or new venture plans. By the end of 1996, the company had come back dramatically from several years of hundreds of million Deutschmark annual losses to break even, with numerous new products, several of them on the Internet, and a greatly improved market image.

The continuous path

From task forces to widespread participation

The problem with task force change is that, even when executed properly with intensive solicitation of opinions throughout the organization, it remains a top-down process. In addition, the temptaton is great for top management to get impatient with the pace of the task force consultation process and switch to top-down turnaround, which makes it even more difficult to get employee-driven support on the frontline.

> **"As long as the initiative for change comes only from the top, you cannot expect employee-driven initiative on the frontline"**

The first step on the continuous path is to shift from task force change to widespread participation. This can be achieved by:

- broadening the range of opinions provided to task forces;
- developing a lateral dialogue with bystanders; and
- integrating the relatively isolated work of task force implementation groups into widespread integrated teamwork that draws traditionalists into participative change.

On the economic dimension, it is necessary to broaden the special mandates of the task forces into new performance agreements that make everyone responsible for change throughout the organization. On the social dimension, it is important to build on individual information sharing to get the full involvement of people in teams taking the initiative for change. Additional change agents are needed: not only the task-oriented types who can design new processes, but also the people-oriented ones who can help others work in integrated teams. The heavy resistors are typically crowded out during the task force phase, while increasing peer group pressure converts the others as participation spreads.

Combining widespread participation with bottom-up initiatives

What one would like is a bottom-up organization that encompasses both the widespread improvement associated with participative change *and* the innovation that emerges from bottom-up initiatives. However, combining widespread participation with bottom-up initiatives is more easily said than done. The former requires that employees immerse themselves in a team effort following prescribed rules of the game, whereas bottom-up initiatives are driven firstly by individual enterprise and only then by a team that forms around the internal entrepreneur.

The path to a combination of widespread improvement with bottom-up initiatives starts more naturally with the former. The discipline of participative integration can be more easily relaxed to encourage bottom-up initiatives. Thus we can combine widespread participation with bottom-up initiatives by loosening the rules of the participative game to encourage the emergence of *intrapreneurs* (internal entrepreneurs).

Four key steps on the continuous path to bottom-up organization

1. Involve bystanders in widespread dialogue to define the change.
2. Lock in a commitment to action and integrate the participative effort with widespread teamwork.
3. Call for bottom-up initiatives within specific value-creating guidelines, with the necessary support for experimentation.
4. Loosen the guidelines further to encourage wider ranging and more innovative initiatives when the external change drivers become clearer.

Clearly these four steps need to be adapted to meet the needs and specific circumstances of a particular organization at a given time. However, an example of a business that followed this continuous path to a more effective bottom-up organization is IBM's customer services organization in South America.

CASE STUDY: THE IBM CUSTOMER SERVICES' CONTINUOUS PATH

IBM had a history of strong country organizations around the world. The move to global lines of business demanded the integration of activities across countries, with all the usual resistance that such a shift generates in the country kingdoms. The case here is about the alignment of the customer services across four countries. The services comprised consulting, outsourcing, software solutions, and support services. Some 1500 people were involved in the countries concerned. The new regional vice president of services started a participative process because he didn't have the authority to do much else. Fortunately for him, IBM had been through so much change by that time that people expected to be involved in any important moves. In addition, it wasn't clear how integration was supposed to be implemented across the countries, so a participative approach made sense. The vice president began by visiting the people reporting to him in the countries to put together a change management leadership team, with a member from each country, to help build the new customer service teams and manage the change there.

Involving people in widespread dialogue to define the change

The vice president started a first round of discussions to familiarize people with the need for, and nature of, the change. "The first thing was to build a personal relationship with the people, to develop a bridge that would generate some trust. It took time. It is one thing to go there and deliver a nice speech. It is another to get the people to open up and listen." Everybody was very polite, but nothing much happened. A big problem was bringing the general guidelines for the new IBM global services organization down to earth and adapt them to the local conditions with very different size scales and working culture. The new matrix structure meant that the number of key managers would more than double unless the structure was adapted to the different local situations.

Despite innumerable discussions about structure and the customer relations process, the new process teams were not functioning with the energy the vice president was looking for: "I can have very nice charts to show you that everything is running fine, but the real action hasn't occurred yet." To find out what was going on, the vice president held informal meetings over breakfast and lunch. People only really opened up when he began to address the question, what's in it for us? "During the first two to three months, we had a very formal reaction, until we gave some signs of real support for their projects: the loan of key resources they needed, consulting people, information technology architects, some key programmers, or analysts. That was the only way they could test that we meant what we were saying about co-operation." Once they began to see that the new rules of the game could work in their favour, the process teams began to coalesce around the change agents.

Locking in a commitment to action within the context of widespread teamwork

The real shift from a country to a line of service commitment, for everyone, including the traditionalists, came with the renewal of people's mandates, what IBM calls the Personal Business Commitments. These involve a very simple, short, written personal statement in which an individual translates his or her business unit's, or manager's, objectives into supporting personal objectives on three dimensions: a quantitative dimension in the form of revenue, profit, and customer satisfaction goals; a people dimension in the form of teamwork objectives; and an execution dimension in the form of an action plan that includes training and personal development. The commitments are supported by the usual range of IBM training programs and promotion ladders, plus performance evaluation on a scale of one to three on each dimension.

To align the new commitments with the lines of business, the vice president tied the 30% variable component of the compensation package to the regional performance on the three quantitative factors (revenue, gross profit, and customer satisfaction). Special attention was focused on objectives and actions aimed at ongoing improvement in the process teams. "The buy-in of people comes not only from the deployment of some tool and some meetings, saying OK we will start to use this process. I believe that processes take some time to really be part of your everyday activities."

A straightforward cascading approach was employed to get the commitments. The vice president developed his budget and action plan with his team and asked them to translate it into budgets for their business units, together with their personal objectives, and so on down to the frontline. These formed the basis of each employee's written Personal Business Commitment, which was discussed individually with the boss and signed by both parties. According to the vice president, this somewhat formal procedure was essential to avoid confusion across the languages and cultures of the different country organizations. What it did was put the initiative for action and process improvement across the countries in the hands of every customer services employee.

It is important to remember, however, that such formal commitments, to be really effective, need a psychological and social dimension. In the words of the vice president: "The formal piece of this process will not be of such a great help if you do not have the psychological commitment of the people. You have to go beyond the formal relation you have in any business to build some kind of human relationship. You have to share things that go beyond the business, while being very careful not to invade a person's privacy, being sensitive to different personalities."

Opening up for bottom-up initiatives

With the new line-of-service process teams up and running, the management team had to confront a number of issues that were not being resolved within the continual improvement framework. At his breakfast meetings with the unit heads, the vice president put these so-called key issues on the table and asked people to call for ideas directly from the frontline. People with ideas were asked to flesh them out first, to explore the idea to see if they could get some results: "Don't come to me if you have ideas or solutions: go ahead and do it. Try it out, and then once you have figured out if it works or not, then come to us. If you need resources or you need decisions, we will try to help you." In the first six months, there were 20 to 25 ideas that reached the experimental project stage and 12 that matured into "projects of significance".

The reason people on the frontline responded so well to this simple call for initiatives was that they too perceived the limitations of participative improvement in responding to complex customer requests that required creative new solutions. Their Personal Business Commitments had opened them up to taking the initiative, and many wanted to go beyond incremental change. At the time of writing, the pace of change, driven by the Internet, market and technological development, in several of IBM's business segments has accelerated so much that there is little time for incremental participative change. Fast bottom-up initiatives are the only way. Business unit leaders are being encouraged to move into action and execute as rapidly as possible. In the words of one vice president in charge of solutions software, "Those who can't keep up have to get out of the way."

Assessing the best path to bottom-up organization for your business

The best approach to achieving a bottom-up organization depends on the circumstances of each business. The advantage of the discontinuous approach is its speed and power, involving the weight of top management taking direct action to foster change. However, this is a two-edged sword: the difficulty with the discontinuous path is the fact that it is a top-down process, sometimes necessary but not conducive to frontline commitment. The discontinuous path tends to work best when:

- Immediate, urgent action is needed, with the top management of the organization working with the task forces and rapidly turning around the rest of the business.
- Senior managers understand that the process requires extra effort to get people to buy in to the top-down changes (and even then there will be those who simply never buy in).
- The top management of the organization is prepared to radically decentralize (often a counter-intuitive move, particularly during difficult times) and encourage entrepreneurship and change.
- Commitment exists to communicate the new approach as widely as possible, spreading best practice and energizing people so that they actively participate in the process and become change agents.

In many ways the continuous path is preferable: instead of moving through a process of top-down turn-around it brings change through widespread participation, which, when time permits, makes it easier to get frontline commitment. When implementing this approach it is important to:

- Stimulate a widespread dialogue that defines the necessary change.
- Follow this up to achieve a firm commitment to action. This is critical if the process is not to drive out the content.
- Create the right climate for bottom-up initiatives by balancing individual innovation with teamwork, creating the right mix of mutual support and experimentation, and ensuring that the whole process works within specific, measurable, value-creating guidelines.
- Loosen the guidelines to encourage wider-ranging innovation initiatives, and so ensure that the process of bottom-up organization is sustained.

Adopting the path that is best for your business at a particular moment is fundamental to achieving the goal of a successful bottom-up organization. Taking the wrong approach is analogous to swimming upstream: it requires much more energy and reduces your chances of getting there.

SUMMARY

Pathways to bottom-up organization

There are four basic change processes to choose from in charting a path to an effective bottom-up organization – a business where initiative, innovation and entrepreneurship grows and develops from the frontline or base of the organization. These four processes are:

1. *Top-down turnaround*, where the senior management of the organization intervenes to effect change directly.
2. *Task-force-driven change*, where change is led through the organization by task-forces involved directly in one or more aspects of the process.
3. *Widespread participation*, where employees throughout the business are involved directly in the change process.
4. *Bottom-up initiatives*, where individuals and teams have the freedom to actively develop and sustain change.

With approaches 1 and 2, resistance is strong and they are essentially directed and controlled closely from the top, cascading down throughout the organization. The challenge implicit in these approaches is to move from top-down direction to bottom-up initiative as smoothly and swiftly as possible. The *discontinuous path* moves from task force change to bottom-up initiative via top-down turn-around. The *continuous path* opens up the organization gradually, moving from task force change to bottom-up initiatives via widespread participation.

BEST PRACTICE

Following the pathways to a successful bottom-up organization

Clearly, specific circumstances and actions vary for every organization that is moving towards a bottom-up organization. However, as the examples in this chapter have highlighted, the pathways are broad and widely applicable, and while the specific actions may vary the overall direction and choices are similar.

Following the discontinuous path

When directing the change process from the top of the organization down (the discontinuous path), four steps are critical to success:

1. **Ask change agent task forces to work with top management to define change direction**
   The first stage is to move from task-force-led change to top-down change designed to turn around the business quickly. As a result, task forces need to work with senior management to define in detail the scope and direction of the change that is required. The new processes and action plans are then presented to the rest of the organization as a fait accompli.

2. **Force resistors out by making buy-in immediate**
   Because of the speed and top-down nature of the changes they are unlikely to foster behavioural change; senior managers therefore need to actively sell the benefits and get frontline employees to buy in. However, while bystanders may become converted later (once their fears are allayed), those that actively resist change need to be crowded out. These people will inevitably be present, and there is often neither the time nor the ability to convert them.

3. **Radically decentralize and offer entrepreneurial mandates to change agents**
   The speed and scope of the turn-around change inevitably results in upheaval as new processes and priorities take effect. The key to moving the situation forward so that bottom-up initiatives are stimulated is to redesign the organization in such a way that decision-making moves nearer to the frontline, raising morale, fostering behavioural change, creating more change agents and converting people to get behind the change process. In addition, decentralizing helps to convert tightly defined objectives for implementation into much more entrepreneurial mandates that appeal to individuals and teams, and also to develop new business opportunities. Clearly, this needs to be matched with greater flexibility and support for experimentation in order to sustain and support the process of change.

4. **Use the evidence and appeal of the value-creating logic embodied in the new organization to convince as many bystanders as possible to convert to change agents**
   Probably the biggest challenge with the discontinuous path is to build sufficient support and momentum for the change process to be sustained. Change directed from the top will always face a struggle to win people's minds and change their attitudes. However, the way that this process can be supported and sustained is to develop decentralized, entrepreneurial agreements with as many change agents and converted bystanders as possible. This can often start by building on high-profile successes as well as by allowing people to experiment and providing them with the freedom and support to make decisions. However, as an inevitable consequence of the top-down start to the process, not everyone will embrace the change or

be able to act as a change agent – it is important, therefore, to accept that this path to a bottom-up organization will not involve everyone.

Following the continuous path

An alternative approach is to broaden task-force-led change into widespread participation, and then focus this to produce bottom-up initiatives. The key steps here are:

1. **Involve bystanders in widespread dialogue to define the change**
    Task forces need to seek the opinions of others, moving from the relatively isolated work of implementation groups into more integrated teamwork and participative change. Additional change agents need to be sought, notably task-oriented agents that can design processes, and people-oriented agents that can support others working in integrated teams. Those people that are fiercely resistant to change need to be crowded out by the overall impetus for change. Other resistors can often be converted by peer pressure during the participative phase.

2. **Lock in a commitment to action in the context of widespread teamwork**
    The special responsibilities and mandates of the task force need to be generalized so that everyone in the organization has an incentive to take responsibility for change. In addition, individual information and tacit knowledge needs to be shared to gain the full involvement of the people and teams that are taking the initiative for change.

3. **Call for bottom-up initiatives within specific value-creating guidelines with the necessary support for experimentation**
    The move from widespread participation to specific bottom-up initiatives is a difficult one. The key here is to challenge people to take the initiative. Clear and workable guidelines, values and objectives need to be established, and the organization needs to support experimentation, innovation and initiative. This support can be provided in a wide variety of forms: from training, development and mentoring programs, to other actions which build a positive, blame-free environment.

4. **Loosen the guidelines further to encourage wider ranging innovation initiatives**
    Once the external factors driving change have become clear, individual innovation and initiative can be sustained by loosening the guidelines – in effect, empowering and enabling people so that more intrapreneurs emerge and succeed.

References

Maletz, M. (1997) Siemens Nixdorf's new dynamism, *Mastering Enterprise*, pp. 334-9. London: Financial Times Pitman.

Strebel, P. (1998) Chapter 13. *The Change Pact: Building Commitment to Ongoing Change*. London: Financial Times Pitman.

Part Two
Energizing the Organization

There are three essential dimensions to an energized organization. The first is a continually evolving set of entrepreneurial bottom-up initiatives that allow the company to exploit emerging opportunities in the marketplace. The second is a network of talent that connects people to each other and to outside partners, so that both entrepreneurial and improvement teams can form to pursue bottom-up initiatives. The third is flexible resources to support the teams in their pursuit of value creation. These three dimensions provide the structure for Part Two.

- Nurturing Entrepreneurial Initiatives (Chapters 3–4)
- Creating Networks of Talent (Chapters 5–6)
- Developing Flexible Resources (Chapters 7–8)

3

Pioneering Spirit

The bottom-up organization has a pioneering spirit: it recognizes new opportunities before they are obvious to others and sustains a strong appetite for experimenting with new ideas. In this chapter **Peter Lorange** explains why pioneering spirit is important and how it can be developed to energize the organization.

Overview

The pioneering spirit in a bottom-up organization enables it to see new business opportunities before they are obvious to everybody else. Put differently, the organization has the capacity to serve its customers in novel ways, not yet obvious even to the customers themselves (Lorange, 1998a). These pioneering organizations typically have an incredible appetite for experimenting with new ideas. They do not necessarily have the organizational capacity in place to build the new business yet, neither the people nor the funds. Still, they allow people to experiment and to test in order to come up with what might be new ways to pioneer the business. For the pioneering organization, success depends on an exceptional innovative drive and appetite, and a willingness to let the members of the organization undertake this. Business renewal is at the center of the firm's attention, both to create its own internal context for breakthrough performance (The Performance Group, 1999) and to grow by proactively seeking new market opportunities and the requisite new competencies.

In this chapter we will examine the pioneering spirit in bottom-up organizations, the commitment to breakthrough performance and the heavy emphasis placed on internally generated growth. In particular we will:

- explore the pioneering challenge;
- describe what is needed to develop and support internal entrepreneurs; and
- examine the key elements of a climate that supports pioneering.

The pioneering challenge

What does it take to create an organizational context with a strong, positive value-based commitment to breakthrough performance? There are three enabling conditions that must be in place:

- A commitment to pioneering at the corporate level.
- An overall objective of building a growth-driven business portfolio.
- A willingness to look beyond existing business unit definitions and think out of the box.

Commitment to pioneering at the corporate level

The key requirement is the development of an overall commitment to pioneering at the corporate level. This means allocation of resources – money as well as key people – to develop new business opportunities. As we all know, the most difficult challenge faced by managers and organizations alike is "how much attention and resources to invest today for today, versus how much to invest today for tomorrow," (Abell, 1993). Unless there is an explicit commitment to today for tomorrow, it will be hard to do any pioneering.

CASE STUDY: THE IMPORTANCE OF CORPORATE COMMITMENT TO PIONEERING

One example can be found in Citibank. Its consumer banking business ran into harder times in the early 1990s in several markets, both in the USA and in Europe, and the approach of cutting costs to maintain competitiveness did not work all that well. They then recognized that what might have been more effective would be the development of more innovative ways of serving their customers. It was then decided that for nine developing markets that Citibank would allocate major resources, including key people, to pioneering business activities for these markets. The new business opportunities were largely seen across these countries in a holistic way, so that innovation happened throughout the firm's overall development market, without reinventing the wheel from market to market (Lorange, 1999). The result was outstanding. By focusing in a top-down mode on entrepreneurial pioneering, they were able not only to maintain their market share but also to expand it.

Building a growth-driven business portfolio

Internally generated growth is probably the key to a firm's longer term success (see, for example, Kröger et al., 1998; Grundy, 1995; Kwestel et al., 1998; Schilit, 1994). Since the human side of the company is obviously of critical importance, the following questions must be addressed:

- What are the major organizational characteristics for achieving rapid internal growth?
- How do leading firms achieve strong, internally generated growth?

Firstly, for internal growth to happen managers of leading firms need to develop a strong ability to *see* new business opportunities ahead of the competition, identifying or creating new customer needs of which the latter is not yet aware. This must be supported by a capacity to *mobilize* the required resources to exploit such opportunities – a combination of the most appropriate team of people, relevant technology and the necessary financial resources.

The growth-driven firm is one that has a clear view of its portfolio of business activities, distinguishing the growth potential dimension from that of its established business. Figure 3.1 proposes a practical approach for a company to assess its business

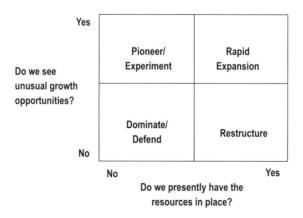

Figure 3.1: *The business development portfolio*

portfolio and its growth-generation potential (Chakravarthy and Lorange, 1991). It is essential to keep an overall portfolio point of view, in the sense that it will help top management to do the necessary top-down "pushing" for portfolio renewal (an issue explored further in Chapter 10).

The successful, rapidly growing firm – the one that sees new opportunities – needs to be truly willing to experiment. It will often have relatively more pioneering activities in its business portfolio than its competitors. A California-based high-technology firm, for instance, estimates that it may have 15 or so activities in the *pioneer* area and three to four *rapid-growth* activities, compared with one in the *dominate/defend* area (Liddle, 1998). A large multinational firm in chemicals similarly has an internal benchmarking rule of six pioneering initiatives for three rapid-expansion scenarios, leading ultimately to one major business to be defended and dominated. For large corporations such as 3M, DuPont and others, an explicit target is to have a fraction of sales come from new business, seen as part of the overall portfolio (Coyne, 1999; Gilmore, 1999). For example, at 3M 25% of the business revenue must come from new initiatives over the last five years. Such firms may also be willing to scale up more rapidly and effectively, by aggressively finding the right path for utilizing a new pioneering business activity that has shown strong initial signs of promise. A capacity to move swiftly is essential. Lew Platt, former CEO of Hewlett Packard, says that his firm's critical core competence is "to take an idea, make it into a product, and bring it to the market quickly", based on an "imaginative understanding of new needs" (Platt, 1998; *Business Week*, 1997; Nee, 1997).

Many companies focus on generating profits by trying to preserve their share of mature markets. They frequently have recourse to drastic measures such as re-engineering, cost-cutting and special, expensive marketing programs for extending established businesses. Here, we are concerned with growth-oriented firms that put a greater than average emphasis on the initiation and dynamism of new businesses, including, but certainly not limited to, extensions of present product lines in existing and new markets. Their overall business portfolio is more even, with new *and* established activities producing a symbiotic balance. However, one key condition for all this to happen is to have within the management team executives endowed with a true entrepreneurial spirit.

Looking beyond business unit definitions

A third requirement is the organization's willingness to look between the established business unit definitions, which is a good way to spot new pioneering opportunities in many cases (Chakravarthy and Lorange, at press). A business unit definition (meaning a definition of core business) is often based on an already established business proposition. However, new opportunities may be found on the outskirts of this definition, or in what one might see as the "white space" between business units. It is important to look at the periphery of an industry to see where it is moving in this respect. It may not make sense to over-analyse the core. Business redefinition typically has to do with business models competing with each other. The periphery, in contrast, is about figuring out how to compete with the core, exploit weaknesses, and how to provide value in new ways. Business redefinition can be described as *gales of creative destruction.*

CASE STUDY: A BREEZE OF CREATIVE DESTRUCTION

An example of this is Norsk Hydro, one of the world leaders in the fertilizer business. They found that, for a long time, fertilizers had been used as part of the preparation of downhill ski slopes, so that the snow would develop a thin, icy crust after an initial melting of the top, fine layer of snow. After several years of procrastination regarding what this actually meant for Norsk Hydro, a group of executives came up with the idea that this might be an excellent means of de-icing airport runways. The problem, however, was that this did not fit into the core business unit analysis of Norsk Hydro. After all, the de-icing of runways is rather different from fertilizing the farmers' fields. After several years of delay, the green light was finally given to develop this new business. In retrospect, this pioneering business has turned out to be a great success.

In looking beyond the existing business units, there are a number of questions that need to be addressed to think out of the box and achieve maximum pioneering drive:

- Are we able to see business opportunities before they are obvious to everyone else? Are there ways we can serve our customers so radically that the customers themselves do not realize yet that they require this type of service?
- Are there entirely new ways to think, while still, to a lesser or greater extent, building on the business perspective of the past, in terms of:
  - extending and modifying one's product offering;
  - breaking into new markets; and/or
  - a combination of these forces?
- Is there a radical way that we can mobilize these growth-providing resources, primarily our essential human capabilities but also financial support, to actually go after and take advantage of pioneering ideas so that they can become a reality through rapid expansion?
- How can we understand the forces at work which slow down mobilization of people and other resources? Is there a way that we can counterbalance these potentially negative, conservative forces?

Having considered the enabling conditions, we now turn to the heart of pioneering, how to develop and support internal entrepreneurs.

Developing and supporting the internal entrepreneur

A commitment to pioneering at the corporate level sets the tone, but the key question for the bottom-up organization is how to nurture the internal entrepreneurs needed in order to achieve pioneering, rapid expansion. It is entrepreneurial individuals within the organization that will drive the process. Typically, internal entrepreneurs will come from the ranks of the general management population (although in theory they could come from anywhere). Developing and encouraging these individuals is vital. The organizational challenge is to create an environment where these individuals can operate with the freedom of action associated with traditional entrepreneurs but with access to the resources of the wider business. For instance, the former CEO of Kvaerner, one of the world's leading engineering companies, felt that a relatively small number of his executives would actually prove to be outstanding in their ability to seek out truly interesting business opportunities and draw effectively on the company's resources to make these deals become a reality.[1] These executives, although at times potentially generating internal controversy, typically enjoy trust and respect, and can count on being supported by the CEO when, occasionally, they might run into internal organizational problems.

How internal entrepreneurs succeed

How does the internal entrepreneur look for new business? There are five guidelines:

1. **Amass facts, primarily technological in nature, in a holistic manner**
    (Baghai et al., 1999)
    These facts should be used for juxtaposition, technology viewpoint against technology viewpoint, technology against markets, and so forth. Facts should be dealt with by zooming in and out. The facts should be interpreted as seeing the world through the eyes of others (including researchers, network partners, and customers).
2. **Work with the market, one's leading customers, and those who appreciate being led by our thinking**
    It is important in this context not to be led by the market, but to understand that the challenge is to *lead* the market. This process needs to transform ideas into workable concepts.
3. **Develop an expansive mindset**
    This is critical for internal entrepreneurs to be successful, and it must be based on reflection: insight is rooted in conversation. A fit with the general corporate values of the firm can also be useful, helping to generate leads to new ideas, and not a source of confinement.
4. **Maintain an open and inquiring mind**
    Above all, internal entrepreneurs are curious, with a truly open mind. For instance, they do not believe that focusing on existing core business is binding. In many large companies, each individual business unit's mission regulates the direction of the businesses. But dynamic opportunities are very often found in the white spaces on the map between the businesses. Here, internal entrepreneurs can play key roles, and they should not be slowed down by turf battles between established divisions.
5. **Establishing connections with the market**
    How do internal entrepreneurs establish this critical link to the market so as to spot the unusual business opportunity? They do, of course, talk to the

---

1. From a personal interview with Mr. Erik Tønseth, former President of Kvaerner ASA.

> "A key challenge for the internal entrepreneur is to develop close links with the market, as it is the market system that works best in inspiring ideas and creating new value"

customer, learning from possible initial failures and initiating actions that will help to hone a workable business concept. This trial and error dialogue can also help develop a clearer picture of the business idea internally, vis-à-vis colleagues. Gradual acceptance, buying in, and even excitement are built. Entrepreneurs create their own track record, their own credibility versus key customers/market segments, as well as the network of internal and external resources. The internal entrepreneur is assisted by the fact that markets are, as a rule, more dynamic than companies and more competitive than any single player. It is the market system, not the hierarchical, bureaucratic corporate system, that tends to work best in creating new value.

Providing internal entrepreneurs with space

What motivates the internal entrepreneur? The need to achieve is vital. The other side of this coin is the recognition arising from what develops into a viable, demonstrated track record of being a proven driver of success. Additional motivation is probably the visibility and relatively direct access to the top – and, perhaps the thrill of living on the edge by doing things first, and asking for permission later. In short, the internal entrepreneur is a different breed – rare, but critically important.

To find, support and retain effective internal entrepreneurs who truly burn for an idea and make it a reality is more critical than is generally recognized by top management (Pinchot, 1985). This is a key task for today's leading CEOs. The starting point is to give the internal entrepreneurs space to do their job. But how do the internal entrepreneurs work, and how does top management give them this space?

> "Internal entrepreneurs are open to anything and anyone that can help their business idea become a reality: they are not bothered by the common "I know best" or "Not invented here" syndromes. They are careful to avoid being trapped in conventional ways of doing business"

Typically, internal entrepreneurs have a good understanding of where the relevant talents are, within and outside their own company. They know who they need to work on their project, and have a strong ability to convince such people to work with them, based on their own enthusiasm and commitment.

In addition to giving themselves space to see things in new ways, internal entrepreneurs will typically also depend on being given space by top management (Stopford and Baden-Fuller, 1994). Partly, this means top management encouraging and supporting them to take risks and to experiment with new ideas, particularly when the sailing gets rough and when it can be seen that sticking one's neck out is a lonely business. This may also mean forgiving them for breaking the rules. Internal entrepreneurs need to be protected against the bureaucracy. Allowing for the occasional failure by showing trust and exercising nonautocratic control is of the essence, as are positive feedback and appropriate praise.

The concept of nonautocratic control is clearly important. It is a way to provide the entrepreneur with direct access to top management, to be close so that support can be provided when requested, whilst *also* providing distance to the entrepreneur, allowing for separation from the established businesses and autonomy. Space thus means a measure of independence while also being part of the overall corporate context.

Networking for internal entrepreneurs

Internal entrepreneurs need effective networking (Chakravarthy and Lorange, at press) among key people at various locations, with the internal entrepreneur playing a catalyst role. (For more on networking, see Chapters 5 and 6.) The internal entrepreneur requires the ability to put together flexible eclectic teams of leading talents working together, often virtually via the Internet. Main constituents of such a team will be external members of the network not formally part of the firm, from sources such as customer organizations, suppliers, consultants, and academic institutions.

A top executive of a leading telecommunications firm stated that, in the past, much development was done in closed, culturally self-selecting teams consisting mostly of engineers in the same age bracket, from similar technical university backgrounds and all from the same parent country. Now much of this takes place in more open teams, with Internet-based interaction and benefits from the insights of many. As a result, the discovery process has opened up, and it is no longer shrouded in the secrecy of internal laboratories. One important result is markedly greater speed.

The successful internal entrepreneur is a master of all this, putting together a team to help launch a business and, later, bring it to fruition. In many ways, he or she resembles the traditional entrepreneur, but has access to the wider resources and skills of the organization. A key characteristic is the ability to draw on the skills base and diversity of the organization to create dynamic project teams which can support rapid evaluation of new business opportunities and, critically, execute start ups. Different management disciplines, different nationalities, different age categories and title levels, and a reasonable balance between women and men – all need to be part of the team, in order to see the business opportunities and to implement them quickly.

CASE STUDY: A CULTURE OF INTERNAL NETWORKING

An example of this is the development of the LC1 yoghurt business at Nestlé. It started with the development by Nestlé researchers of an ingredient that helps strengthen the immune system when consumed regularly. The problem was that as a commercial venture, this new finding had no business value per se. Only after the French and German Nestlé marketing organizations saw the opportunity to put this ingredient into yoghurt to boost the health features offered in their yogurt business, did it become a commercial success. Through internal networking, which brought research, the market forces, and the central SBU entity together, they were able to quickly see a confluence of the ideas, so that a pioneer business emerged. Internal networking made this happen (Rogers, at press).

In creating successful networks there are several key issues to be resolved by the CEO, focusing on organizational structures and networks:

- What can the CEO do to provide a network that will support the drivers for growth, the internal entrepreneurs?
- How can the CEO help with the creation of ad hoc organizational growth-focused units with multifunctional teams, composed of people with dramatically different backgrounds?
- How can the CEO help create such networks so that a truly higher level of energy and personal conviction can flourish, in contrast to a hierarchical control culture? How can the CEO cut out the bulk of the bureaucratic controls and eliminate unnecessary procedures?

Selection of the right people is particularly critical and can often represent a tangible focal point for the CEO in creating a truly innovative and totally different organization. Emphasis should be more on the CEO's choice of people than on the systems and the processes. These people must be able to function despite what will always be an element of bureaucracy. The CEO must look at the mindsets rather than the skills. While the people that are recruited must at least be able to establish and maintain their respect and effectiveness vis-à-vis their colleagues in the network, the crucial issues are their mental flexibility, the adherence to growth values, and the ability to work in a totally transparent manner.

The CEO can also have an impact on the physical design of the organization so as to achieve more openness, creating meeting places and favourable conditions for people to get together in a relaxed atmosphere where they can think freely and multidimensionally. The physical layout of rooms, with no fixed bases or desk structure, plays a potentially significant role. The CEO can use timing and location – where people are at a given time – to become an active resource for the organization, not an isolated, inactive asset, encapsulated in an office. Lack of walls and partitions can help the CEO to foster a design for the organization that allows for maximum communication, including a radically improved informal communication dimension. Perhaps one of the most interesting examples of this is the Danish corporation Oticon, which described itself as the "Spaghetti Organization".

CASE STUDY: OTICON'S SPAGHETTI ORGANIZATION

Oticon, a leading hearing-aid company, is probably best known outside Denmark for its pioneering development of the paperless office and its radical organizational restructuring into the "Spaghetti Organization". Founded in 1904, Oticon was the first hearing instrument company in the world. By the 1970s, it was the world's number one manufacturer of behind-the-ear hearing aids.

But by 1974, Oticon's market share began declining as people started using in-the-ear models. By 1987, it had dropped from 15 to 7% and the company was starting to lose money. That's when Lars Kolind became CEO. His first move was a classic cost-cutting exercise. He pared the company down, shedding staff and raising efficiency. He refocused the business on its key markets. By 1989, the medicine seemed to be working and Oticon returned to profit. But Kolind knew that the changes were not enough. "It was clear that we could not survive over the next five years without taking a radical step," he remembers. "Where was our competitive edge? Nowhere."

On New Years day 1990, Kolind produced his manifesto for change. In future, he believed a company's success would be increasingly reliant upon creating the right working environment – one where employees behaved as entrepreneurs rather than as part of a large organization. He believed that formal organizational structure, titles and hierarchies stifled innovation and initiative. He launched the 300 Project, so-called because it aimed to increase productivity at the company's Copenhagen headquarters by 300% over three years. He hoped it would trigger a breakthrough in creativity and innovation.

Kolind created a new organizational model based on the idea of replacing permanent departments with a network of continuously changing project teams. He called his new creation the Spaghetti Organization. Any individual who came up with a good idea was free to assemble a team and act as project leader. Each project, however, then had to compete with all the other projects trying to get off the ground at any time. An employee had to attract sufficient resources and support for his or her project, or it perished. At times, there are up to 100 projects on the go, forming and disbanding as tasks are started or completed. Individuals invariably contributed to more than one project at a time. Although Oticon has recently moved back to a work traditional organization, the Spaghetti Organization was a great example of pioneering.

Refocusing management processes to support the internal entrepreneur

Traditionally, planning, budgeting and control systems have played prominent roles in directing and impacting the operating activity patterns of a company, and this will of course continue (Lorange, 1996; 1998b, 2000). However, these processes can be bureaucratic and inflexible for the internal entrepreneur pursuing ultra-rapid growth. The ability of a company to critically re-examine management processes and systems is therefore another critical way of providing space. Perhaps it is more a matter of how the dialogue is actually practised between top management and the internal entrepreneur, as the following example illustrates.

The CEO says to the executive leading a pioneering initiative: "You have my go-ahead with the task to test whether we have a business or not, based on the new product proposition put forward. You have *carte blanche* to pick up to 10 top people from where you want within and outside the organization, and you have a budget of

$1 million – within the broad parameters we have discussed, *you* decide how to use it. After eight months, you let us know whether we have a business or not. And, by the way, customer actions – purchases or testimonials – will be key! You will not be required to file a weekly budget progress report; just let me know if something extraordinary happens."

Here we see all the elements of the new approach: a focused initiative that is given space, and not hampered by existing management processes. The entrepreneur is only required to state "go" or "no go" at the end of a clearly defined time period. A properly focused interactive and iterative approach to the top-down/bottom-up dialogue is therefore crucial.

Learning environment for internal entrepreneurs

In conventional, established business situations, such as in the dominate/defend case mentioned earlier, a key to success might be to offer even more value to the key customer through continuous improvements and/or at lower costs. The firm develops business plans, budgets and controls to guide these activities based on putting together an overall budget, picturing the business from a set of complementary functional inputs. If, subsequently, something goes wrong, a detailed analysis of the source of the deviation follows, actions are taken to ameliorate the problem, and a new, revised plan and budget are issued. This implies a Cartesian learning approach: to understand each of the pieces, fix those that need to be fixed and then put them back together. This has indeed dominated much of our management approaches to learning in business.

The problem with the Cartesian approach to learning is that when it comes to pioneer situations, when speed of learning and implementing is of the absolute essence, it probably works too slowly. Perhaps we can draw analogies from the fast learning mode of a child. According to the work of the pioneering child psychologist Piaget (for details, *see* Hedberg, 1981), children learn by forming a total – but of course incomplete – picture of a phenomenon. When they experience that reality does not work according to their picture, they simply form a new total picture, discarding the old one, and with no inhibitions or preconceived limiting beliefs. After a number of such increasingly realistic pictures, they end up getting it right. The same process could characterize the learning that goes on in ultra-rapid pioneer businesses. Rather than getting mired in analysing the detail, they maintain the overview and simply reformulate the business concept until it works. This can be much faster.

> **"The key is to see anything that goes against you as a vehicle to try again, and to build on what went wrong, rather than as an outcome in itself. One must think in terms of opportunities, not problems"**

Similarly, when it comes to scaling up a new business and maintaining the first-mover advantage we can learn from Harold Leavitt's (1986) work on pathfinding in psychology. Rather than seeing what might be considered failures when things do not work, such experiences might simply be seen as stimuli to what would be analogous to trying another path among the trees in the forest. This approach involves more aggressive trial-and-error as a standard, without the executives involved feeling the stigma of failure. It should also be pointed out that most internal entrepreneurs actually have a fear of being too slow, of falling behind. This fear of failure can also be turned around and built on in a positive way, as an inducement to constructive learning. Both of these points have special resonance for the new-style dot.com businesses, which lend themselves to rapid prototyping and fast execution. Typically, they exhibit nonlinear behaviour, with the ability to reformulate their business plans at a moment's notice. This is one of their chief advantages over traditional bricks and mortar businesses. What many of the new-style web-based businesses have in common is a willingness to experiment, which allows them to move up the learning curve at break-neck speed. This sense of urgency – and adventure – is a key characteristic of the dot.com world.

In summary, internal entrepreneurs are essential. A company culture that will give them space and support – a breakthrough performance culture – is equally important. Network features of the organization, mainly networked teams, drive the creation of new value. Management processes must be focused on driving growth, rather than on compliance with bureaucratic practices that merely take time and drain energy.

Creating a climate for pioneering

A critical task for the CEO is to create a climate in the organization that is conducive to a pioneering spirit (The Performance Group, 1999). We will look at five such factors, some of which directly support seeing new business opportunities, while others are associated more with creating a climate for the better mobilization of resources. On the creative "seeing" side, we will discuss the handling of risk-taking, innovation culture and dealing with mistakes. On the implementation side we will discuss communication and reinforcement of success.

Risk-taking

How can the CEO help create more of a conducive climate for experimentation and innovation, encouraging his or her people to step out of the comfort zone? How can the CEO help cultivate an attitude of thinking out of the box? There are three inter-related approaches for CEOs:

- They must be willing to back up the risk-taking personally, stand behind it, and be loyal to people, even in adverse times. There are immediate, negative consequences for an organization's risk-taking capabilities if the CEO walks away from the battleground.
- They must be willing to appoint and tolerate disruptive people who have a track record of thinking in unconventional ways.
- They must play on the uncertainty of outcomes and survival as exemplified by the need to put pressure on the organization to ask for results. This lack of

patience, rather than a deliberate impatience, is also essential for the development of a better risk profile.

Building an innovation culture

What about developing a more conducive, innovative context? What about creating a tradition for thinking the unthinkable, thinking outside of the box? The CEO might encourage people to look upon their jobs differently, not as organizational tasks covered by a job description but as a mandate to create the largest possible space in which the capabilities of a person can flourish. The key is to make the space as large as possible, thereby forcing people to work at the edge of what they are qualified to do (Gould, 1994). By widening the space, by inspiring one's people to use more of their own resources, by insisting on multijob assignments, the innovative flame can be further kindled. There is much that the CEO can do here by breaking down the walls that can stifle innovation, encouraging openness and dampening fear. Innovation can be encouraged by energizing people and giving permission, not control.

Dealing with mistakes

Mistakes are typically sources of contention within most organizations. People fear the consequences of making a mistake, and such fears – more or less justified – can lead to stifling and acceptance of the status quo. It is important for the CEO to make sure that failures do not lead to punishment but that they become a source of learning. The CEO must instill a cultural dimension that gives people the right to fail as well as also insisting on learning from such failures.

Communication

Communication is essential for mobilizing the organization. This means ensuring that teams work, often under great pressure, with a lot of complementary, eclectic people pulling together. A feeling of being heard, being part of an open network and experiencing the positive effect of this on their own confidence, is critical to everyone. Such an open, flexible attitude stimulates the flow of ideas and the creativity to implement better.

Reinforce success

Linked with this will be the CEO's attempt to create more pride in work by initiating celebrations. Developing this feeling of pride by positively reinforcing success and celebrating milestones that are achieved is very important. It is important to avoid complacency and the issue of positive praise should not be underestimated: it is a key characteristic of the CEO's job for stimulating growth.

These five factors contribute to the creation and strengthening of a breakthrough performance climate. They stimulate the context for both creative "seeing", and the radical mobilization of resources for implementation. The CEO is responsible for both and must therefore focus on all five factors. This should be achieved through formal channels, but at the same time, as noted earlier, in today's flat organizations networking is one of the most important roles of the CEO.

 # SUMMARY

Pioneering spirit

To develop a pioneering spirit capable of delivering breakthrough performance requires an open, forward-looking culture and a unified organizational perspective as necessary preconditions. All in all, it adds up to the need to perfect our ability to attract internal entrepreneurs, to stimulate them to excel and to create a context in which they can succeed. This pioneering attitude is essential to building the firm of the future. Too much effort is put into defending the status quo or the past. Too little effort is put into the development of business for the future, towards a pioneering approach. Too few companies realize that pioneering is indeed the *only* secure way to defend themselves in the future.

A pioneering spirit can therefore be created by fostering a positive context based on the dictum that *good can always be done better*, and a healthy dissatisfaction with the status quo. While top management must clearly play a role in the creation of such a breakthrough performance climate, the internal entrepreneur will be essential. Without such drivers, it is hard to see how breakthrough performance can happen. It is absolutely critical that the pioneering internal entrepreneur is proactively and comfortably at work. Pioneering spirit does indeed mean pioneering internal entrepreneurs.

In this chapter, we have focused on how to develop a pioneering spirit. A fundamental key to this is a mindset that emphasizes how to *see new business opportunities* – preferably early, before they are obvious to everyone else. Equally critical is the ability to effectively *mobilize organizational resources* to take advantage of such growth opportunities.

Pioneering can therefore be achieved by:

- Ensuring commitment at the top, developing a view of one's overall business portfolio, as well as specifically verifying for oneself that there are enough pioneering and rapid expansion business initiatives there, looking beyond today's business units for new opportunities.
- Most important is selecting and nurturing internal entrepreneurs to spearhead the internally generated growth initiatives – those rather rare general managers who can see new business opportunities *and* mobilize organizational resources to achieve growth. The internal entrepreneur must be

given space to operate – both by having sufficient independence within the organizational hierarchy and by considering themselves close to the CEO when there are issues that need to be clarified. They operate naturally in a networked reality and are fast learners.

● Nurturing an organizational climate that supports pioneering and breakthrough performance.

 **BEST PRACTICE**

Assessing pioneering spirit in your organization

Because pioneering spirit is a vital but largely *intangible* resource, it can be difficult to assess the extent to which it exists or needs to be developed. It can therefore be helpful to consider some of the following issues:

● **Do managers have a strong ability to *see* opportunities ahead of the competition?**
  In considering this issue it is worth reflecting on whether the business tendency is to extend the product offering, break into entirely new markets, or undertake a combination of both.

● **Does your business portfolio include new and existing products? Are they in balance?**
  The issue here is to avoid becoming obsessed with maintaining share of a mature (or declining) market. Old and new products can be symbiotic, resulting in the portfolio as a whole being greater than the sum of its parts.

● **Do managers have the space to mobilize the resources needed to exploit these opportunities?**
  Here, the issues are whether – and how easily – managers can mobilize the resources needed to achieve growth. Put another way, how strong and pervasive are the forces *preventing* resources being mobilized?

In answering these questions it is useful to consider each business or product against the business development portfolio in Figure 3.1. Other issues to consider include:

- Is there a commitment to pioneering at the corporate level?
- How well developed are internal networks for knowledge enhancement, transfer and learning?
- Are people looking at the space between businesses, the opportunities that lie on the *edge* of existing business unit definitions?

The final question is who are your internal entrepreneurs, and what additional support do they need?

- Are internal entrepreneurs encouraged and supported?
- Are they successful in identifying opportunities ahead of the competition?
- Do entrepreneurs have the *space* to mobilize the resources they need?

The strength of personal networks can be decisive in delivering internally generated growth. It is useful, therefore, to assess what more can be done to facilitate the free flow of ideas and information necessary to foster innovation and entrepreneurship. By focusing on selecting the right people and influencing the physical design of the organization, the CEO can help to develop a pioneering organization.

References

Abell, D. (1993) *Managing with Dual Strategies – Mastering the Present; Preempting the Future*. New York: Free Press.

Baghai, M., Coley, S. and White, D. (1999) *The Alchemy of Growth: Practical Insights for Building the Enduring Enterprise*. Reading, USA: Perseus Books.

Business Week (1997) H-P Pictures of the Future, *Business Week*, July 7, 1997: 100–109.

Chakravarthy, B. and Lorange, P. (1991) *Managing the Strategy Process*. Englewood Cliffs, USA: Prentice Hall.

Chakravarthy, B. and Lorange, P. (at press) *Nurturing Organic Growth: Multilevel Entrepreneurship*.

Chakravarthy, B. and Lorange, P. (at press) *Nurturing Organic Growth: Strategic Processes*.

Coyne, W.E. (1999) *Technology Management at 3M*. Presentation given at IMD, Lausanne, Switzerland, January 13, 1999.

Gilmore, A. (1999) *Business-Integrated R&D*. Presentation given at IMD, Lausanne, Switzerland, January 14, 1999.

Gould, R.M. (1994) *Revolution at Oticon A/S: The Spaghetti Organization*. IMD case no. OB 235.

Grundy, T. (1995) Breakthrough Strategies for Growth. London: Pitman Publishing.

Hedberg, B. (1981) *How Organizations Learn and Unlearn*, in *Handbook of Organizational Design*, eds Nystrom, P.L. and Starbuck, W.H. vol. 1. Oxford: Oxford University Press.

Kröger, F., Träm, M. and Vandenbosch, M. (1998) *Spearheading Growth*. London: Pitman Publishing.

Kwestel, M., Preston, M. and Plaster, G. (1998) *The Road to Success: How to Manage Growth*. New York: John Wiley & Sons.

Leavitt, H.J. (1986) *Corporate Pathfinders: Building Vision and Values into Organizations*. Homewood, USA: Dow-Jones Irwin.

Liddle, D. (1998) *The R&D Imperative: What is wrong with R&D*. Presentation given at Forbes CEO Forum, Phoenix, Arizona, May 7, 1998.

Lorange, P. (1996) Strategic Planning for Rapid Profitable Growth, *Strategy & Leadership* **24**(3): 42–48.

Lorange, P. (1998a) The Internal Entrepreneur as Driver of Business Growth, *Perspectives for Managers* **49**(8).

Lorange, P. (1998b) Internally Generated Growth – Strategy Implementation: the New Realities, *Long Range Planning* **31**(1): 18–29.

Lorange, P. (1999) The Internal Entrepreneur as a Driver of Growth, *General Management Review*, Calcutta, **1**(1): 18–44.

Lorange, P. (2000) Ultra Rapid Management Processes, in *Management 21C*, ed. Chowdhury, S. Harlow: Pearson Education.

Nee, E. (1997) What Have You Invented For Me Lately? *Forbes*, July 23, 1997.

The Performance Group (1999) *Breakthrough Performance Through People*. Surrey, UK.

Pinchot, G. III (1985) *Intrapreneuring: why you don't have to leave the Corporation to become an entrepreneur*. New York: Harper & Row.

Platt, L.E. (1998) *Rules for Survival in the Brave New World of Total Connectivity*. Remarks given at the IDC European Forum, Paris, September 7, 1998.

Rogers, B. (at press) *The LC1 Case*.

Schilit, W.K. (1994) *Rising Stars and Falling Fads*. New York: Lexington Books.

Stopford, J.M. and Baden-Fuller, C.W.F. (1994) Creating Corporate Entrepreneurship, *Strategic Management Journal*, **15**(7): 521–536.

4

Growth Catalysts

For pioneering initiatives to flourish, top management has to stimulate growth opportunities with a growth catalyst – an organizational arrangement that encourages people to pursue growth. **Jacques Horovitz** describes five common growth catalysts, plus some common approaches to growth that are not catalytic and should be avoided because they destroy value.

CASE STUDY: TACO BELL

Taco Bell's growth from the mid-1980s to the mid-1990s illustrates perfectly how growth in a company can be fuelled by organizational catalysts whilst also becoming dysfunctional (in the case of Taco Bell, ultimately leading to its disposal by PepsiCo). John Martin joined Taco Bell (a $700-million company) in 1983 and found himself at the helm of a chain of around 1500 Mexican fast food restaurants, 60% franchised. His plan to wake up the company and make it dance to parent PepsiCo's demanding beat included the following:

- *Defining what business to be in - fast food, not Mexican food - and offering the best value.*
- *Defining stretch objectives - more than 250 extra units per year, while reducing costs and price by 50%.*
- *Giving autonomy to the restaurant general manager (RGM), with full profit and loss responsibility. This included giving RGMs the freedom to take ownership and grow, including kiosk extensions to the business, in school points of sales and other initiatives. The plan also included an expanded role of market manager, who would not only supervise 6 to 12 restaurants but would be allowed to develop his or her whole market. To avoid too much control on the autonomy of the RGMs, market managers were given 20 to 60 RGMs to supervise. (In effect, this meant they had no time for preventing things from happening.)*
- *Flattening the organization to reinforce autonomy through a rigorous information system, the goal of the CEO being to have 10 000 RGMs reporting to him directly.*
- *Installing safety nets to ensure that customer satisfaction, employee satisfaction and business results were known at all times.*

As a consequence the company grew six-fold in less than 10 years to reach $4 billion in 1994. From the traditional 1500 stores, it had grown to 10 000 points of access. However this growth started to get dysfunctional when:

- *It moved away from fast food to other variations on Mexican food (Chevys) or non-Mexican fast food (Hot-n-Now drive thru' hamburgers' bought in 1991 and sold in 1997).*
- *It expanded abroad in 21 countries with just 100 restaurants (100 meant it was far too thin on the ground to benefit from economies of scale).*
- *It started using the brand as an umbrella for traditional restaurants, and other new concepts (too broad).*
- *It had points of access in geographical markets with diminishing returns.*

As a result, in 1997 PepsiCo decided to divert resources from all its restaurant business including the disposal of Taco Bell which was draining its resources.

Overview

Growth is a natural path for businesses. It is expected by shareholders for value appreciation. It is hoped for by employees for career development. It is wished for by management for new things to do. It is a necessary competitive tool for companies (not to grow is to regress). It is sometimes desired by customers who are delighted by a supplier who can fulfil their wider needs. But growth is not automatically beneficial to the long-term prospects of the organization. Companies need to ensure that it is the right sort of growth and occurs in a controlled way. The wrong sort of growth can easily become dysfunctional and threaten the stability of the business. This is especially true of the bottom-up organization, which can all too easily be pulled in many different directions. Senior management has to provide an environment that stimulates new ideas for growing the business, while at the same time preventing the organization from spreading itself too thinly. The most effective way to do this is through growth catalysts.

Growth catalysts are organizational arrangements that energize the organization by providing a stimulus and outlet for bottom-up activity. This chapter reviews:

- common organizational arrangements that are employed to catalyse growth; and
- dysfunctional approaches that destroy value for shareholders, employees or customers, which must be avoided if bottom-up growth initiatives are to succeed.

Growth catalysts

In a bottom-up organization, growth can come from several different directions as shown in Table 4.1.

Table 4.1: *Modes of growth*

	Existing products/ services	New products/services
Existing geographical market	✓	✓
Existing customer segment	✓	✓
New geographical markets, same customer segment	✓	✓
New customer segment, same geography	✓	✓
New customer segment and new geography	✓	✓
Unrelated customer group	✓	✓
Existing channels	✓	✓
New channels	✓	✓

If these growth modes are to produce results, they must be supported by growth catalysts. Several corporate arrangements are used as catalysts to elicit growth within companies, including:

- strategic ambition;
- autonomy of units;
- breaking the rules of the game;
- stretching core competencies; and
- customer focus.

Strategic ambition

Strategic ambitions, typically pushed by shareholder expectations, often encompass growth objectives and bold goals. Since in most multibusiness companies the planning process is a mix between top-down and bottom-up process, there is a lot of room for business units to initiate growth projects under an "umbrella" of top-down-expressed growth objectives or goals. This umbrella can take different forms, for example:

- a specific growth objective expressed in sales, market share, return on asset or return on equity leaving the strategy to make it happen to the business units;
- a more qualitative "strategic intent", or mission, defining in broad terms what business(es) the company wants to be in and leaving the specific product(s) and market(s) definition to the business units.

Take for example the mission statement of ISS Group, a leading service company (mainly industrial cleaning) of 12000 employees based in Denmark. It reads as follows: "To manage and deliver ranges of high-quality services which add value for our customers and meet the need for clean, healthy, efficient and comfortable environment for people at work and at leisure."

This mission leaves ample opportunities for operational growth well beyond what ISS has been known for initially: cleaning offices. In the same vein, Disney has grown immensely under the umbrella of family entertainment – from cartoons to theme park, retailing, resorts, cruiselines, TV broadcasting and live entertainment.

Companies have also benefited from another way to spur on growth – through a vision of the future. Vision (i.e. the next dream) is another qualitative top-down contributing factor to eliciting proposals for growth. An ISS annual report defines its next dream as "To be the leading and most innovative international service enterprise." Leading can be interpreted as number one in market share. International can mean present in all markets etc.

A similar sort of approach has been used to good effect at General Electric (GE). When, in the 1980s, CEO Jack Welsh decided that for a business to be part of GE, it had to be either number one or number two worldwide, it provided enormous incentive to get proposals from the units to reach that dream.

Business unit autonomy

Autonomy of business units describes the relative autonomy given to business units to achieve overall goals or specific growth objectives. The autonomy is expressed in the specific products, markets, and customer segments that a unit may choose to develop within the broad context of corporate goals and strategic ambitions. The more businesses a company has, the more autonomy it typically gives. The bigger the company, the more autonomy will arise. Usually, provided profit, cashflow or other measure of economic performance are met within the broad definition of strategic thrusts, a business unit will be allowed to develop and grow continuously. It could even be argued that if a company wants to energize its organization, top management should have as big a span of control as possible (i.e. direct reports) in order to prevent the centre from interfering too much with operations – or saying no to new growth opportunities.

ISS, for example, has a corporate staff of 80 people to manage a 120 000-employee business. It fosters not only autonomy but also entrepreneurial freedom. In each country, for each business, the head of that business has the title of managing director and is more or less left alone to develop that business. As another example, the turn-around at the sports apparel company, Adidas, is due partly to its reorganization from a centralized, functional organization to a decentralized organization by global business units by sports category, and regionalization of sales responsibility. The company has tripled its sales over the last five years.

Autonomy is sometimes portrayed as creating unnecessary competition among the business units who fight for the same customer. However, all in all, favouring the independence of a unit has more advantages than drawbacks even if there is some cannibalization and overlap. This strategy is applied in e-commerce in what is called the "clicks and mortar" approach. By opening up a new competing Internet channel, retailers aim to increase their overall sales rather than substituting one channel for the other. At Gap.com, for example, you can buy clothes over the Internet. You may also buy them in the store or pick up at the store what you bought on Internet. The Internet site reinforces what is in the store. The store promotes the Internet site. In 1999, Gap.com added $100 million in sales to the company – and the store's growth has not declined.

Breaking the rules of the game

Another growth catalyst involves redefining the business. This can open up huge opportunities for new initiatives. Many companies are in mature sectors. Yet some of those companies achieve superior growth performance because they have broken the existing rules of the game. In the USA, Carmax, for instance, has broken the rules of the game for a car dealership by providing a "supermarket-like" self-service (no hassles from sales people) for used cars. Schwab has broken the rules of the game of brokerage (twice) by providing a low-cost, 24-hour service to investors first physically and now on the Internet. Chrysler and Renault broke the rules of car design by introducing the minivan, sales of which have grown eight times faster than the car industry as a whole. Virgin Atlantic Airways has made significant inroads in long-haul travel by providing breakthrough service in the airline industry, with new services on the ground as well as lower prices. A quantum leap in value can also come from new products (the 3M Post it note), or new business models (Dell direct).

Stretching core competencies

Every company has resources – including technology, physical or human assets or a customer base. Unless they are put in motion, those resources stay idle. Companies that develop skills in leveraging their resources in an active manner can open up opportunities for bottom-up initiatives. In this way they can add new products or services to their existing lines, new customer segments, or new geographical markets in their current business. As they grow and develop, some may go further and develop core competencies, i.e. capabilities that can be applied to new businesses. "Miniaturization" at Sony can be applied to home entertainment. But as a core competence it extends beyond the home, as exemplified by the company's current success with the portable PC and, perhaps in the future, mobile phones. For Disney, a core competence is story-telling, which provides a lever for new products.

> **CASE STUDY:-DISNEY**
>
> *Disney is in the business of family entertainment. However, one of its core competencies is story-telling. Leveraging that core competence fuels growth throughout the organization, as different units grab a story and conjugate it for their own business unit. The story-telling competence acts as a catalyst for developing new products and new markets. So what starts with a cartoon (film division) can then be used for a new show (theatre division), leading to a new parade or attraction in the theme park (parks division), which brings repeat customers. The catalyst creates new products in merchandizing (in the Disney Store business unit) bringing back customers for repeat purchases, and could end up being used in the rights division to develop merchandize for other manufacturers. In this way, the organization triggers new opportunities for all those business unit managers, energized by a core competence that they can use successfully for their own growth.*

A company that has developed these difficult-to-imitate competencies (often expressed in customer benefits terms that can be applied to different businesses) opens itself up to growth through diversification beyond the simple introduction of new products in the same market. By nurturing those core competencies throughout the organization – through bottom-up project work, job rotation, internal promotion, co-ordination between units, training, cross-fertilization and benchmarking – the company unleashes additional energy to grow and develop beyond its current limits.

Customer focus

Many companies have grown simply by spotting the complementary needs of their customers and trying to bring an operational solution to those needs. For example, a big share of the growth of Vivendi, an international leader in water and water treatment, has come from its work with municipalities. Towns have first asked the company to bring water. As Vivendi got to know how to do business with munici-palities, the company noted that they had other problems in managing city services – e.g. transportation, hospitals, jails, health – and little by little Vivendi proposed new services that were welcomed by the cities. This would not have been possible without a close relationship with the customers. This intimate knowledge that was fed back internally led to the new service proposal.

The closer a company works with its customer, and the more open it is to listen-ing to that customer, the more chances there are of finding growth opportunities. Only frontline and operational people in close contact can come up with those ideas. It relies on a customer focus being ingrained into the culture of a company, i.e. that the general attitude is to look at the company from the outside and not from the inside.

Dysfunctional approaches to growth

The five growth catalysts discussed above can be used to stimulate growth in bottom-up organizations. However, there are also a number of dysfunctional growth triggers to be wary of. Bottom-up organizations are particularly prone to divergent initiatives that spread resources too thinly. Growth catalysts focus energy, but dysfunctional growth triggers dissipate it. Dysfunctional growth methods include:

- creating short-term growth to boost short-term profits;
- investing in decreasing marginal returns on growth;
- pushing the growth umbrella too far;
- moving abroad because someone is willing;
- moving abroad without preparation;
- expanding vertically to control resources;
- stretching the mission; and
- excessive growth.

Creating short-term growth to boost short-term profits

A classic problem for companies is the desire to boost the bottom line in the short-term, without adequate thought about the longer term implications of growth. In some organizations, performance measures encourage managers to pursue initiatives that are ill conceived. Bottom-up organizations require senior management to create an environment that recognizes and rewards managers who display behaviour that fits with organizational goals. The organizational culture is critical. In a now-famous video, GE's Jack Welch distinguishes four types of managers:

- Type 1 is trying hard but does not get the results yet. He or she will be encouraged.
- Type 2 is getting the results with the long-term strategic goals and values of the company – he or she is a winner in GE's culture.
- Type 3 does not get results no matter what he or she does. Process is more important to him or her than performance. He or she is a loser in GE's culture.

- Type 4 gets results but does not care about the long-term goals, strategic fit, and the values of the company. He or she will be let go in GE's culture.

There are many Type-4 managers who, either for self-interest, or lack of vision, or both, will be tempted to follow that path. This behaviour is often observed before a company is sold or acquired. Promotions to boost traffic, short-term advertising which destroys image long-term, no investment in tomorrow's business, and cutting costs in customer service, sales training, IT investments etc. may boost short-term growth sales and profit but will result in longer term loss of value.

This type of value-destroying growth is the easiest to spot but the most difficult to stop especially if a company faces problems in other businesses and is happy to get some "cash cows". In fact in companies where people move fast from one job to another, from one country to the other, it is very difficult to keep track of who was responsible for what; the next manager often inherits a situation in which he or she has to continue a discount or promotion, or cut costs or reduce profitability for a while to put the business back on strategic track. Doing this can make the manager look bad. To avoid such dysfunction, Type-4 managers should be discouraged; track records should be kept after a manager has left and incentives can be given on long-term growth.

Investing in decreasing marginal returns on growth

Sometimes the way business units are set up, and the profit-and-loss responsibility attached to them, forces managers to look for pockets of growth with decreasing marginal returns. This is either because the market segments they seek are of smaller and smaller size, or the cost to get the extra growth points goes up. For instance, say the manager of a retail group in a particular country has a sole objective to grow his business profitably in that country. At some point, he could be tempted to invest in new stores in smaller and smaller catchment areas. Even if each new store meets ROI (return on investment) criteria, each store's positive contribution to the whole will be less and less. Capital budgeting projects are rarely, if ever, put on a worldwide list to get the best no matter what country they represent. Organizational responsibility often reduces the scope of analysis to the country area or division concerned. Avoiding such dysfunction requires discipline in allocating funds on the whole portfolio of business/regions rather than letting each unit reinvest.

Pushing the growth umbrella too far

In this case, an "umbrella" denotes a common denominator under which extensions of product lines are often proposed. As noted earlier, such an umbrella can positively energize a company and its business units to come up with new growth prospects. For instance, Virgin has used its brand as an umbrella to diversify into airlines, financial services, travel, cosmetics, and soft drinks. The thinking there is that the values, personality and character of the brand name will be a good vehicle to promote new consumer products. In the case of Virgin, playing the underdog, the newcomer, the unconventional, the beater of dinosaurs, and the pirate in new markets provides a useful umbrella. This audacity will presumably attract consumers and will, of course, be reinforced in advertising. However, abnormal growth may also arise from such a strategy if the umbrella becomes too small to shelter new product lines or when new product lines destroy the harmony of the umbrella.

The Club Med brand represents holiday resort villages. In 1990, the company bought an airline. Although no attempt was made in the beginning to put the same brand name on the acquisition, it was generally known that it belonged to Club Med. It did not work. In 1992, the company launched its cruise ships, Club Med I and II. One was sold in 1998 and the second one has been faltering. In this case, the umbrella brand did not work. This is probably because few customers who love Club Med for its resorts go on cruises, and perhaps because the core cruise customers have a negative image of Club Med as a brand.

Sony also provides a good example. The company misused its umbrella mission "home entertainment". In the 1990s, this umbrella led the company to acquire Columbia pictures with a resultant monumental loss. Sony discovered the hard way that managing entertainment through hardware (cameras, TVs, CD players) was not the same as managing entertainment through software.

The lesson here is that it is tempting to go one bridge too far – either by using the brand image as the umbrella or using the customer database or the salesforce. In the 1980s, banks started selling a lot of products through their branches. But with hundreds of different products, how can the agent and the counter clerk know all the products? The branch network, then, is too small an umbrella for so many products. Whether it is a brand, a mission statement, a core competency, or a goal, its scope should not be overtaken by individual projects. Only by continuous discussion of the umbrella – what it is, and what it is not – is it possible to qualify or disqualify growth prospects before they become failure.

Moving abroad because someone is willing

Reading companies' annual reports, it is common to discover that some of their international sales and marketing offices seem to be located not in mainstream countries but in seemingly isolated places. Often they will have set up shop in a small market before the big markets are covered. These offices may be too isolated, physically or culturally, to provide meaningful inputs or control. The explanations for such establishments are often to be found in accidental meetings between a senior executive and someone who was willing to start the business locally. We may see French retailers mentioning a store in the French West Indies or la Reunion, for example, even though they have not covered Toulouse or Bordeaux. Not only is this a distraction from mainstream investments, it can also be time-consuming.

CASE STUDY: GPS' ACQUISITION OF VISION EXPRESS

When GPS bought Vision Express – a UK retailer of prescription spectacles – the latter had a dispersion of stores: one in Russia, eight in Argentina, one in Germany, four in Sweden, six in the Philippines, five in Lithuania, nine in Latvia, six in Hungary, 20 in

Italy, 130 in the UK and 10 in Belgium. This simple description does not make the international strategy obvious. It wasn't. It had been developed by the founder of Vision Express as he was meeting people at cocktail parties and on planes. GPS' first job was to close stores in "odd" places and concentrate on fewer countries. Explicit criteria for selecting countries and modes of entry, and sticking to them, can avoid such problems.

Moving abroad without preparation

We have seen that lack of geographical focus can be the cause of uncontrolled growth. Another common problem can occur even when the right criteria markets and countries are chosen: if the move has been ill prepared, it can create chaotic (too slow, too fast, too soon) or unprofitable growth. Crossing borders requires some preparation in terms of knowledge of the market, competitors and ways of doing business. It requires the company to take its implicit domestic know-how and make it explicit in order to transfer that expertise, leading to an effective replication (and adaptation) of the successful formula that has existed in the domestic market. Does the company know where its expertise and know-how lies? Is it formalized in such a way that it can be transferred? Does it have people who are knowledgeable enough about the domestic operation, and open enough to local adaptation, to be sent abroad?

CASE STUDY: EURODISNEY

EuroDisney is an intriguing case of international growth with some hiccups at its start. Disney chose to open a theme park near Paris. Except for its CEO, who was a Californian and whose skills were mostly political, the top team came mostly from Disney's Florida theme park; most of the team consisted of seasoned, experienced Orlando executives. Altogether, there were some 300 expatriates. They brought with them their certainties and implicit acquired know-how, which they transformed into policies for the European version: high prices – we don't care about intermediaries to sell – our brand is strong – we won't serve wine with lunch – people eat all day – we don't need extra seats at restaurants. In this particular case, there was too much direct transfer and not enough adaptation without sharing knowledge or allowing locals to interfere. This resulted in a big loss during the first two years. Only when all expatriates were replaced by locals did the company start to adapt. Probably the seasoned executives had forgotten how it was when they started Orlando, and were "too seasoned" to listen and adapt. Sending younger blood from the USA – with a more open attitude might have served the company better.

Expanding vertically to control resources

There is a big temptation sometimes to grow by integrating backward or forward to control the value-added chain. However, this often results in less than optimal solutions. On the backward side, such growth ranges from creating simple in-house departments for printing, advertising, design and pay, to fully-fledged integration of suppliers. On the forward side, it ranges from a few retail spots to enhance the brand to fully-fledged distribution channels. How many airlines in the 1980s and 1990s created their own catering, their own hotel chains, resort spots, mostly without much success?

The logic beyond such moves – often implemented by acquisitions – is one of either control ("we cannot master our distribution and convey the right image to end consumers or keep price integrity or provide a total solution to the customer") or cost-reduction (especially when buying suppliers). However, in order to preserve the sales level that comes with such acquisitions, the integrated acquired companies or the in-house departments would need to have total freedom. In practice, however, they often have additional constraints: not to sell to competitors; an internal transfer price often not comparable to market price; a level of service to the parent which is not at its best (especially if there is no outside market). Again, if not mastered, this is a way to grow which does not lead to the best results. For the integration of the value chain to energize growth, its units really need to get as few corporate constraints as possible in order to continue to foster competitiveness. (Chapter 6 presents a more detailed discussion on how bottom-up organizations can get energy from value chain integration).

Stretching the mission

This situation is typical of retailers who cannot get extra sites or market share through geographical growth in their domestic countries. In such cases, they start to add new products and services to their offer. For instance, Carrefour cannot expand in terms of the number of hypermarkets in France. So beyond buying one of its competitors (Promodes) in 1999, it started getting into new fields that are remote from its basic mission: food, household products and appliances, and apparel. Thus it has diversified into jewellery, vacation and travel, financial services and, more recently, optics. Whereas, at corporate level, the strategic logic is leaning more toward investing in new countries (Far East, South America), from the standpoint of the general manager responsible for sales and profits in France, product diversification is his only avenue for growth. At some point, however, such a local all-encompassing strategy could create a backlash against Carrefour. An image of domination could arouse negative feelings from consumers; alternatively, diversification in domains where core skills are so different that it does not offer competitive advantages could result in less than optimal economic performance.

Excessive growth

Innovative growth is often fuelled by agreements that in themselves will lead to problems later. They include joint ventures, distribution, franchising or licensing agreements which allow a company to grow fast. So fast that at some point, it is not manageable. In its early developments, Benetton, through its independent agents, granted the right to sell its products to so many retailers that they ended up being on top of each other in the same street. On the positive side, it did a lot of free adver-tising for the brand with so much store frontage. On the negative side, catchment areas that were too small created problems for the retailers.

When the product is very innovative, it is tempting to be innovative in the market with distributorships. However when the market is inundated, distribution will tend not to invest too much in rigorous marketing as demand works by itself. Thus, after a while, growth is likely to stall because of a lack of marketing, logistics and selling investments. This process is happening now with mobile phone manufacturers.

 # SUMMARY

In the bottom-up organization, top management has to stimulate growth opportuni-ties by creating a meaningful frame of reference and stimulation for entrepreneurial activity. This requires the use of a growth catalyst – an organizational arrangement that encourages people to pursue growth. There are five common growth catalysts, that can be used to foster positive growth and increase long-term value:

- strategic ambitions;
- autonomy of units;
- breaking the rules of the game;
- stretching core competencies; and
- customer focus.

But there are also eight common dysfunctional growth triggers that are not catalytic and should be avoided because they destroy value:

- creating short-term growth to boost short-term profits;
- investing in decreasing marginal returns on growth;
- pushing the growth umbrella too far;
- moving abroad because someone is willing;
- moving abroad without preparation;
- expanding vertically to control resources;
- stretching the mission; and
- excessive growth.

 # BEST PRACTICE

By looking at what acts as a growth catalyst, and those factors that can create dys-functional growth, senior management can combine the catalysts to stimulate a con-tinuing flow of entrepreneurial initiatives (Figure 4.1).

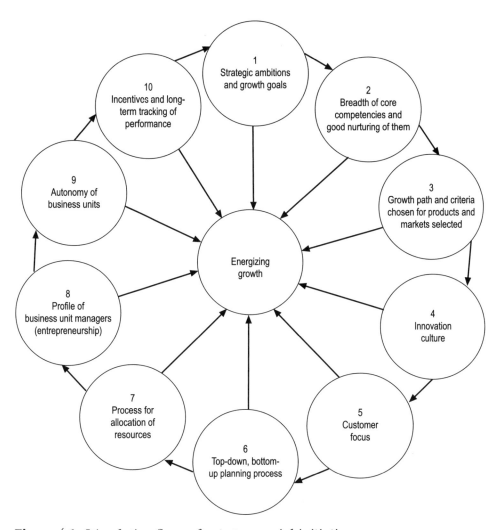

Figure 4.1: *Stimulating flows of entrepreneurial initiatives*

The key is to recognize that a bottom-up organization cannot be energized from the centre. Rather, the top management team should stimulate and challenge the wider organization to pursue growth initiatives by using appropriate strategic themes and/or organizational arrangements. To do so, senior managers have to take responsibility for the cultural assumptions and signals to managers – both formal and informal.

The vital steps in doing so are:

- setting growth goals;
- identifying core competencies;
- selecting growth paths and criteria;
- fostering an innovation culture;

- maintaining customer focus;
- a top-down, bottom-up planning process, including clear explanation of decisions;
- creating a transparent process for allocating resources to growth initiatives;
- identifying and rewarding entrepreneurial competencies;
- providing autonomy to business units; and
- creating and adjusting incentives and performance measures.

The enablers reinforce one another. The more of them in place the greater is the bottom-up energy.

5

Craft Networks

Craftwork is the application of personal know-how or tacit knowledge to create value (Nonaka, 1991; Nonaka, 1988; Polanyi, 1967). In this chapter, **Andy Boynton** explains how bottom-up organizations use the principles of craftwork to release know-how and energy in networks of knowledge workers.

CASE STUDY: CRAFTWORK IN ITALY'S BELLUNO PROVINCE

*To see craft at work in the new economy, go to Italy's Belluno province. This moun-
tainous region near the Austrian border produces many of the world's high-price spectacle frames. For generations, the people of Belluno have been making spectacles and
sharing ideas about the intricacies of spectacle frame design and production. If you
wear glasses by Liz Claiborne, Calvin Klein, Yves Saint Laurent or Giorgio Armani, the
frames were probably crafted in one of Belluno's small towns.*

*If estimates are right, the Italian province supplies 25% of the $2-billion market for
spectacle frames priced $100 and up – in the USA, Belluno has Luxottica Group ($1.7
billion in sales), Safilo Group ($270 million) and Marcolin ($75 million), as well as
some 800 smaller suppliers working in scattered alpine villages (Klebnikov and Morais,
1996). Today, the region's disparate, yet highly interconnected, network of small craft
manufacturers and their suppliers give the world what it wants: top-quality novelty
products or services at fairly reasonable prices. This re-emergence of craft is possible
because in today's new markets, novelty – style, innovation, and unique features – caps
the list of customer wants and needs. It also provides a powerful model for releasing
energy and knowledge in the bottom-up organization.*

Overview[1]

The origins of craftwork date back to early human history, when people first made
useful objects by hand. As civilized societies emerged, craftworkers fashioned lavish
goods for the wealthy and powerful. In the Middle Ages, craftworkers were instru-
mental in creating the cities and towns of Western Europe. This led to the rise of the
powerful guilds that shaped the years from the twelfth to the fifteenth centuries.
Highly skilled craftsmen such as carpenters, wheelwrights, masons, blacksmiths and
weavers were knowledge workers. They possessed the experience, intuition, insight,
and tools of their trade which allowed them to carry out work of unequalled quality,
intricacy and utility. They acted on their own initiative, providing a model of bottom-
up organization.

The technological developments of the eighteenth century, and especially those of
the late nineteenth century, led to a decline in the power of craftworkers and the
emergence of machines. But the unique and personally-owned knowledge and capabilities of the craftworkers were the forerunners of today's knowledge workers. Key
to craftwork is the recognition of the critical faculty of the person doing the work to
make judgements and observations about what is required – without unnecessary
interference from those above. Companies are energized through the empowerment
and networking of the modern day equivalent of craft workers – be they software
designers or customer service staff. At the same time, some use traditional craft skills
to differentiate their products from mass-produced alternatives. In both cases,

---

1. This chapter draws heavily on Boynton and Victor (1998).

rediscovering the culture and network environment of craftwork offers a key to the effective functioning of the bottom-up organization.

This chapter looks at:

- the return to craftwork;
- how to compete with craft;
- the ingredients of effective craft networks; and
- what comes after craft.

The return to craft

Today, firms are turning back to the competitive value of craftwork as an end in itself. To respond to changing and unique customer wants and needs, they are relying more and more on their workers' talents, experience, skills and intellects. In many industries the search for innovative, novel products or services is driving a return to the traditional craft culture. Ernst Thomke, a senior manager at Bally, the Swiss manufacturer of high-quality leather products, has this to say about craft: "Crafts-manship, labour, quality are in exquisite harmony when loving devotion is their common denominator. In a Bally wallet, this begins with the designer's inspiration, moves on to extreme care in the choice of leathers, and ends with perfection achieved by the meticulous execution of every single step involved in a traditional craft. The result for customers is a unique product that embodies all the values of a famous brand name."

Thomke's words may portray craft at Bally, but craft extends well beyond the Ballys of the world. Craft is thriving in many firms and economic regions where the skills, judgement and experience of people are creating unique value for consumers.

Novelty is increasingly important. The days of mass-marketing are numbered. Increasingly, companies succeed by offering tailored bundles of value to carefully targeted market segments. Whenever and wherever customers seek a combination of unique features, customized content, or greater variety of products or services, there is an element of craftwork involved. Automobiles, designer clothes, watches and jew-ellery, leather products, tools and machinery, financial advice, software, and consult-ing solutions are all examples where customers seek novelty in significant numbers. In many ways, the idea of market novelty is consistent with the classic market posi-tion of differentiation – often called "product or service leadership" – wherein a firm tries to garner a premium price with a product or service that customers see as unique, customized or otherwise valuable. Today, however, differentiation is as likely to come from a different level of service as from product features.

Craft is one way to close the gap between the increasingly diverse and turbulent demands of novelty markets and the capacity of individuals in a company, much of which may have gone untapped for some time. Where rules, procedures, standards or automation are great at creating standard, replicable products or services, firms meet the demand for a wide range of unique products in the novelty market by turning to the skills of their people. They leverage craftsmanship.

Companies are returning to craft in diverse places. Large financial institutions rely on the experience of a flexible, knowledgeable and skilled craft-like workforce. The firms find they can compete with craftworkers more effectively than by codifying rules and procedures that are rapidly obsolete. This application of craftwork is becoming more prevalent as the demands for personalized services, new markets, and regulatory upheaval increases. In major manufacturing firms such as Sony, craftsmen on the factory floor, with their flexibility and knowledge, are taking over the automated work of rigid machines. Boston's financial district and Japan's factory floors are a long way from the workshop world of Switzerland's Bally and Italy's Armani, but craft is emerging wherever people's skills are needed to create products, solve complex problems, or perform work earmarked by personal insights and intuition. Craft networks are at the heart of successful bottom-up organizations.

Competing with craft

But why is going back to craft the right move for so many companies today? It is precisely because the new, global markets are fiercely contested, highly volatile and – by virtue of their size – likely to be more profitable, that managers can win with the innovative, tailored solutions of craft. The primary challenge is to create value from a craftworker's personal know-how, often called "tacit knowledge". The trick is to connect people to leverage their knowledge and insights in the face of fast changing novelty markets. To take advantage of every ounce of a person's abilities, many successful firms today give their professional – or craft – workers a dazzling array of information technology tools: Internet search engines and push technologies, elaborate corporate intranets, powerful spreadsheets and graphic packages, and a dizzying array of personal information and time-management technologies.

Craftwork leverages tacit knowledge

Tacit knowledge results directly from craftwork. It is knowledge stored or bundled in an individual worker's mind, essentially a combination of experience, judgement and intuition. Tacit knowledge is a powerful resource for the individual, but is difficult to share. With tacit knowledge, craftworkers know more than they can tell. Like the skill one has to ride a bicycle, tacit knowledge is real but hard to describe. Such knowledge is gained through first-hand experience – learning by doing. As individuals work in a craft environment, they gain knowledge from doing, and the tacit knowledge accumulates. The individual figures out intuitively how to respond to shifting customer demands and diverse market needs using a set of tools at their disposal, senses the urgency to react to a novel market, and has the freedom and motivation to do so. The challenge for craft managers is to get the most from this individual expertise to drive bottom-up initiatives in their firms.

Three advantages of craft

Knowing how to use craft depends on understanding its three major advantages:

1. A craft worker is the ultimate sense-and-response mechanism.
2. Craft offers the most predictable and, perhaps, the most manageable form of learning.
3. Craft is the basis from which all organizational knowledge is created.

The ultimate sense-and-response mechanism

A craftworker's ability to address changing market conditions and meet the needs for novel solutions is the number one asset for a firm seeking a novelty position. The individual craftworker immediately senses a new production requirement, a different customer need, or a sudden exception to a rule (each of these representing a valuable opportunity or a potential loss). Drawing on tacit knowledge, the craftworker can organize an effective, timely response. This tacit knowledge enables individuals in the company to adapt quickly, then respond appropriately and flexibly to unique, unpredictable, changing market product or service requirements. The most responsive system yet devised is the human system; its ability to respond to the challenges of many markets is unparalleled.

CASE STUDY: BUCKMAN LABORATORIES INTERNATIONAL

Buckman Laboratories International, Memphis, Tennessee, is a speciality chemical maker that does business in more than 90 nations across the globe. These days, Buckman can no longer afford to ship carloads of standard product. The company has to offer fast, tailored, often unique solutions to specific customer needs. As a result, it provides its craftworkers with a well-designed electronic network to augment their personal skills and insights. Using a global web of electronic forums, virtual conference rooms, online libraries and e-mail, Buckman has been able to capture the collective experience of its frontline sales and professional workers and bring this experience to bear to a wide pallet of customer problems. This combination of leveraged experience, judgement and creative solutions gives Buckman the power the market seeks.

By accessing K'Netix through IBM PC Company's ThinkPad 755s, Buckman's frontline sales people can literally ask hundreds of employees across the globe any question, virtually around the clock. Buckman has leveraged its skilled craftworkers' knowledge for huge gains over the competition: experience has been captured and expertise has been shared. In short, the organization's craft experiences and skills have been leveraged effectively. Over the past decade, Buckman's sales have grown by 250%. Buckman did not rely on traditional sources of advantage by spending more on R&D, sales or a hiring. It grew because it became a smarter organization that knows more collectively about the customer and the market than its competition does.

The most predictable and manageable form of learning

As has been shown, craft rests on the idea that people learn by doing. Tacit knowledge is a cumulative process. The more tacit knowledge individuals in a company have, the better the company can respond to new market demands. A firm that connects and harnesses the tacit knowledge of its people innovates better and finds unique solutions. Clearly, this does not mean an either/or choice between people and computers. Both have advantages over the other. It simply highlights the point that different balances between the two offer alternative competitive advantages. Indeed, one of the mistakes made by western car companies in the 1980s was to over-automate their production facilities.

As people work, they get smarter. They develop better skills, intuition and judgement. As individual workers improve, the quality and efficiency of their work improves too. After several decades of experimentation with robotics and other automation technology, many Japanese industrial firms value their craftworkers more than ever before. At Toyota, for example, the new rallying cry is: "People are flexible, machines are not!" The reality is that computers do what we tell them to do. (In time, it is possible that artificial intelligence will begin to change this.)

Consider a typical management challenge facing a company: the company wants to improve its information capabilities. So it decides to buy a new information technology (IT) system. Consider what happens: the company struggles to pick the right system. But too many managers think that the right IT system will solve all their information needs. Time is lost. Money runs out. Ask yourself: which asset at the company will learn more quickly how to improve customer service under novelty market conditions – the craftworker or the computer? Which asset allows the company to respond better, not to preprogrammed demands, but to constantly shifting demands? Which asset senses an immediate, barely perceptible change in the market and adjusts itself accordingly?

Managing networks of craftworkers, with their focus on learning and knowledge creation and retention, is vastly different from putting a new IT system in place. Craftworkers learn from new experiences, adjust their responses and invent new solutions. This is impossible for a carefully codified computer-based information system. With the right person *and* the right IT system, firms discover new marketplace value. But the creation of that value begins with the individual craftworkers, and the manager's job is to help them mount the most effective response.

CASE STUDY: MONSANTO

The chemical and biotechnology company Monsanto discovered the value of using IT to support its networked communities of craft practice after it lost a major contract to a competitor (Maglitta, 1995; Stewart, 1995). Trying to understand what happened to make them lose the contract, managers at the company's St Louis headquarters learned something that stopped them cold: a sales representative halfway across the globe, in a completely different business unit, had overheard gossip about the impending contract loss, but time zone differences and various organizational boundaries had kept the knowledge secret until it was too late. Monsanto's management quickly spotted the problem. The knowledge of the contract shift was in the company, but no one could get to it. It sat in the head of one sales professional, not in the guts of the organization.

A pilot IT program was introduced to network hundreds of Monsanto's sales people who share gossip and news on a Lotus Notes database that is also used by the firm's major account executives and intelligence analysts. The database is modelled on work done by Ceregen, a biotechnology unit in Monsanto's $2.2-billion (1994 sales) agricultural group. Ceregen's online database is accessible to all of Monsanto's 6000 employees. As employees happen upon economic news, draft reports, or tap in notes about their work, they continuously update the system. Such knowledge has always existed in the firm, but now it is centralized rather than scattered, pigeonholed or otherwise hidden.

Monsanto has taken advantage of today's IT to create a network of knowledge that can be dipped into for higher worker productivity and deeper company knowledge. This knowledge doesn't dwell in hard-wired procedures and training manuals; it purrs in a repository of softer, tacit understandings of customers, competitions and new technologies. Like Buckman, Monsanto became a whole lot smarter by managing craftwork in an innovative and holistic fashion.

The basis from which all organizational knowledge is created

The point boils down to this: the storage of craft know-how is the essence of knowledge creation. It is the birthplace of new ideas. The demanding practice of a craft demands a lot of the individual workers. To make their work easier and more efficient, they want to accumulate knowledge. As work proceeds, they develop new approaches and routines, better judgement, and a feel for how a particular task should be accomplished. Craftwork therefore begets knowledge, which, in turn, is applied to the work at hand. The cycle is endless. It is the essential motor of the bottom-up organization. It is the force that energizes the company, animating it in a changing business environment.

CASE STUDY: OVERCOMING CRAFT'S LIMITATIONS: THE CASE OF CIGNA[2]

As we have seen, managers who understand the essence of craft can gain important competitive advantages. Take Cigna, the Philadelphia insurer. In 1993, the insurer's property and casualty division was a miserable performer, having lost $251 million from its active USA portfolio. This devastating loss occurred even though Cigna employed capable craftworkers who worked in close proximity to their customers. Missing from the firm, however, was a way to reuse and replicate valuable information. That's why Cigna decided to focus on seeking new ways to capture tacit knowledge within its network of expertise.

Cigna assigned home-office managers the additional job of building and maintain-

---

2. This case is based on Stoddard and Jarvenpaa, 1994.

ing a knowledge base, housed in the software each company underwriter used to process customer insurance applications. Now, for example, when a California nursing home inquires about coverage, a Cigna underwriter can call up the company's custom-built software, locate the nearest earthquake fault, and let the computer program tell them exactly what guidelines to use in assessing risk factors. As the claims department generates new knowledge, or as hardworking underwriters happen upon new insights, Cigna's home-office managers can now evaluate the information for possible reuse and replication. Information deemed important is programmed into Cigna's software.

The cost for the insurer has been small: company underwriters and claims officers are constantly generating new knowledge anyway. Home-office managers have adjusted their roles only slightly, and time invested in the project is minor. But the benefits for the company have been immense. The quality and efficiency of underwriting, perhaps the most critical and difficult process for an insurer, have both been increased greatly. In short, Cigna has converted tacit knowledge into property that is individually and communally owned. Under craft conditions, enlarging tacit knowledge is a firm's greatest challenge as well as its greatest chance for profit. At Cigna, that meant multimillion-dollar profits.

Effective craft networks

There are three keys to building effective craft networks. First, *hire the very best people* the market has to offer – and put them to work in close collaboration with each other in a tightly networked communities of practice. To succeed in any craft enterprise, a manager must hire the very best people, invest in their professional development, and create an atmosphere where they can survive and flourish.

Second, managers must create a context where excellence in personal achievement is the norm. The very best craftwork places become "*hot groups*": self-motivating, highly desirable, and highly productive collections of experts. Hot groups that attract and retain the best talent available, because to work anywhere else would be settling for second best, characterize all the leading high-tech firms.

Thirdly, the essence is creating truly *networked communities of practice* among the craftworkers. Communities of practice take shape over time. They develop as craftworkers pursue their work together, but management can encourage or hamper them. Within these communities, firms build up knowledgeable, social networks of workers who perform similar tasks and do similar work. At the centre of every community of practice are accumulated stories, collaboration and social networks. The resulting networked linkages allow tacit knowledge, previously locked in a craftworker's mind, to be shared by the larger community: language, stories, information channels and knowledge repositories can all be shared. Communities of practice can reduce craft's limitations, while increasing its possibilities.

Consider the situation in a large, service-driven insurance company. Everyday, the firm's service representatives handled a wide variety of service calls. Each representative had personal knowledge of the firm's products and services, and offered customers a sense of intimacy and comfort. This scene recurred whenever a customer approached the firm. Observing the firm's service representatives in action, it was clear that communications in the group were customer-driven and focused on solving problems. In essence, the firm's service representatives were craftworkers, responding to a novelty market. Often, these workers communicated by listening to stories and talking about similar problems. On more than one occasion, a service representative said, "Remember the problem you talked about last week? The one about insurance for the vacation home and rental property? Maybe your customer's problem is similar to that one."

In this insurance company, networked collaboration leads to collective action. No longer does an individual representative provide customer service alone. Each service representative has the time – and the network of all the insurance company's representatives take the time – to collaborate in resolving customer issues. Such collaboration may appear to be a naturally ocurring phenomenon and a fairly obvious feature of the work environment, but this network plays a significant role in a company's ability to take effective action. It may fall outside a firm's structure and outside the scope of a service representative's work, yet it can be leveraged for advantage.

Strength comes from networked social ties. The very fiber of a community of practice is its social network. Craftworkers share an understanding and a deep knowledge of the confusing, demanding world of their work. In the insurance company, for example, service representatives offer a large number of customer services. These services can change frequently. Each customer brings unique, complex demands. To succeed, the insurance company has to understand the nature of its community of practice: the service representatives have the knowledge that makes it possible for them to deal with complex problems in improvisational ways.

The insurance company provides its representatives with only a portion of what they need to know, so representatives must make do with whatever they have at hand. Often, they pick up the information needed to meet market demand in their social network, where they share stories and experiences, all with an eye to providing the kind of customer service the insurance company purports is its strategy. Individual workers become bound in a tight network of knowledge exchange, which provides the insurance company with additional resources and more capacity to meet market ambitions.

Beyond craftwork: leveraging the learning

Not every firm will find craft networks powerful as they are not applicable to every organizational process or critical activity. Nevertheless, tacit knowledge can be leveraged for competitive advantage whenever a firm needs bottom-up initiatives. If customers want novelty (products their way), if they require innovative services, or if they demand goods that follow new market trends, a smart company will consider a return to craft.

However, the product or service created by craftwork often becomes desirable to more people in more places than the firm can provide. The idea catches on, the product becomes a standard desire or requirement, and the orders and requests flood in. To this opportunity, the manager must bring something different from what even the very best craftwork can manage – scale, speed and low delivered costs. When the market shifts and the opportunity for rapid and large-scale growth presents itself, craft may no longer be the right capability at the right time. In such a case, if the craftwork has been well managed, the community of practice highly effective, and the tools well used, there will exist an immense and potentially valuable store of learning.

Craftspeople, with experience, learn more and more clearly how they do their work. With time and repetition, this learning goes beyond intuition, and becomes clear and simple in their minds. Such articulated knowledge can then be shared readily. Unlike the tacit knowledge that resides in sensing, intuition and skill, articulated knowledge is explicit and repeatable. Articulated knowledge can be described in steps and actions. When a master craftsperson teaches an apprentice the basics of cabinet making, or using graphic design software, he or she is communicating articulated knowledge. This articulated knowledge is a potential goldmine for the company that is prepared to gather and leverage it. With articulated knowledge, a new form of work is possible. This work can use the repeatability and clarity of articulated knowledge to bring scale economy and efficiency to the competitive arena.

 **SUMMARY**

Taking advantage of networks of skilled workers to resolve complex and strategic business challenges is at the heart of energizing the bottom-up organization. As the examples of Buckman, Monsanto and Cigna illustrate, firms can leverage craft knowledge to outpace competition. In each, IT helped capture the knowledge generated by craftwork. Craftworkers in these firms became more experienced and insightful. They became smarter. In other words, they captured the knowledge byproduct of craftwork, stored, codified and reused it, then reconfigured again and again. This process of capturing the knowledge as a byproduct represents a bottom-up approach to knowledge management. Craftworkers learn in communities via a process of osmosis. Technology offers both a conduit and a repository for that learning. Networked linkages also allow craftworkers to function as the eyes and ears of the bottom-up organization, attuned to changes in the market. Figure 5.1 shows this diagramatically.

The key to managing craftwork is to:

- Create truly *networked communities of practice* among the craftworkers. Within these communities, firms build up knowledgeable, social networks of workers who perform similar tasks and do similar work. At the centre of every community of practice are accumulated stories, collaboration and social

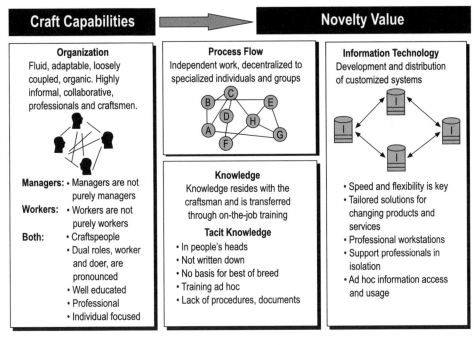

Figure 5.1: *Craft networks drive bottom-up value-creation*

networks. The resulting networked linkages allow tacit knowledge, previously locked in a craftworker's mind, to be shared by the larger community.

- Use technology to leverage craft knowledge. Technology speeds up the exchange of learning acting as a conduit to other parts of the organization, but also creating a repository of knowledge. Over time, smart craft leads to smart bottom-up organizations.

 **BEST PRACTICE**

The experience across hundreds of industries suggests it is possible to observe how communities of bottom-up practice develop over time, how managers support them or allow them to wither, and how they can add to a company's knowledge and its profit if given the chance. Experience suggests three factors enhance the ability of a community of practice to accumulate new knowledge.

Stories act like storage units

In networks of bottom-up initiatives, stories are a kind of organizational memory. The story represents the codification of individual knowledge and experience. With such codification, the service representatives in the insurance company example can draw on their fellow workers' knowledge. Each representative is then better able to meet customer demand over and over. Knowledge is reused and replicated, the first step along the path to greater market advantage.

Control by results, not process

Focus on the *results* of work, and propagate few rules or procedures to control how work is done. Managing for craft is allowing the talents of people to get the work done, and worrying about results first, second and last. Because it is impossible to predict the nature or pattern of a craftperson's work, a craftworker's job must be defined broadly and should be based on individual skills, experience and expertise. Such a job cannot be reduced to a narrow set of finite, definable tasks. A context needs to be created in which the natural variety of craftwork can be used to respond to a variety of market demands. The best people to decide how to do the work are the craftspeople, and it is important not to constrain their creative talents.

However, control over the quality of the outcome of the work is where the focus should be. By focusing control on output, not process, the talent of craft is unleashed to produce the best results possible. Only in this way can an organization acquire the depth and breadth of routines that will allow it to compete successfully in global novelty markets. Control under craft comes from the firm's shared understanding, not from organizational controls and procedures. Managers should encourage and enable workers' conversations. They should avoid dictating organizational responses to the market. Successful companies, instead, capitalize on their craftworkers' market adaptations. Control with craft comes through attention to workers' social context, not through a firm's typical levers of control, procedures and processes.

Build networked information channels around how people do work

Network information channels should be aligned and realigned to serve whatever work is at hand. At many companies, information-flow channels dictate who has access to important knowledge and who is allowed to respond to given market conditions. Under craft, these channels cannot be predetermined and predefined. They must be flexible, yet fast, individually constructed, yet efficient. The skilled craftspersons solving an engineering problem, building a complex spreadsheet, or running a simulation all have one thing in common. They must be able to get the information they need when they need, not the information the organization's systems and communication channels select for them. Craft requires information empowerment. Ten years ago, such a set of requirements would have been impossible to meet, so contradictory would have been the demands. But today, with the advent of the Internet and intranets, with their vast resources of information and people access capabilities, and software designed around group dynamics (groupware, client-server and object-oriented technologies), flexible information-channel design is possible. Such design is mandatory in a craft context.

References

Nonaka, I. (1991) The Knowledge Creating Company, *Harvard Business Review* **69**(6): 96–104.

Nonaka, I. (1988) Creating Order Out of Chaos: Self-Renewal of Japanese Firms, *California Management Review* **29**(3): 57–73.

Polanyi, M. (1967) *The Tacit Dimension*. New York: Doubleday.

Klebnikov, P. and Morais, R.C. (1996) Italy's Second Risorgimento, *Forbes*, April 22, 1996.

Boynton, A. and Victor, B. (1998) *Invented Here: Maximizing your organization's growth and internal profitability*. Boston: Harvard Business School Press.

Maglitta, J. (1995) Smarten Up! *Computerworld*, June 5, 1995: 84–86.

Stewart, T. (1995) Getting Real About Brainpower, *Fortune*, November 27, 1995: 97–99.

Stoddard, D.B. and Jarvenpaa, S. (1994) *CIGNA Corp., Inc.: Managing and Institutionalizing Business Reengineering, Case 9-195-097*. Boston: Harvard Business School.

6

Boundary-crossing Networks

Bottom-up organizations are continuously under pressure to satisfy the increasing expectations of customers. This means closer working relationships between customer and supplier, with a corresponding need for creative energy on the interface. In this chapter, **Thomas Vollmann** shows how to manage networks that cross company boundaries, so that they create greater value and competitive advantage.

CASE STUDY: EXXON CHEMICALS AND NEDLLOYD

The relationship between Exxon Chemicals and the trucking firm, Nedlloyd, illustrates the principle of boundary-crossing networks. The partnership started with an Exxon plant in Italy deciding that it was spending far too much time shopping around for trucking firms to transport chemicals from their plant to various destinations. The factory wished to form a partnership with one hauling firm to do all transportation of its products. This was not possible since no one firm in Europe covered all routes that were necessary for the outbound freight from this factory. But Exxon persisted, and finally asked Nedlloyd, a firm it had worked with closely over a number of years, to plan and co-ordinate all outbound shipments. This meant that Nedlloyd in turn had to contract with four other hauling companies to cover the routes that it did not already service.

The other hauling firms were initially nervous, but they are now quite satisfied with the arrangement. The prices are fixed, with only periodic negotiation. A number of cost drivers were identified and are recognized by all parties. If any of these change up or down by more than a certain percentage, then the prices are renegotiated. The value delivered, however, is not fixed. Exxon has several key performance indicators to measure the delivery performance, such as on-time delivery, cleanliness of the trucks, safety, and customer satisfaction. These have continued to increase over time, at no additional cost to Exxon. There is also competition among the five hauling firms to achieve best overall performance. These firms in turn are happy with the contract. They know what work they will have, and they are able to better anticipate the demand for their services. As a result, they have reduced clerical work, the selling is simplified, and they are able to better utilize their trucking fleets. Exxon has now expanded this approach with Nedlloyd to cover the outbound freight of all its European chemicals factories.

Overview

One of the most important reasons for energizing an organization is to better satisfy customer needs. What this often means in practical terms is better linkages with customers – including business process re-engineering of processes that cross company boundaries. Thus when Albert Heijn, the largest Dutch retailer, asked Heineken to deliver beer in 24 hours instead of four days, the two firms needed to re-engineer the processes that connected them. This required new information systems, new internal processes at Heineken that do not follow functional organizational lines, and new ways of selling and buying in both firms.

This chapter explores the major issues facing companies as they implement supply/demand chain management to create talent networks across organizational boundaries. To do so, it focuses on the following five questions:

• What is supply/demand chain management, and what are the leading edge practices for achieving major breakthroughs?

- How is demand chain management linked to market segmentation, and what are the implications for creating new relationships with key customers?
- What is outsourcing all about? How should this popular concept be seen in the right context for a particular firm?
- What are the changes in information systems and other supporting infrastructure to achieve true demand chain management?
- What are the new roles – ways of working – in the traditional functional areas most impacted by demand chain management?

Supply/demand chain management

The term "supply chain management" is used by a growing number of businesses as they seek to connect various activities associated with the flows of materials from the suppliers on to the customers. It assumes that the focus is in one direction. But this view is shortsighted in several ways.

Supply chain management starts from the suppliers and moves forward to the customers. Demand chain management, on the other hand, starts from the customers and moves backwards through the selling organization to the suppliers. The difference is much more than semantics. In the demand chain approach, the explicit needs of particular customers (segments or individual) are recognized. These needs become the fundamental driving force for the bundles of goods and services that are produced by each player in the chain (Figure 6.1). Because the driving force is customer needs, it is understood that these needs are not static. In fact, the upstream players in the chain should be continually searching for improvements that allow end consumers to become more satisfied – and all firms in the chain to become less vulnerable to

Demand chain management starts with the customers and works back

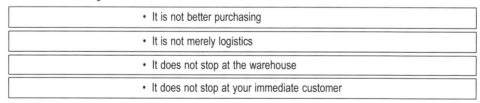

• It is not better purchasing
• It is not merely logistics
• It does not stop at the warehouse
• It does not stop at your immediate customer

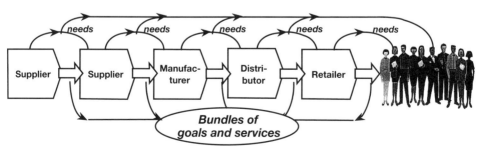

Figure 6.1: *Demand chain management – the critical difference*

competitive threats. This is illustrated in Figure 6.2, where the multitude of relations is depicted. Here it should be clear that the common view of competition (one business unit versus another) is shortsighted. In fact Figure 6.2 shows how chains compete for the final consumer. Chain competition means that the firms linked in a chain become mutually dependent. As a result, zero sum thinking between customer and supplier needs to be replaced with collective/co-operative thinking. Figure 6.2 also illustrates another important issue. The multitude of relations means that each firm needs to select those on which it chooses to concentrate. Customer partnering is a grandiose idea, but in reality a company needs to choose a small number of suppliers and customers with whom it can invest the time and organizational energy to form true partnerships (10 appears to be a practical maximum).

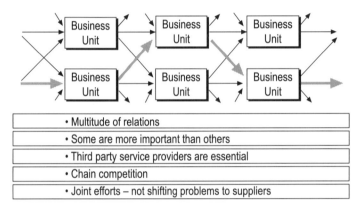

Figure 6.2: *Demand chain management – moving up the value chain*

From supply chain to demand chain management

Demand chain management requires major changes or transformations. The term can be defined by saying that transformation is not about just doing the same things better; although necessary, it is not enough by itself. Transformation requires organizations to do better things. This involves breaking out, to change the rules, to set up new relations, and to focus on those improvements that will create long-term dominance in a marketplace. In demand chain management, this implies new ways of working with suppliers and customers, a focus on how the chain can compete, and a keen understanding of what kinds of improvements will create major advantages – either in cost-savings or in value-creation.

Transforming a demand chain requires a combination of strategy and infrastructure. It is necessary to know clearly what you wish to achieve in a partnership (not some vague ideas of mutual friendship). But then it is necessary to do the hard work of changing the detailed infrastructure to turn the strategy into reality.

In the Albert Heijn–Heineken example, Heineken needed to change the ways it processed orders, scheduled production, planned physical distribution, and invoiced Albert Heijn. Similarly, Albert Heijn had to change the way information was collected from its retail stores, how that information was collated before passing it to suppliers, the ways goods were received in its warehouses, and the processing order receipts. Both firms needed to change jointly the way one sold and the other bought. Negotiation became a periodic process, rather than an ongoing one. "Ordering", as such, ceased. Forecasting was replaced by explicit knowledge of what is needed downstream, and salespeople no longer push excess inventories into the pipeline at the ends of accounting periods.

Demand chain partnering as a staircase

The relationship achieved with a particular supply or customer partner needs to be seen as a logical progression or series of transformations. That is, some things need to be done before others, providing a base or platform for the next step. Figure 6.3 shows an example – a large, multinational firm wishing to develop a regional approach to its supply/demand chain management. The figure shows the series of transformations the multinational and one of its major suppliers go through in a process that lasts several years.

Figure 6.3 begins at the bottom where the customer firm wishes to consolidate its purchases for Europe with one supplier, which will supply 18 plants in Europe. The action is consolidated purchasing, and the objective is to reduce purchasing cost. For it to be worthwhile for the supplier, the action on its part must achieve economies of scale. The two actions and the two objectives – if achieved – result in a win–win situation. The mechanism for achieving this result requires only a minor extension to the traditional purchasing–sales approach.

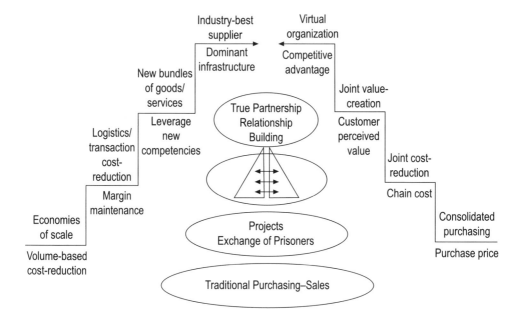

Figure 6.3: *The transformation stairstep: subcontracting to partnership*

But after the initial partnership achievements on both sides, the question becomes "What's next?" For the multinational customer, perhaps the next logical action is joint cost-reduction, with the added objective of reducing chain cost. For this to be viable for the supplier, the action might well be some combined work on logistics/transaction cost-reduction, where the supplier also wishes to maintain its profit margin. That is, the two firms work together to take cost out of the chain – but this is not achieved by squeezing the supplier's profit. In order to accomplish this objective, the mechanism now needs to be joint work on projects aimed at the total cost of the chain. Each firm sends someone to work full-time at the other company for a period in order to redesign the processes and information systems, which connect the companies. This is often called an "exchange of prisoners".

Figure 6.3 shows two more steps on the staircase: their action programs, objectives, and mechanisms for achieving them. The key point is that true partnerships require an aggressive improvement agenda, which in turn needs to be based on a well-co-ordinated series of transformations. For participating companies the energy comes from focusing on what *we* need to do – not what *they* need to do.

Cost savings plus value enhancements

So far, the focus has been on achieving a series of transformations to reduce the overall costs in the chain. But it is equally desirable to develop transformations that increase the value provided by the chain. Some of these include ways to speed new product development, such as working with customers in early supplier involvement. Here, the design knowledge and other competencies of the suppliers are leveraged in the design stage – rather than using the traditional process where the customer specifies exactly the work to be carried out by the supplier.

Another example of working on value enhancement is to create a wider variety of bundles of goods and services – those where the particular needs of customers are better satisfied. Instead of a "one size fits all" approach, solutions are customized for each major customer. So although a jar of brand-name coffee might be exactly the same on the shelf of two competing supermarkets, the bundles of goods and services that support the product delivery (e.g. ordering, invoicing and delivery) could be very different. Similarly, in a recent example when a major hotel chain asked a telecommunications firm to provide a worldwide contract for telecom equipment, this required a customized solution. The solution implies a different way of selling, a unique sales support mechanism, a logistics approach to support the unique customer needs, a field service mechanism, changes in manufacturing, and even new approaches to purchasing. In fact, a unique, customized demand chain was required.

In the long run, value enhancement needs to be seen as a desire to help your suppliers and customers make more money. This ensures that the best suppliers and the best customers will wish to work with you – and not with your competitors. If your firm in turn can partner with the smartest and most demanding customers, it will learn faster than the competitors. The only proviso is that the demanding customers need to demand the right things – not just price reductions with no interest in taking the actions to create price reductions. Smart partners know the differences between prices, costs and margins. Margins need to be preserved. Chain costs must be reduced. Prices become the passenger – not the driver.

Transportation cost

Many firms mistakenly believe they are minimizing transportation costs when they play one transport carrier off against another creating a fierce competition among their suppliers. Nothing could be further from the truth. In fact, transport vehicles are much more efficient when not running half-full, and if the planning for these vehicles can be consolidated and planned with some time discretion, major savings can be achieved. For example, Skanska, the Swedish construction company was able to reduce the costs of in-bound freight to its building sites by 45%, by consolidating all transport with one trucking company and by providing a few more days of advanced planning information to their supply chain partner companies.

Demand chain management and market segmentation

Demand chain partnering needs to be seen in a strategic context. The choice of partners and the way in which demand chains are exploited for mutual benefit is central to how firms need to compete in today's marketplaces. But making these choices – and living through the necessary changes – exacerbates centrifugal forces.

Choosing customer partners

A firm's choice of customer partners is more complex than just working harder with its largest customers. To get organizational energy from the relationship it is vital to choose smart – rather than stupid – partners. It may sound unduly harsh to talk about customers in such unflattering terms. But there are plenty of examples of stupid partnering. Here are some sure signs of partner stupidity – to be avoided:

- Customers that only want to discuss prices are not serious partners.
- If all the work is to be done by one side, instead of joint business process re-engineering, the payoffs will be small.
- If the customer wants the supplier to install consignment stocks – to cover its own ineptitude and lack of planning – this will not produce good results.
- If a customer cannot execute flawlessly – meet the schedule, quality standards and planning horizon required to plan/co-ordinate information systems linkages, and guarantee no surprises – then anyone who partners with such a company will end up paying for the mistake.

The choice of which suppliers and customers to partner with implies a commitment of time and resources. This requires a considered decision. In some cases, it is not from the largest customers that a supplier can learn the most. In other situations it is important to classify, or segment, customers. This might involve one group of large customers which allows the firm to keep the equipment occupied and another that offers some interesting possibilities for developing the competencies for the future.

The link to market segmentation is illustrated by the following example: a food ingredients manufacturing company was interested in demand chain management. Each of the marketing and sales units in the individual business units were asked to identify what they saw as the key challenges facing them. In particular, what did they need to do to win the orders? which customers were most important? and why? The first business unit to respond was one producing a series of speciality chemicals for the flavouring of many food products. Its immediate answer was that the most important challenge came from a particular customer that was now entering the European market. This firm was the dominant player in the US market – and many people expected it to similarly dominate the European market before too long. It was now working with 15 suppliers in this part of the business, but wished to reduce the supplier base to three or four. The business unit of the food ingredients supplier wished to be one of these preferred suppliers.

The desire to be selected was based not just on the volume of the account. This was a "smart" customer. It was asking the right questions, such as:

- Tell us your cost drivers through activity-based costing and we will find ways to work with you to reduce your costs (naturally, we want to have a share of the savings).
- We wish to have uniform application of your flavouring so that our entire product has uniform taste and we use a minimum of material. We want to work with your R&D people to achieve this result.
- We want you to formulate the flavourings for our products with ingredients having low-price volatility. In this way you will not be coming to us with unpleasant surprises based on your costs of operation.

The most interesting aspect of working with this company is that the demand chain necessary to best support this smart customer was not at all the same as that required in other business units. Each of these business units needed to define the marketplace – as *it* saw it – and thereafter to define the appropriate demand chain to support it. This is especially true of the dictate of flawless execution. The ingredients manufacturer needs to execute flawlessly in *every demand chain*. If it cannot do so it becomes a "stupid partner".

Moving up the value chain

Another form of market segmentation is seen in the case of companies that take on more and more of the activities that were formerly performed by their customers. For example, telecommunications firms used to sell to regulated monopolistic customers. These customers knew a great deal about telecommunications technology and could combine equipment from multiple sources, fix operating problems, and anticipate their technical needs. But today there is a different class of customers for the telecommunications companies. There are new players who wish to put up mobile phone networks in the newly deregulated telecom environments. These firms do not know a telephone switch from a refrigerator – and do not care. For them, the telecom firms need to move up the value chain, providing a new bundle of goods and services. It is the Nokias and Ericssons who need to decide what is to be in a base station, where to put them, what kind of antenna to put on top of a church or mountain, and when expansions need to be made. Moreover, these telecom firms need to understand the different objectives of the customer segments. The state monopolies had plenty of money; to the newcomers, cash flow is everything.

CASE STUDY: A MEDICAL EQUIPMENT COMPANY

Another example comes from a company in the medical equipment business. At one time, it sold X-ray machines to the radiology technicians in a hospital. Now the machines are sold to a business manager who first wants to know: How much does it cost? What is the economic life? What is the payback? Will you finance it? Next he wishes to know: Will this piece of equipment include information systems that link to patient record keeping and patient billing? Does it integrate with the scheduling of patients and other pieces of hospital equipment? Next questions include: Is the X-ray data in digital form that can be integrated with other data for disease diagnosis? And finally, if we are sued for malpractice, will this equipment help us keep a digital record that could form the basis of a good practice referral?

Again, the result is new segments and new requirements to satisfy them. The competencies, resource base, and talents required by the key employees needed to shift dramatically. At the same time they needed to decide what they no longer needed to do themselves. The firm here defined a series of 11 noncore technology clusters, and they are presently developing partnerships with suppliers who can in turn move up their value chains. The supply partners in the noncore technology clusters will - over time - need to develop their abilities to work with the medical equipment manufacturer at the product design concept level.

Moving up the value chain means developing the resources and competencies needed for the new market segments. It also implies outsourcing (see below). Essentially, moving up implies new requirements, but it also implies focusing on those most important. The firm that moves up needs to also decide what present activities can be successfully provided by others. If not, the firm runs the risk of spreading itself too thin.

Seeing customers moving up the value chain has profound implications. The most important include:

- If your customers shift up, then you will probably need to do so as well.
- The bundles of goods and services you provide can change radically.
- The bundles become increasingly unique.
- Each player in the chain needs to define his or her core competencies.
- The interdependencies in the chain are increased.
- There are higher switching costs for each firm to change partners.
- This implies a strong need for the partnership to function well - and fairly.

- Each firm will need to change its ways of working.
- The information and other infrastructure needs will also change significantly.

Outsourcing

Outsourcing also needs to be seen in a strategic context. Outsourcing of production competencies is very different to outsourcing the company cafeteria. One needs to understand the key difference between outsourcing and subcontracting. In the former, one gives up the assets, the people, the infrastructure, and the competencies. That is, outsourcing implies divestiture. Clearly the process of implementing outsourcing decisions creates tension on the frontline, which can sap the energy of the organization. The impact on those people who are no longer required (as well as those who stay and those who are added) is severe. In order to chart the right course for outsourcing, it is important to clearly understand and share the particular rationale for the decisions made – which tend to be unique depending on the situation faced.

CASE STUDY: OUTSOURCING DECISIONS AT DUPONT

One of our first examinations of outsourcing practices came from a request from the European headquarters of DuPont. A senior executive was concerned because in the American plants a particular activity was considered "core" business – so it was not under consideration for outsourcing. But at the same time, several European facilities had concluded that the same activity was "noncore" and therefore should be outsourced. Pursuing this issue led to the conclusion that the core–noncore issue can be overly simplified. Deciding what to retain and what to outsource is indeed an important idea, but equating this to core–noncore can result in tautological conclusions.

In fact, it does make sense for one business unit or division to outsource an activity and another in the same company to not do so. To some extent the issue comes down to choices as well as to the marketplace faced. If the customers are moving up the value chain, then it is necessary to follow and deliver the enhanced bundle of goods and services. This, in turn, leads naturally to deciding what can be outsourced. The outsourcing decision is also based on the availability of suppliers who can readily provide an activity currently done internally. If there is no good supply alternative, then the decision for outsourcing is moot.

There is also a question of economics in these decisions. In some cases, the particular activity is not in itself of great interest to the firm, but because the quantity of this work is so high, there are large economies of scale. Transportation issues may also influence the outsourcing decision. If the product is bulky, or there is a great deal of it, or the suppliers are a long way from the company, then outsourcing may not be a viable alternative. Finally there is a definitional issue involved in all this. In the case of DuPont, one activity being considered for outsourcing was compounding of polymers. The key question becomes: What is compounding? In some markets, compounding was becoming the way to deliver "designer plastics", while in others compounding was a routine mixing of ingredients into standard products.

CASE STUDY: OUTSOURCING AT A MEDICAL EQUIPMENT COMPANY

Take the example of the medical equipment company discussed earlier. A closer examination of the outsourcing decisions reveals the centrifugal forces at play. The original rationale for outsourcing was not as clear as it became over time. At first, the company wished to reduce complexity - and decided that buying assemblies instead of individual parts would accomplish this objective. They also believed that their manufacturing operations were saddled with high overheads, and that through outsourcing they could reduce these costs. The decision of which suppliers to partner with was based on asking those suppliers with the most complex/expensive parts to deliver the entire assemblies instead.

This approach undermined the commitment and energy on the frontline. The response of the workforce was highly negative, since the outsourcing seemed aimed at replacing their work by work performed by less expensive suppliers. Whether the quality would be equal was a subject for long debate. More importantly, the company truly underestimated the efforts necessary to transfer implicit knowledge to the suppliers. For example, the company assumed that the supplier could assemble with no problems - when in fact expertise in assembly operations had been developed over a long time period. The purchase of required components was another problem: the supplier could not obtain the same terms as the medical equipment company, but taking on the procurement of all components severely compromised the concept of buying assemblies. Complicating things even further were incompatibilities between systems in the two companies for computerized design and manufacturing. In fact, the supplier firm had to increase their design competencies dramatically in order to perform as needed. Finally, there was an entire set of issues associated with the bill of materials - who designs it, maintains it, and for how long? - maintenance parts, and life cycles.

The beacon of light in this example came from stepping back and developing a set of explicit outsourcing policies. That is, it was necessary to codify and clearly communicate a strategy for outsourcing - one that begins with the marketplace. This led to defining the shift up the value chain of the customers, and the needed response by the medical equipment manufacturer. This view allowed the company to identify what was, for them, core and noncore. In fact, it was more the question of what was noncore than what was core - which was most helpful. This involved searching questions such as do we really need to make display devices? should we be in the metal cutting field? is this technology medical or nonmedical? is our competitive advantage based on this technology? can we find good (smart) suppliers for this technology?

The outsourcing policies were designed, and a set of implementation steps was articulated. In essence, the implementation was seen as a staircase process, where key changes were necessary for both the suppliers and the medical equipment firm. Over time, the company wished to form partnerships where the supplier would pass through four critical transformation stages: first, the supplier would work from detailed item specifications. Here the drawings and specifications for individual parts now made internally would be given to the supplier and the task would be to duplicate the parts. In the second stage, the supplier would develop the bill of materials for assemblies and their component parts. The third-stage transformation was for the supplier to design major modules of the products. Here, the only instructions given to the supplier are the functional requirements of the module in support of the overall requirements of the particular product. Finally, the suppliers were to develop the ability to work at the functional specification stage, where product ideas are conceived and converted into the major modules to be produced by the suppliers.

The changes required by both suppliers and customer in climbing this staircase are enormous. They are ongoing, and the medical equipment manufacturer has had to tame their original enthusiasm for outsourcing. They have had to develop processes for qualifying suppliers, for thereafter evaluating success, for finding new ways to work together, and finally for updating their thinking on the outsourcing policies themselves. In some cases it has not been possible to follow the staircase model. Moreover, the existence of suppliers who meet the criteria is very limited. This turns out to be more of a supplier development approach than a supplier evaluation approach.

Information systems to support boundary-crossing

This section addresses the practical aspects of supporting boundary-crossing networks. It is a good idea, but how do you actually do it? Unfortunately, the answer is with a great deal of hard work. It is necessary to change the ways in which people work in companies, and to change the underlying infrastructure – in this case, the information systems. Too many individuals mistakenly believe that if they integrate information within their company this will enable them to integrate the flows of information through the demand chain. This is just not the case. Figure 6.4 shows the problem many companies face. They have an material requirements planning (MRP), manufacturing resource planning (MRPII) or enterprise requirements planning (ERP) system, such as those shown as operating in the customer and supplier of Figure 6.4. With this approach, how long does it take for a problem in manufacturing in the customer company to be compensated for in the supplier firm? With this up-over-down system the answer is usually "weeks". In fact, the boundary-crossing approach is to connect the two firms in their execution systems – as shown by the dotted relationship in the bottom of the figure. This implies a response in minutes or hours rather than days or weeks.

Customer-driven systems

Demand chain management requires a unique bundle of goods and services for each market segment. One part of the bundle is the information systems that support the unique bundle. In today's highly competitive environment, customers are receiving ever more highly customized bundles of goods and services. Another way of saying this is that the number of unique market segments is rapidly increasing. Being able

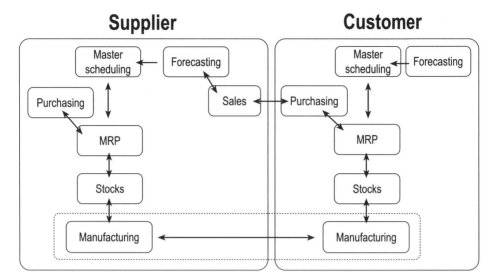

Figure 6.4: *Transforming the information flows to eliminate up-over-down processes*

to accommodate these diverse demand chains requires a highly flexible approach to the design of information systems. Moreover, since one mark of best practice in demand chain management is an aggressive improvement agenda, expect constant evolution in the bundles. Many times the improvements will focus on better information linkages between the companies in the demand chain.

Being able to provide highly customized information system linkages between companies is not an easy task. The requirements are often very different to those associated with preparing summary analyses of historical results. In demand chain management it is often necessary to plan and co-ordinate very detailed flows of materials. For example when a car manufacturer works in the just-in-time (JIT) mode with their supplier of seats, the approach is not only to pass along long-term forecasts of demand – or even the expected usage for the next week. Proper JIT requires that the automobile manufacturer continually communicates the exact build schedule – something like 35 hours out – to the key suppliers. The seat manufacturer is not told how many green seats are required next week, but the sequence – green, blue, blue, red etc. The seat manufacturer does not pull these from inventory, but makes them and delivers them in exact sequence. The worker on the line picks up the next seat in his or her stack of seats: it is blue: here comes a blue car. This mandates flawless execution in both firms – as well as the information systems to support it.

The building system at VW will be different from that at Ford. So will the supporting information systems. The seat manufacturer for the two plants needs to be able to respond to both sets of requirements – and to be able to understand the summary resource requirements for his factory. This implies a robust information system and an ability to interface with many kinds of other information systems. For the customers, they also have to meet certain requirements for the design of their information systems (in addition to executing flawlessly). The signals sent from the customer to the supplier need to be clear, unambiguous, and readily translatable into the supplier information systems. Both firms need to operate with a continuous improvement concept. The demand chain should be continually enhanced, with chain cost being reduced and customer perceived value increased.

Front-office systems

One way to clearly see the boundary-crossing advances in information systems is to consider the rapidly growing set of information systems that better connect firms to their customers. These tend to be called front-office systems, as opposed to back-office systems, which run things inside the company. The increasing use of Internet technology here allows customers to do business 24 hours a day in ways that support unique needs. Thus, for example, a camera manufacturer has an Internet site that can be addressed by the person whose camera needs repair. Through a set of user-friendly questions and pictures, the exact camera model can be identified, as well as the problems the user is having with his or her camera. In a significant number of instances, the owner can repair the camera simply by following directions. When this is not the case, the owner is told exactly where to send the camera. When it gets there, the problem diagnosis has already been done – and any new parts could have been pre-requisitioned. The net result is that the camera can be repaired in far less time, with higher productivity of the repair staff. Moreover, the patterns of necessary repairs can drive design improvements in the next generation of products.

There are many other examples of Internet-based front-office systems, including home shopping. A large increase in this market segment is inevitable, and firms clearly need to develop their long-term thinking/strategy for how best to use this information technology. The choices also imply additional kinds of potential boundary crossings. For large consumer products companies, it may or may not make sense to go into electronic shopping with home delivery on their own. It well may be that some kinds of alliances will be the best channel in these markets. The players could well include the post office/package delivery services, which have existing systems and infrastructure for the physical delivery as well as for the billing mechanisms. Another player might be the large petroleum station chains that could provide a convenient pickup point for the customers to collect their orders. Still another might be the major supermarkets, who already have the variety of products, which facilitate a large choice for the consumers.

But these ideas also make sense for business-to-business selling. The passing of paper orders – or even orders by connected information systems – does not make sense for all customers. If the order volume is not too high, again Internet ordering makes a great deal of sense. This approach can be configured to be interactive so that the order is received – in full and correctly the first time. This is often a rarity with existing information systems in many companies. For example, at one telecom company, the time from when an order is first started until it is correctly received at the factory is often in excess of 40 days. There is just no reason for this, and the costs to the demand chain – are far too high.

Implementing robust information systems

The demands are severe for implementing information systems that support highly individualized ways of dealing with customers and suppliers. The objective is to create a series of highly effective demand chains which allow our customers to find *us* easier to do business with than any competitor. But a series of demand chains – particularly one that is continually evolving – requires ongoing work on information systems to support these demand chains. This cannot be done without some repetitive use of information systems, or at least elements or modules of those systems.

In fact, the task is not too unlike that facing the manufacturer of specialized machines for the printed circuit board industry. There the design needed to be seen in modules, where particular modules or building blocks are assembled to create a specific machine to serve a market niche or customer need. In the case of information systems, it is necessary to develop some system building blocks or approaches where we can be fairly robust in terms of the ways to interface with customer requirements. At the same time, if *we*, acting proactively, define a set of ways to connect efficiently to the information systems to achieve individualized sets of demand chain benefits, then perhaps the customers and suppliers will work with our design concepts for how to support demand chain boundary-crossing.

Another maxim for the company concerned with highly customized demand chain relationships is to avoid long-run development of monolithic systems. In today's world, many companies have indeed found it necessary to implement large ERP systems, in many cases to overcome the Y2K problems. But any system that takes several years to implement is bound to end up solving yesterday's problems – not today's, and certainly not tomorrow's. Don Marchand, author of Chapter 13, recommends what he calls a six-by-six approach: no information system project should take more than six months to implement, nor more than six person-years of effort. Software packages are the absolute preferred solution, and the information systems group needs to have the competencies to be able to implement virtually any package with ease.

New roles and ways of working

The last major question facing firms as they implement demand chain management is how to deal with the new roles and ways of working that are required. The changes are significant, and implementing does not occur without stress and pain. At the end of the day, boundary-crossing networks require new thinking and serious "unlearning" before energy can be unleashed to create value.

New thinking

Perhaps the most profound change in boundary crossing networks based on demand chain concepts is in the ways people need to think about the objectives. The suppliers and customers are not adversaries. They are partners and all need to work for their collective good. It will never be possible to eliminate totally the competitive/adversarial relationships, but it is important to try – hard. Zero sum thinking is just not useful. The double objective is always to reduce the costs in the overall chain and to increase the value generated by the chain. It requires that 99% of the attention and effort be devoted to making a bigger pie and only 1% spent on deciding who gets what share of it. Conflicts are to be expected in any relationship. They should not be avoided or papered over when they occur. Rather, they should be viewed at least as potential learning experiences. Mechanisms need to be put in place for conflict resolution, so that the people feel that whatever problems come up can be solved equitably.

Price needs to be seen for what it is. Price should become the passenger, not the driver. That is, the partners should all make adequate margins, which makes the price the result. At the same time, for this to occur, the partnership needs to create better value for the price paid by the end consumer. This is the promise of demand chain management: all partners should be able to make better margins in this relationship than in others. They *need* to, since the partnership requires hard work. But the work should pay off. It should be more competitive than alternative demand chains, because this chain works smarter than others do. Moreover, the others will catch up, so it is necessary to stay ahead by continually improving the cost and value performance of the chain.

The focus on cost instead of on margins means that it is necessary to model the costs and benefits of the entire chain. The partners in the chain need to see clearly how actions in one part of the chain affect the results in others. It is also important to focus on non-value-adding activities for the entire chain. The key question to be asked continually is whether some activity adds value from the end customer point of view, or if it is merely there because the partners do not trust each other to do what is necessary. A related question often raised is how are cost savings to be divided among the partners in the chain? There can be many schemes. The two most popular are to let the cost savings accumulate where they fall or to split them 50/50. But under the really best practice, the savings are usually reinvested in better design, faster new product innovation, lower prices for the consumer, or greater advertising. This is in everyone's best interest providing that margins are maintained. That is, cost savings can indeed be reinvested. No one is hurt, the market is expanded, all sell more, and the competitors find it increasingly hard to match the combined performance.

New buying and selling

The changes in buying and selling are profound in good demand chain partnerships. Negotiation is a periodic, rather than a continuous, process. The focus is on other things. The day-to-day work is changed completely. In fact, for many companies the number of people in these activities goes down dramatically. More importantly, for those who take on the new roles, the jobs are fundamentally different and highly energizing. Sales people no longer stuff the pipeline trying to convince purchasing people to buy more than they need to make a quota. Purchasing people no longer treat representatives from suppliers like enemies, where the game is only price. The collective brainpower of the suppliers needs to be applied to *our* problems and it is *my* job to see that *I* achieve it.

Ordering is basically not a very intelligent idea. In far too many cases, orders are issued as late as possible to minimize inventory investments and cash flows. The suppliers are kept in the dark as to what to expect, in order to "increase bargaining power". Next year's contract is only provisional, and is held over the head of the supplier. All this increases chain costs unnecessarily. If the information linkages are right between the customer and supplier, then ordering is not necessary. The supplier does not have to guess or forecast: the supplier knows what is needed, and when it is needed, and it should be up to the supplier to make sure that the customer gets it in time. Perhaps the customer should only pay for the goods when used (consignment stock), but then it is important to recall the imperative for "smart" partners.

Finally, it is important to understand that if you have a dog but wished you had a cat, no matter how hard you kick the dog, it will always be a dog and not a cat. The plain fact is that the changes required for demand change management to be implemented are huge. Some people will just not be able to make the adjustment. Moreover, sometimes there can be a matter of bad chemistry between people in partner companies. If that is the case, the sooner the problem is recognized, the sooner the necessary changes can be made – even if they are painful.

SUMMARY

Energized organizations require networks of talent that cross company borders, especially those between customer and supplier. In particular, energized organizations can use demand chain management to initiate a series of transformations. This requires more than just doing the same things better – it requires doing better things and breaking out to change the rules, set up new relations, and focus on those improvements that will create long-term dominance in a marketplace. In demand chain management, this implies new ways of working with suppliers and customers, a focus on how the chain can compete, and a keen understanding of what kinds of improvements will create major advantages, either in cost savings or in value-creation.

Transforming a demand chain, then, requires a combination of strategy and infrastructure. It is necessary to know clearly what you wish to achieve in a partnership (not some vague ideas of mutual friendship). But then it is necessary to do the hard work of changing the detailed infrastructure and ways of working to unleash energy and value creation.

The key elements are:

- Viewing demand chain partnering as a staircase. The relationship achieved with a particular supply or customer partner needs to be seen as a logical progression or series of transformations.
- Demand chain partnering needs to be seen in a strategic context. The choice of partners and the way in which demand chains are exploited for mutual benefit is critical.
- Outsourcing, too, needs to be seen in a strategic context. Outsourcing of production competencies is very different from outsourcing the company cafeteria.
- Sophisticated information systems are required to support highly

individualized ways of dealing with customers and suppliers. The objective is to create a series of highly effective demand chains that make life easier for the customer.

● Underpinning the whole approach are new ways of thinking about the demand chain. This involves a shift from an adversarial style relationship to one that actively seeks collaboration.

BEST PRACTICE

Boundary-crossing networks may well be the best competitive game in town. The competencies gained in working together across company boundaries are often the best means of reducing costs and increasing value for the end customers. But the need is to develop a true win–win attitude, where parochial interests are reduced for the overall benefit. Both partners should be able to maintain – and even increase – their margins. But doing so must not depend on one trying to gain advantage at the expense of the other.

Boundary-crossing networks based on demand chain management require a new agenda. This defines what is truly important. That is, what do the partner companies need to focus their attention on once the partnership is alive and well? One key issue is how to develop and foster multiple communications channels between the bottom-up initiatives in the partner companies. The exchange of prisoners is one good start, but multiple others need to be created and fostered. It is important for the engineers from one company to talk to those of their partner companies. But this needs to be more than bull sessions. The time of these people is valuable and needs to be planned carefully. Visits to partner companies should be orchestrated carefully and after each one all parties should evaluate what can be done to improve and further energize this activity.

The fundamental goal in any boundary-crossing network is improvement. An aggressive improvement agenda is imperative to create energy. The issue is not what has been done, but what are *we* going to do next? In good demand partnerships, such as that between Wal-Mart and Procter and Gamble, or that between Chrysler and its suppliers, the partnership evolves through successive stages of increasing co-operation and value-creation. All of this is critical to the continuous improvement of the demand chain network.

Last, but not least, is the need for unlearning. Senior managers need to concentrate on determining which existing practices need to be stopped. Equally important is to determine which existing performance measures need to be changed. For example, a large consumer-products company is now basing the bonuses of its executives more and more on regional performance, rather than on individual country performance. It is only in this way that the team will truly play as a team.

7

Reconfigurable Organizations

Why build up organizational structures that are out of date as soon as they are formed? In this chapter, **Jay Galbraith** shows how a bottom-up organization should be designed to make it reconfigurable and easily adapted to exploit opportunities as they arise.

Overview

The energy in a bottom-up organization depends on the extent to which resources can be focused on emerging opportunities. The business environment is changing so fast that more flexibility is required to refocus resources and maintain the energy of the organization. Flexibility was always desirable, but today the changes are more frequent, the execution needs to be faster, and the responses need to be directed along a larger number of dimensions. The design principles underlying this flexible organization are:

1. The organization must change as fast as its business changes, if not it falls behind.
2. The organization must be as complex as the business, if not, it is vulnerable.

> "If bottom-up organizations are to exploit opportunity they need a design that can be changed constantly without Herculean efforts. An organization is *reconfigurable* when it is designed from the beginning to be quickly and easily changeable"

For most companies, the consequence of following these design principles is to create an organization that can be changed quickly and easily. This organization is the *reconfigurable organization* that is designed from the beginning to possess a built-in capacity for change. This chapter discusses reconfigurability – a key feature of an energized bottom-up organization – and examines the requirements in terms of:

- design
- structure
- processes
- reward systems
- people management.

Designing a reconfigurable organization

The renewed interest in reconfigurable organizations

There has always been an interest in flexible organizations. We can find references to *organic organizations* (Burns and Stalker, 1961), *lateral forms of organization* (Galbraith, 1973), and *matrix forms* (Davis and Lawrence, 1977). But these forms were often confined to the R&D function, or project-oriented industries like aerospace. When applied outside these situations in command- and control-oriented companies, these flexible forms did not lead to success. However, with shortening lifecycles, greater strategic space and the faster speed of response described above, there is renewed interest in flexible organizations (Volberda, 1998), sense and respond organizations, adaptable organizations, and agile organizations – or what I prefer to call the *reconfigurable organization* (Galbraith, 1997). This renewed interest derives from the fact that companies today compete with their organization. When product advantages do not last long, competition revolves around the ability to continually create and implement new advantages. That ability requires an organization that is designed from the beginning to be continuously reconfigurable. The more flexible or reconfigurable the organization, the greater the advantage.

Along with the renewed interest in flexible organizations has come an interest in new organization models. In the past, management crafted a winning business strategy and erected barriers to entry to sustain their advantage. Next, management created an organization structure around functions, products, markets or geography that was designed to deliver the success formula. To complete the integrity of the organization, planning and budgeting processes, information systems, new product development processes, compensation systems, selection and promotion criteria, career paths, performance appraisals and training and development sequences would all be designed and aligned with each other and with the organization's strategy and structure. Such an aligned organization would execute the strategy with as little friction as possible. This thinking resulted in organization models, such as the McKinsey Seven S model or the star model (Figure 7.1).

It is now suggested that alignment becomes a disadvantage in times of rapid change. Digital Equipment is offered as an example of a company that had alignment of its strategy and organization. They had so much alignment around large computers and proprietary architectures that they were unable to reconfigure themselves around client–server computing and open architectures. Thus it is suggested that success and

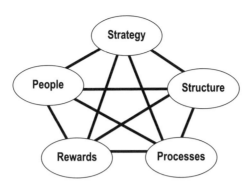

Figure 7.1: *Star model*

alignment in today's business model can prevent the rapid adaptation into tomorrow's model. There is some truth to the assertion that success and alignment can slow adaptation. But in my view, it was Digital's past success in vax minicomputers that slowed the response to desktops and UNIX. It is the success syndrome, and not alignment, that prevents the needed change. In the end, it is the persistence in yesterday's strategy against new competitors with new and superior business models that is the undoing of yesterday's top performers.

Equally important is the effect of not having alignment among organizational policies. The alternative is misalignment, and with misalignment come conflicting activities, units working at cross-purposes and a loss of organizational energy over many frictions. Instead of a new organizational model, we need new types of strategy and organizational alignment. We need to align bottom-up organizations around continuously changing strategies. This alignment results in the reconfigurable organization. We also need an alignment around the innovation process that results in creating new business models (Galbraith, 1982). This chapter is focused on the former type of alignment.

Structure

The structure of the reconfigurable organization consists of a stable part and a part that can be easily configured and reconfigured. The example of the food company mentioned earlier illustrates this. The company's original structure is shown in Figure 7.2. It is the usual functional structure for a single business with cross-functional teams to focus on the business's two product lines.

After completing the series of strategy changes mentioned above, the company had reconfigured itself into five additional teams each focused on the health segment, new channels, new customers and new categories. The structure is shown in Figure 7.3.

The company has reconfigured itself from a functional structure with product teams, to a *multistructure* based on functions, products, segments, channels, customers and categories. It is a multiple profit-and-loss structure that can be changed flexibly to any dimension that will support the next strategic advantage. Whilst there is probably a limit to the number of miniature business units that can be in place at

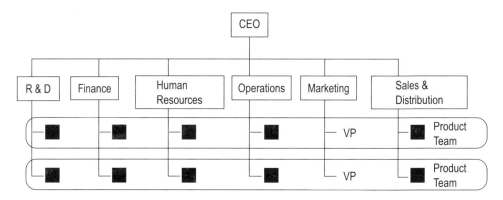

Figure 7.2: *Product team organization*

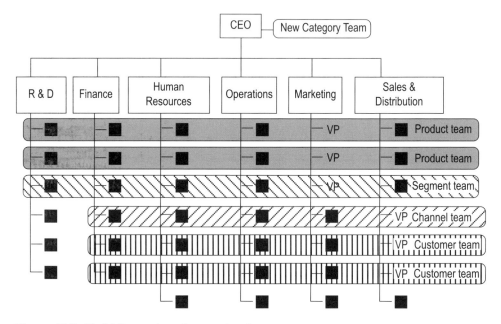

Figure 7.3: *Multidimensional organization*

any one time, the company is creating the capability to organize any way that it wants to. Instead of choosing to organize by function or product or market segment to implement a sustainable brand advantage, the company is organized by function, product, segment, channel, category *and* customer to implement a series of changing short-term advantages.

In this example, and for single businesses in general, the functions are the stable part of the structure. The functions serve as homes for specialists who reside in the function, and as hosts for generalists on rotating assignments. The teams or miniature businesses are the reconfigurable part that can be added, combined or dropped as circumstances and strategy requires. However, also necessary for reconfigurability are the other aligned elements of the star model shown in Figure 7.1.

Processes in the reconfigurable organization

There are four types of systems and processes supporting a reconfigurable structure:

1. The information and accounting system.
2. Horizontal processes.
3. Vertical resource allocation processes.
4. A timely management decision process.

The information system and the decision process are unique to the reconfigurable organization. The horizontal and vertical processes are not.

Information and accounting system

The multidimensional organization requires a multidimensional information and accounting system. Each product line, segment, category, channel and customer are *profit-measurable* at the food company. They are referred to as miniature business units because the company is the only true profit centre. However, each team has profit goals and needs to be profit-measurable. This information system needs to be designed so that it can provide multidimensional profit-and-loss statements for products, channels, customers, segments and so on.

Horizontal processes

The horizontal processes are the usual ones for order fulfilment, product development, customer relationship management and so on. These processes, like the functional homes, are stable parts of the reconfigurable organization. So while products, segments and channels may come and go, the teams all use the same horizontal processes to reduce complexity.

Vertical resource allocation processes

The vertical processes are those that support decisions around allocating the limiting resources. In the past, money was the limiting resource, and budgeting was the process for allocating this resource, which limited what a firm could do. However, other resources can constrain action over some time periods. The food company experienced supply shortages of, and spikes in demand for, the new low-fat products. So supply chain information was needed to support the decisions to allocate logistics and supply resources. Today the limiting factor for many companies tends to be types of talent. Consulting firms in 1998 did not have enough SAP programmers and program managers. In Europe they would convene different groups of managers to weigh the demand for and supply of programmers. The idea was to get together the information and the group of people that gives a total firm perspective and the authority to make the decisions. The firms are becoming adept at identifying the limiting talent category and convening the appropriate group to decide on the allocation to clients and projects. In this case, each group is different and represents a reconfigurable hierarchical decision process.

Management decision processes

The management process for deciding on the allocation of the limiting resource is mentioned as a fourth process because of its importance. Even though it is tied to the vertical process, the management decision process is a make-or-break feature. The execution of a reconfigurable organization increases the level of conflict and decreases the time to resolve it. At the food company, new low-fat products would reduce sales of existing products. Product managers for existing product lines would want to constrain the introduction of new products. Then there were issues of which products to ship through the overloaded distribution system, whose customers to send partial deliveries to, etc. Having comprehensive information support helps, but it is the quality and timeliness of the management problem-solving process that determines success. The decisions and the resulting goals and objectives then become the basis for the reward systems.

Reward systems in the reconfigurable organization

Reward systems need to be as flexible as the strategy and structure. These reward systems and the accompanying human resources practices represent a shift away from rigid, hierarchical job-based systems to more fluid competency- or person-based systems (Lawler, 1994). In more stable organizations, the job was the basic building block. People were hired for a job. People were paid based on job descriptions and job evaluation systems. In flexible organizations, however, jobs are changing continually. Most work is becoming project work; it is therefore better to focus on individuals and their skills and competencies as the basic building blocks.

Compensation systems

Compensation systems for reconfigurable organizations are becoming skill-based and contain more variable performance-based components. Before, we "paid the job not the person". Today, we pay the person, not a job that changes continually. People are receiving fixed salaries based on their skill sets. Indeed it is these sets of skills and competencies that are basic building blocks in rapidly changing organizations. The incentive for the individual is to acquire more skills and to learn. This incentive aligns the individual's interest in acquiring new competencies with their organization's interest in acquiring new capabilities. The rigid job-based systems of the past often discouraged people from taking a transfer to another function to learn a new skill.

Performance-based rewards

Performance-based rewards are becoming more variable and are based on more comprehensive, subjective assessments. Investment banks and consulting firms are the models. At the completion of each project or deal, the project leader assesses the team that worked on it. The team members also evaluate the leader and other team members. A managing partner collects these assessments along with an evaluation from the customer. The team as a whole is assessed against the goals of the project. People are assessed on their contributions to the goals, their customer orientation, their teamwork, the use of their networks and many other factors. The assessment has quantitative and subjective components, but it is conducted rigorously. Managing partners can spend 20–25% of their time evaluating performance. (The issue of performance-based rewards and open company values are explored further by Piero Morosini in *Competing With Information*, also published in the IMD Executive Development series.)

In this manner the performance assessments and feedback are completed frequently. Performance is assessed on multiple dimensions, including teamwork and networking. The assessments are performed by multiple people and include peers, subordinates and customers. The people who observed a person's performance directly make the assessments. The process is a rigorous one: performance criteria are articulated and known; people are trained in how to make performance assessments; and a person's acquisition of skills are assessed in the same way. It is the peers and team members who also know when someone has mastered a new skill. This type of reward system operates at the speed of the business, and rewards the adaptation and learning of new skills as well as the translation of these skills into high performance.

CASE STUDY: MCKINSEY & COMPANY

McKinsey & Company has been one of the most successful international consultancies of the 1980s and 1990s, earning on average 20% more revenue per consultant than several of their main competitors. The company has also developed an enviable reputation in the area of strategic consulting, with former McKinsey personnel leading businesses such as IBM and American Express at one time or another.

Maintaining this enviable performance is achieved by fostering a nonhierarchical meritocracy, where commitment to the highest standards of quality and open learning are standard across the company's 70 offices worldwide. One of the ways in which the company maintains their meritocracy is the "up-or-out" approach, where McKinsey consultants are promoted to the next level within a specific time period, or they are invited to leave the company.

McKinsey's up-or-out policy is implemented across all of the firm's offices, using a standard evaluation document called Evaluation Performance Review *(EPR). Each time a project team starts an engagement, a comprehensive performance-based system begins. The key features are:*

- *During the first week of the project, the team's engagement manager spends a few hours with each team member to agree on what kind of performance they expect in the specific context of the client and the engagement that is about to start.*
- *A complementary document, available to everybody in the team, describes in detail what kind of behaviour corresponds to each performance level.*
- *Halfway through an engagement, or after a couple of months for longer engagements, the engagement manager will undertake an interim evaluation of each McKinsey team member, completing a draft EPR for each member of the team and discussing it in detail (and in private). Strengths, successes and performance gaps are highlighted, and corrective actions or modifications are considered.*
- *At the end of the engagement, the final EPR is prepared by the manager and discussed with the evaluated individual as well as the person leading the engagement.*

This system forms the basis for promotion, and while it has its occasional errors McKinsey's EPR approach more than fulfils its primary purpose, which is one of high-stakes coaching and learning as much as evaluation.

People management in the reconfigurable organization

In the reconfigurable organization, the human resources policies are also based on competencies rather than the job. People are hired to fit the company culture and practices, and a fit between the person's personality and the company culture is sought. These are features that change slowly and for which a fit is most important. The basic competencies and attitudes of teamwork, interpersonal skills, interest in personal growth and development are also sought. The selection process is intensive: it requires interviews, tests and simulations to determine the fit and competencies.

> **"The flexible, bottom-up organization is built around flexible *people*. Individuals who like change and who like to learn new skills are attracted, selected, developed and rewarded. Individuals develop in their specialities or across specialities in the business"**

Reconfigurable organizations require both *specialists* with in-depth knowledge and *generalists* who like to be multiskilled. The generalists then follow a track of rotational assignments to build their knowledge and their networks. Training is continuous and targeted at communities of interest for specialists and cross-functional groups for generalists. The purpose is to simultaneously build know-how and "know-who". The human resources practices fit with the changing strategy and structures of the reconfigurable organization.

SUMMARY

Reconfigurable organization designs

The reconfigurable bottom-up organization is one that is designed from the beginning to be quickly and easily changeable. It consists of structures, processes, rewards and people practices that fit with the strategic flexibility required to be successful in the marketplace. The new strategy and dimensions of organizational alignment are shown in the star model in Figure 7.4.

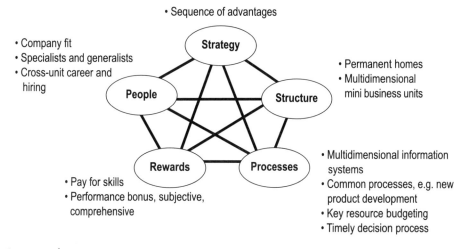

Figure 7.4: *Star model of a Reconfigurable but aligned company*

All of the organizational elements are aligned with a strategy that is based on creating a continuous stream of short-term advantages. Then the structure, processes, rewards and people practices are aligned among themselves. When combined with the elements described in the other chapters in Part Two, the organization will have built-in energy for change on the frontline.

BEST PRACTICE

It is important to understand how flexible your organization is, as well as how flexible it needs to be. The star model provides an ideal framework for this assessment and the following questions drawn from the text highlight areas to consider.

Strategy

- *How old are the strategies that are in place? When were they last reviewed?* Persisting with yesterday's strategies when faced with new, superior sources of competition will lead to inevitable decline.
- *Is the success syndrome preventing needed change?* Companies that have succeeded with a specific business model can be reluctant to change it, often on the grounds that "if it ain't broke, don't fix it". This ignores the fact that it might be about to break, or incapable of surviving if the market situation alters, as it inevitably will. The danger here is that success will slow adaptation.
- *How well aligned is the organization? Is there an organizational culture and approach that can deliver this flexibility?* Clearly strategies, policies, structures and processes all need to be aligned and pulling in the same direction, but more than that the organization needs to be able to align around continuously changing strategies.

Structure

Successful reconfigurable organizations possess both *stable* and *flexible* parts, and it is worth reflecting on the extent to which both exist in the organization. Stability is generally achieved through the business functions, which are often home to specialists and generalists on rotating assignments. Reconfigurability around other dimensions like product, segment, channel or customer is provided by the other elements of the star model: processes, rewards and people.

Processes

- *Are the information and accounting systems sufficiently multidimensional?* These systems need to routinely provide a range of information for products, channels, markets, customers, suppliers and other key elements of the business.
- *Are the horizontal processes (e.g. order fulfilment) and the vertical processes for resource allocation (e.g. budgeting) working well?* These two processes should form the stable part of the organization; any problems with these processes will routinely weaken and destabilize the organization, undermining flexibility.
- *How can the quality and timeliness of the management decision-making process be improved?* A reconfigurable organization demands a decision-making and problem-solving structure that is adaptive, and capable of dealing quickly and successfully with new challenges.

Rewards

Reward systems need to be flexible in the reconfigurable organization, and it is useful to consider:

- whether compensation systems overall are skill-based, with a variable performance-based element; and
- whether performance-based elements are derived from comprehensive assessments.

People

In building the reconfigurable bottom-up organization, it is vitally important to select people that fit with the organization's culture and approach, as well as for their technical skills. Consider the extent to which the organization has a blend of specialists and generalists; how knowledge and best practice techniques are spread; how training and development are pursued. The human resource management policies of the company need to be clearly aligned with the requirements of a flexible, reconfigurable organization.

References

Burns, T. and Stalker, G.M. (1961) *The Management of Innovation*. London: Tavistock.

Davis, S. and Lawrence, P. (1977) *Matrix*. Reading, USA: Addison-Wesley.

Galbraith, J. (1973) *Designing Complex Organizations*. Reading, USA: Addison-Wesley.

Galbraith, J. (1982) Designing the Innovating Organization, *Organization Dynamics*, Winter.

Galbraith, J. (1997) The Reconfigurable Organization, in *The Organization of the Future*, eds Hasselbein et al. California: Jossey-Bass.

Lawler, E.E. (1994) From Job-Based to Competency-Based Organizations, *Journal of Organization Behavior*, **15**: 3–15.

Volberda, H. (1998) *Building the Flexible Firm*. Oxford: Oxford University Press.

8

Competence-sharing across Boundaries

The sharing of competence is central to making knowledge and intangible resources flexible in the bottom-up organization. In this chapter, **Piero Morosini** argues, on the basis of evidence from globalization initiatives, that flexible execution is vital for success. Critical to energy in the bottom-up organization is the ability to learn faster than the competitors, and transfer that learning across cultural, organizational and individual boundaries.

CASE STUDY: ASEA BROWN BOVERI

ASEA Brown Boveri (ABB), the Swiss-Swedish industrial giant, is one of the most lauded companies of recent years. Headquartered in Zurich, Switzerland, ABB is the world's leading power engineering company employing over 213 000 people in 50 countries. It is broken down into 35 business areas with 5000 profit centres ("5000 perceived companies," says CEO Göran Lindahl). ABB came about from the merger of the Swedish company Allmänna Svenska Elektriska Aktiebolag (ASEA), then led by the redoubtable Percy Barnevik, and the Swiss company, Brown Boveri. The merger was announced on 10 August, 1987. Barnevik became the CEO of the resulting ABB and revolutionized its organization and performance until being succeeded by Goran Lindahl in 1997.

Its initial organizational design was admired widely by academics and practitioners alike, but what has proved crucial is not the elegance of the organizational architecture, but the company's ability to make the potentially unwieldy structure work. ABB's execution capabilities have successfully carried the company through at least three radical organizational transformations since 1987.

Overview

Some of the business initiatives best embodying the very essence of globalization have a dismal track record, and herein lies a dramatic paradox. For example, a well-documented body of literature, impressive both in the variety of approaches utilized and in the depth and scope of the underlying empirical analyses, distinctly suggests that the failure rate of all mergers, acquisitions and alliances is well over 50%. Strikingly similar findings have been reported in the case of other major global undertakings, such as re-engineering and large-scale change programs. In the field of management, traditionally fraught with contradictory approaches and seemingly opposing views around single phenomena, such empirical evidence has enjoyed a surprising degree of consensus during the past 30 years.

The situation described unveils only part of the story. Indeed, its profound paradoxes become fully evident only when we realize the enormous difficulty that academics, practitioners and managers seem to have in identifying with some degree of consistency the major reasons why most globalization programs seem to fail, and how to increase their success rate. Indeed, the numerous and widely differing theories that have been put forward to explain such failure rates have in common scant or nonexistent empirical support. Thus, for example, *strategic* approaches fostering merger and acquisition activity based on the existing relationship between the firms, or on the strategic "fit" between the acquirer and the target, have found little empirical support based on performance. Also, *organizational* approaches postulating specific links between a firm's structural categories and the underlying performance of its globalization activities have found no significant empirical correlations to date. Similar considerations can be made of *finance-* and *marketing-based* approaches, which, particularly in areas such as mergers and acquisitions, have abounded.

Confronted with the stubbornly high failure rates of these kinds of global initiatives, a number of researchers and practitioners have concluded that new, holistic and pragmatic approaches deserve serious consideration. In particular, this chapter introduces the notion of "competence for execution", the ability to continuously learn and communicate across organizational, cultural and market boundaries. This is critical to making knowledge and intangible resources flexible in the bottom-up organization. The chapter is divided into three sections:

- the importance of execution;
- the nature of competence for execution; and
- how to build effective execution capabilities.

The importance of execution

The notion of core competencies is now well-established. In their influential article published in 1990, academics C.K. Prahalad and Gary Hamel introduced the concept as ". . . the collective learning in the organization, especially how to co-ordinate diverse production skills and integrate multiple streams of technologies." They argued that NEC constituted one archetypal example of a company that grew exponentially during the 1980s, largely because it had focused on its "core competencies" early on. In the case of the NEC of the 1980s, it had identified three core and interrelated streams of technological and market evolution, and had built on those single-mindedly, entering numerous alliances during that period in order to learn and absorb other companies skills around those core competencies. Thus the solution to the complex dilemmas of global growth, according to Prahalad and Hamel, implied a company's fundamental awareness of its own core competencies and a strategic plan to concentrate and grow around those.

Similar to most previous attempts to explaining why and how companies obtain specific performance results in global competition, Prahalad and Hamel's approach relies too much on formal, analytical responses to address a complex managerial phenomena, overlooking the pragmatic aspects of implementing global strategies, whether these are based on core competencies or not. Thus, Prahalad and Hamel's article ignores the enormous implementation challenges involved in co-ordinating, integrating and continuously learning around multiple streams of competencies. Even apparently sophisticated formal strategies based on sound analyses can become dangerously simplistic, fallacious and even detrimental when managers attempt to implement them in a rapidly changing and unpredictable global environment.

For example, the crucial core competencies of a bottom-up organization are likely to change over time. What matters is that the company is able to adjust itself and execute its strategy in changing circumstances. We refer to this capability as the "core competence for execution" in a corporation. Indeed, this author's recent research findings suggest that the success of companies as diverse as McKinsey & Company, General Electric or ABB has more to do with their systematic ability to *execute* well-thought-out global strategies in the real world, than with the intrinsic analytical and intellectual value of those strategies per se.

We have seen that, in its original formulation, the notion of core competencies crucially included a company's ability to seamlessly circulate key streams of knowledge and co-ordinate critical resources across boundaries. Our recent research findings suggest that these "soft" abilities are essential for the performance of bottom-up initiatives in a global firm. By contrast, it could be argued that any other stock of core competencies which a corporation might be lacking at a given time period (i.e. specific technological or functional set of competencies) can simply be acquired through mergers and acquisition (M&A), alliances and/or licensing agreements in an increasingly deregulated global environment.

Sony's 1989 acquisition of Columbia Pictures gave it an access to the entertainment industry it had singled out as a key (but missing) strategic competency to complement its portfolio of consumer electronics competencies. Also, through a set of acquisitions during the late 1980s and early 1990s, Benetton, the Italian clothing manufacturer and distributor, acquired new competencies which turned it into a leading global player in plastic sporting equipment manufacturing and marketing, such as roller-blades and skis. Similarly, Olivetti, an electrical typewriter producer until the early 1980s, established an international network of acquisitions and strategic alliances during most of that decade. This allowed it to transform itself into a PC manufacturer. During the 1990s, Olivetti carried out over 60 new acquisitions – of which Telecom Italia was the largest – and as many divestitures, to transform itself into one of Europe's largest telecommunication companies. The business arena abounds with examples of global companies absorbing new technology- and market-based core competencies via mergers, acquisitions, alliances or other similar agreements.

Some academics and executives increasingly highlight implementation difficulties as the key reasons behind the lack of success of most company's globalization efforts. Thus, specific organizational structures and processes, or cultural differences in management styles and nationalities, are viewed as barriers, boundaries or risk factors preventing a company's global co-ordination of resources and communication. These boundaries can be vertical (e.g. vis-à-vis suppliers or customers) or horizontal (e.g. between a company's R&D and marketing departments), encompassing geographic borders, or being embedded in national and/or corporate cultural divides. However, our recent research suggests that although managing across these boundaries can be an extremely difficult endeavour for any global corporation, company executives often find recourse to these boundaries as an excuse for performance shortcomings, or failure to properly execute global co-ordination tasks on a global scale.

For example, the notion that national cultural distance represents a boundary detrimental to the performance of global business is well-entrenched in management theory and practice (the case of cross-border M&A being a classic in this area). However, the first empirical test of such notion in the case of cross-border acquisitions recently reported that, contrary to previous management theories, the higher the national cultural distance the higher the cross-border acquisition performance (Morosini et al., 1998). Such results suggest that, while the ability to co-ordinate across national cultural boundaries may unleash significant potential for multinational corporations, management prejudice, inability or unwillingness to handle these boundaries might be preventing a company's stakeholders' from reaping the full benefits of global co-ordination.

Indeed, in the same empirical study it became clear that execution factors were much more dominant for performance than strategic variables. A problem common to conventional approaches to global business has been to systematically underestimate the execution aspects.

The nature of execution

By "execution", we mean a specific set of pragmatic mechanisms that firms utilize in order to strengthen their organizational identity and continuously learn and communicate on a global scale, across organizational, cultural and market boundaries. Our research suggests that global firms combining both a strong identity and the ability to seamlessly learn and communicate across boundaries innovate faster, co-ordinate internal resources better, and integrate networks of alliances more efficiently than their competitors. Moreover, execution mechanisms rely heavily on a company's tacit knowledge, cultural metaphors and subjective values, which can be traced back to a firm's unique history and specific context, and often take considerable time and effort to develop. However, the fact that execution mechanisms rely heavily on these complex, unique and tacit norms and values makes a firm's competitive advantages based on execution difficult to be replicated by competitors. By contrast, technology- and process-based streams of competencies that can be largely codified or formalized explicitly are easily transferrable (or acquired) across companies.

Today's fast-changing and interconnected environment poses new and increased sources of complexity for a company operating on a global scale. As most of these changes result in new situations for which there is often no historical or systematic data available, the company's managers will have to rely significantly on their own first-line experience and intuition to make rapid decisions and to act on them. In such an environment, strategic approaches overly based on analytical tools or, even worse, planning systems based on forecasting techniques, scenario analyses etc. understandably have little value. On the one hand, today's global corporation relies on its ability to respond quickly to brusque and unforeseen changes in its competitive environment, and to do so continuously, within broad strategic parameters and clear end-goals. On the other hand, national cultural differences and related complexities are likely to further complicate a manager's ability to adequately grasp and respond to rapidly changing situations, thereby enhancing the value of his or her pragmatic intuition and expertise.

Paradoxically, in order to handle today's technologically sophisticated global marketplace, a company requires more, not less, managerial intuition than in the past – along with sound technological and technical skills. Continuous technological change, and the persistence of national cultural differences within the foreseeable future, suggests that this mixture of technical abilities and cross-cultural managerial intuition will continue to be increasingly valuable for the global corporation well into the twenty-first century.

In the remainder of this chapter, we will refer to tacit knowledge as "gnosis", the Greek word to describe intuitive knowledge, or knowledge gained through subjective experience. My recent research findings suggest that the core competence for execution, or the way in which a global corporation co-ordinates critical resources and collectively learns from its environment, is embedded deeply in its subjective fabric of values, group metaphors, tacit norms, cultural symbols and other gnostic characteristics. These uniquely pervade the way a company acts, makes decisions, co-ordinates resources and communicates in the widest sense. Thus, underlying sound strategic goals and technical knowledge, the gnostic content of a firm's execution routines makes them difficult to transfer and replicate by other firms, and determine a company's unique organizational identity.

The central elements of execution

Whereas implementation can be regarded as the universe of ongoing activities that a firm carries out, research carried out at IMD suggests that execution can be characterized by a given set of pragmatic mechanisms within the following five areas:

1. *Building blocks*: these are organizational tools and formal rules that are available in an explicit and codified way within the firm. They comprise factors such as a company's:

    - official internal language;
    - set of corporate values or mission statements;
    - internal reporting and control systems;
    - personnel and incentive policies for employees operating across national borders; and
    - operational and financial performance rules and measurements.

2. *International assignment policies*: these are the concrete mechanisms that firms utilize to rotate employees across national borders, and to support personnel directly involved in global co-ordination tasks. They differ from personnel policies as a building block in that the latter are constituted by explicit documents or rules, whereas international assignment policies reflect what the firm actually does. For example, a document containing a firm's specific incentive policies for expatriate managers forms part of its building blocks of globalization. However, the length, number and level of managers which are actually sent by a firm on overseas assignments in a given year is one element that characterizes its international assignment policies for that time period.

3. *Communication mechanisms*: these refer to the nature, frequency and structure of the communication flows between a firm's top management and their upper- and middle-managerial ranks with operating responsibilities across national borders. They also include the communication flows between those upper and middle managers and the lower-level employees within their respective units.

4. *Co-ordination mechanisms*: in a given firm, these are constituted by the set of periodic, formal and informal project teams, taskforces, group councils etc. operating across functions and national borders, with specific operating, technology transfer, benchmarking, best-practice or knowledge dissemination purposes.

5. *Leadership*: we predominantly refer to the execution orientation of a firm's top executives indicated by his or her level of direct involvement in communicating a company's vision and strategic goals to the upper- and middle-managerial ranks with operating responsibilities across national borders, as well as identifying, coaching and evaluating those managerial ranks.

The central elements underlying the competence for execution in a corporation are shown schematically in Figure 8.1. These elements are important because they interact in a holistic way, generating more than the sum of its parts. This "more" is given primarily by the level and strength of *shared company values* that this interaction generates, and the amount of gnosis gathered through this interaction, involving complex phenomena, such as local cultural contexts, technological innovations, and internal and external processes and methods.

ABB provides a case in point to illustrate how a global company can energize a bottom-up organization and derive competitive advantages based on its competencies for execution.

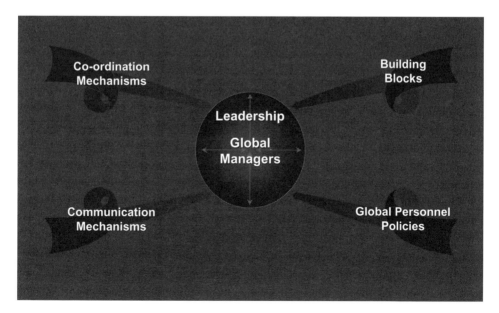

Figure 8.1: *Key capabilities that sustain competence for execution*
Professor Piero Morosini. IMD International Copyright 2000©

Building effective execution capabilities

During the period 1988 to 1999, ABB more than tripled its revenues to about $25 billion, with dramatic increases in profitability, productivity and international coverage and market capitalization. During those years, ABB's organization has been referred to and followed as a model ideally suited for the postindustrial age. The fact that this company was initially formed after the 1987 merger between Sweden's ASEA and Switzerland's Brown Boveri, and subsequently expanded through a string of cross-border M&As and alliances (totalling well over 200 by the eve of 2000) has undoubtedly given it some of its initial impetus to develop significant capabilities across boundaries.

As well as looking at ABB's impressive global achievements since its inception, it is important to examine how this company has already managed to overcome significant internal and external crises during its relatively short existence. Following a period of unparalleled growth under Percy Barnevik's 1988–96 CEO tenure, the company faced a profound crisis following major currency devaluations across the so-called "emerging economies" in 1996, as well as the rapid deregulation of electricity markets across most of the industrialized world during the late 1990s. With sales and share prices tumbling in 1997, many company observers took the opportunity to highlight the excessive risks of ABB's strategy of rapid expansion in Asia and Eastern Europe during the first half of the 1990s, as well as its having put too much emphasis on mature manufacturing business, while global deregulation was rapidly tilting the scales in favour of more value-added and service-based offerings to electrical utilities.

However, Göran Lindahl, who succeeded Barnevik as CEO in 1996, was about to carry out the most dramatic transformation yet in the company's history. In just over two years, ABB turned itself into the world's largest process automation player, through combining its internal automation businesses and carrying out large acquisitions abroad. It also divested its noncore transportation businesses, and restructured its mature power generation businesses through an autonomous joint venture with Alstom. ABB has also invested heavily in creating a customer-centred solutions business, where it provides a range of services, software and hardware offerings for the new situations arising in electrical distribution after global deregulation. The shift in focus can be seen in the sheer scale of this transformation: during the past five years, through lay-offs or divestments, ABB has eliminated 25 000 jobs in mature electrical equipment manufacturing in Western Europe and the USA. In these same geographic areas, the company has hired over 10 000 software professionals. After 1996, ABB had simultaneously embarked in a major internal reorganization, strengthening key global processes such as financial services and knowledge management, while maintaining an extremely decentralized global network of 5000 profit centres under a 200-strong headquarters. By early 2000, ABB was again showing strong sales growth, record profitability and double-digit earnings growth, almost doubling its market capitalization during 1999.

What is behind ABB's kind of resilient capability to continuously reinvent itself? What allows it to manage effectively these radical transformations across challenging boundaries and critical situations? Although ABB's organizational design was cited early on as a clear source of competitive advantage for the company, the supposedly unique federation type of principles underlying ABB's design had been pioneered many decades ago by companies such as Royal Dutch Shell, Cable & Wireless, General Electric and IBM.

Instead, ABB leaders point out that the unique advantages of a truly globally managed company is grounded on its *practical ability* to make co-ordination functions work in practice, across cultural, organizational and operational boundaries.

How did ABB actually make it happen across boundaries? In the culturally unfamiliar former Communist countries of Eastern Europe and Russia, for example, ABB built up a multibillion-dollar business from scratch, acquiring companies at a rate exceeding one per month immediately after the fall of the Berlin Wall in 1989. However, most firms that tried to implement similar initiatives in their organizations (even prior to ABB) failed to obtain similar performance results, even when counting on global managers of higher calibre and international exposure.

Building blocks

ABB actually did it by excelling at the five key execution areas (see Figure 8.1). First of all, the company set in place a few key building blocks for global co-ordination right after the 1987 merger between ASEA and Brown Boveri. These were:

- a common company language (English);
- a company's constitution (explicit in ABB's "book of values");
- a unified reporting and control systems (ABACUS, introduced successfully across ABB's 5000 profit centres 18 months after the 1987 merger);
- clear career policies for ABB's 500 global managers; and
- clear company performance rules and measurements.

Beyond the mere existence of these building blocks, what set ABB apart from other cases was the direct involvement of top management to "walk the talk" and ensure that these key blocks functioned in a consistent way. For example, one important principle in ABB's book of values at the outset of ABB's 1987 merger stated that:

We must strive to have managers who are "givers": they attract and develop talented people and thus provide internal candidates not only for themselves but also for other parts of ABB. We cannot afford "receivers" who always need to recruit from someone else or externally. We must promote a "giver" mentality among our managers so that we can maintain our policy of normally recruiting and promoting from within the group.

This principle, which was key for ABB to be able to expand in Eastern Europe while maintaining a 200-strong headquarters, is embedded firmly in the company's promotion and incentive policies. Every year, the company's CEO and executive committee personally revise and decide upon every global manager's compensation and career advancement.

International assignment policies

Another key area to make a complex multidomestic design work in practice concerns the personnel and international assignment policies for the key global managers group. From an execution perspective, these managers have to make practical day-to-day sense of ABB's global pool of resources, providing every BA with a worldwide strategy, achieving financial results and profitability targets, monitoring risk management, making mergers, acquisitions and investment decisions, co-ordinating global R&D, product development, market allocations, transfer pricing decisions etc. In short, quite a demanding list by any corporate standards. Explains Barnevik:

At the top it may be complicated. I and my people at the top have to understand the power plant business which involves billion-dollar projects running over five years ... emerging markets build-up ... and the different national cultures we operate in. But the thousands of managers in Italy, and Mid-west America, and China, or wherever, they need to know their countries. They're all part of a network, they reap the benefits out of that.

As a result, it is not difficult to see why the ability to identify, recruit, develop and nurture people with the broad cultural skills and technical knowledge required from an ABB global manager becomes one of the paramount execution challenges for the multidomestic organization. However, to adequately address efforts such as their Eastern European expansion, ABB did much more than resorting to the familiar long-term expatriate assignments or short-term rotation and trainee programs common to several multinationals. Rather, it made extensive use of innovative mechanisms that allowed it to pre-position key resources long in advance and gather understanding of culturally distant locations. Barnevik explains that one such mechanism is *cloning*:

... management candidates in Ukraine were too state-oriented. Job assignments were often not based on ability but political reasons. So we looked for younger Ukrainians in the group, maybe someone who was working in Germany and Italy before. So one or two years before concluding the deal, we had 10 to 15 candidates working in the Western world, younger champions who could be catalysts inside the Ukraine organizations. Some of these become senior managers ... Then you build on the base you have in Central Europe. [With the progressive turn-around of other areas, such as] the Czech and Polish businesses, [suddenly you have] 15 000 people there now [1996]. That gives you quite a pool of talent, people who can help build the business further east.

One crucial advantage of organizational cloning (and more generally a consequence of developing local people and capabilities early on) is that an acquired company can be restructured with greater speed while keeping intact its national character and inside local networks. Thus, as early as March 1996, ABB Nevsky, a joint venture based in Saint Petersburg, Russia, could win a US$100 million contract from Omskenergo, an electric utility in Omsk, to refurbish its power station jointly with Russian power engineering companies. Under the contract, it was agreed that new-technology 55-MW gas turbines would replace a less efficient, more polluting oil-fired plant. To win this contract, it was crucial that ABB was perceived as a thoroughly local player, managed by Russians, relying on local manufacturing and technological capabilities and contributing loyally to the domestic economy.

However, many local champions often end up isolated or cut off from the company's global network of resources, or find it difficult to secure smoothly the required functional, technological and human support in order to turn around an acquisition or make an alliance work. In addition, corporate and national cultural differences can significantly complicate co-ordination and communication efforts internationally. Under ABB's decentralized organization, one execution response to this challenge was to promote a comprehensive program of internal adoptions in support of the company's global expansion. Barnevik observes:

Senior managers in a well-developed market like Germany, Sweden or Finland adopt a country. That's their baby. They develop it, help it, support it, build export business, buy companies. Then, five years from now, the adopted businesses can stand on their own feet. You have to nurture them along. These are things that broaden your horizons beyond your country. Let's say, for example, that an ABB company in Milan building generators takes responsibility for a company in southern Poland, and helps them: accounting, language, organization, supply, quality assurance, pricing, the whole thing. And then I say to them: "OK you are measured in lire on your profit in this generation plant but you're also measured 25% on how well your adoptee performs in Poland."

Through international assignment policies such as cloning and adoption by 1995 ABB was employing over 10 000 people in Eastern Europe and Russia, generating close to $1.5 billion in the area.

Communication mechanisms

Another crucial execution area concerns the intensive communication mechanisms that took a variety of forms and reached numerous ABB constituencies, from day-to-day routine communications to regular group executive committee meetings and continuous visits to ABB subsidiaries.

During the early stages of the ABB merger, communications reached a climax during the annual global manager meetings. Their purpose was to foster and consolidate common company values, business practices and key achievements across ABB's multicultural global managers group, while at the same time building an *esprit de corps* across internal and cultural boundaries under the CEO's leadership. Similar kinds of intensive communication mechanisms, involving the CEO and top management, can be observed at the heart of General Electric's aggressive growth programs overseas. Barnevik remarks:

Communicating to these global managers is the whole thing. And the reason for having these four hundred top people meet regularly, is to have the group executive committee go through all the key issues, hammer them home, show cases, motivate them, lift them up, show them that we are the best, we take the lead, creating cultural success and belonging together. And now, this is done in other areas . . . they do it all over the place.

Co-ordination mechanisms

During the period 1988 to 1996, ABB pioneered and implanted a number of co-ordination mechanisms to continuously share best practices, establish internal benchmarks and align key managers in the complex transformation programs, breaking boundaries and initial resistance to change at an early stage.

One example of such mechanisms is the fixed consortium. It consists of a cross-cultural team formed with the explicit objective of carrying out a large and complex project, such as building manufacturing and distribution capabilities for electrical components and equipment anywhere in the world. It typically includes employees representing all the operational, technological, functional and country knowledge capabilities that are required to complete a large, complex project. By working co-operatively across national, cultural and internal company boundaries, as well as teaming up with suppliers or competitors as required, members of a fixed consortium can design and deliver innovative solutions, creating significant technological and cost advantages. Barnevik explains:

We combine our global managerial resources to form international teams which can effectively carry out large and complex projects. In one recent case, we formed a team with managers from Italy, Sweden, Switzerland and other countries, to build a major project in Italy. Their combined talents could convince the Italian government to support our project, and involve Pirelli as a local partner. In addition, we were able to cut the total costs of the project by 25% by forming this consortium.

Leadership

Underlying a firm's execution capabilities is the quality of leadership qualities, starting from the top. Beyond the media hype that surrounded ABB's global transformation from 1988 to 1996, the company's top leadership truly was distinct in its strict adherence to a few managerial principles and simple business values. Thus, ABB leaders such as Lindahl or Barnevik often resorted to expressions such as "management is 5% strategic thinking and 95% execution," or "senior executives must manage with their fingers in the pie, not surround themselves with layers and layers of other managers." They supplemented this kind of talk by combining a clear strategic vision with spending over 200 days on the road every year, visiting ABB subsidiaries all over the world and building direct communication with several managerial levels and key customers.

Such a mixture of a "thinker" and a "doer" – explicit knowledge and gnosis – found within the same individual constitute a key characteristic of leaders in companies such as ABB, General Electric and Daewoo. They bring to mind the ancient military figure of the Strategos, or the war fleet commander, intimately involved in the execution of strategy.

Three successful transformations

Although its initial organizational design was widely admired by academics and practitioners alike, ABB's execution capabilities have successfully carried the company through at least three radical organizational transformations since 1987:

1. *Co-ordination between national structures.* Right after the 1987 merger that created ABB, the local dimension of its matrix organization included both regional and country structures, with four major country heads as members of the 12-strong executive committee. Some members of the latter combined both global and local responsibilities, but co-ordination between these two dimensions often led to conflicts and time-consuming negotiations. However, the four country heads had discretion to conduct massive restructuring inside their major ABB operations.
2. *Regional simplification.* During the early 1990s, regional trading blocs erupted in full force, with the electrical engineering industry facing increased cross-border competition in public bidding from power utilities, and the explosive growth of large infrastructural projects across each region. To respond better to the new challenges, in 1993 ABB created three regions: Asia, Americas and Europe; Middle East; and Africa. Three regional heads in the executive committee replaced the four major country heads. The executive committee was reduced to eight members after the number of global segments was reduced to four.
3. *Global simplification.* After 1996, the regions were increasingly interrelated and integrated. ABB's new CEO, Göran Lindahl, eliminated the regional and subregional structures in the ABB matrix "after having fulfilled their mission to co-ordinate ABB's expansion in their respective areas." Only global and country dimensions remained after this reorganization, simplifying greatly communication and co-ordination on a global basis. Under this new organizational fine-tuning, in case of disagreement or conflict between these two dimensions, the global interests will prevail over local ones.

SUMMARY

The key point of execution in a bottom-up organization is not the success of any particular mechanism utilized by a successful firm, but a company's ability to continuously learn and adapt a series of execution capabilities that suit particular local contexts of a global organization, and to develop managers capable of co-ordinating resources across organizational and cultural boundaries in concert with the firm's values and objectives. Five types of mechanism are important:

- building blocks of organizational policy;
- international assignment policies;
- communication mechanisms;
- co-ordination mechanisms; and
- leadership.

ABB's initial multidomestic matrix structure has hardly remained rigid throughout the company's relatively short life. During its momentous transformation efforts, the key to the company's ability to continuously adapt to its changing environment has remained its execution capabilities to make a complex design work smoothly across organizational and cultural boundaries, both generating and supporting bottom-up energy. In this sense, it is interesting to note that throughout ABB's radical transformation, its highly decentralized global network of 5000 profit centres has remained intact, as in a reconfigurable organization. (See Chapter 7).

ABB's case also highlights the lack of any fixed recipe for how a company should approach its journey towards developing global execution capabilities. Indeed, the art is not in the concept, as it takes time, determination and subjective experience to develop the necessary capabilities to manage across boundaries. However, this is the very reason why companies that move quickly and determinedly to build execution capabilities can reap the upside of global co-ordination in a bottom-up organization in ways that are unique and difficult to replicate by competitors.

 **BEST PRACTICE**

The challenge is to create execution capabilities across boundaries as a key part of your global strategy bottom-up organization.

Global cohort of talent

The first step for companies such as ABB and General Electric has been to identify, attract, develop and retain a key group of 500 global managers.

Simplicity

Specific building blocks must be introduced if a company aims to manage successfully across boundaries. These building blocks are relatively simple, e.g. a common company language, a common performance measurement. Yet their conspicuous absence is one key reason behind the dismal track record of large-scale global programs.

Building common values by "walking the talk"

Relentlessly creating common values amongst a company's key managerial levels is one of the central tasks of a global company's senior executives. However, these values are ultimately instilled by example, by doing and observable behaviour.

Sharing competences by rotation and co-ordination

Unleash bottom-up energy in your company by destroying long-established hierarchies. But replace those hierarchies with small teams, common values, communication and co-ordination mechanisms.

References

Prahalad, C.K. and Hamel, G. The core competence of the corporation, *Harvard Business Review*.

Morosini, P. et al. (1998) National Cultural Distance and Cross-border Acquisition Performance, *Journal of International Business Studies*, March 1998: 137–158.

Part Three

Focusing the Energy

If not co-ordinated, the bottom-up initiatives in an energized organization create centrifugal forces that can pull a company apart. On the other hand, too much control will kill the initiatives. Achieving the right balance – focusing without losing the energy – is a subtle exercise, a true test of managerial skill. Part Three looks at how to focus energy in the three quintessential roles of managerial leadership:

- Finding Direction (Chapters 9–12)
- Orchestrating Activity (Chapters 13–15)
- Integrating Commitment (Chapters 16–18)

CHAPTER 9

Balancing Bottom-up with Top-down

Critical to focusing the energy in bottom-up organizations is developing and maintaining an overall perspective, keeping in balance a broad range of initiatives that fit with the overall business portfolio, to find strategic direction. In this chapter, **Peter Lorange** builds on the themes outlined in Chapter 3 and considers the key issues of balance and control facing energized bottom-up organizations.

CASE STUDY: THE PARTICIPATIVE, TOP-DOWN PORTFOLIO MANAGEMENT STYLE OF
JACK WELCH AT GENERAL ELECTRIC

*No-one has created as much shareholder value as Jack Welch at General Electric (GE).
His top-down strategic style is built on four principles. First, an effective top-down strategy must be rooted in high – even enormous – energy. Above all, one must react fast.
It is not what one predicts, but how one reacts. Secondly, one must build and maintain
the organization – above all, be able to energize others in a portfolio context where
all have essentially the same information, not least due to the realities of the Web. Third,
a top-down view must be built on the evolution of one's strategy, allow for trials and
errors – it will never be perfect. Finally, execution is all – namely to actually take the
hard portfolio decisions that will be needed, and to carry things through to fruition,
across the entire organization.*

*GE's portfolio consists of 10 product groups that are constantly changing, with more
than 100 acquisitions in 1998, and numerous divestitures. There are clear criteria
behind this portfolio strategy composition:*

- *Size matters, i.e. be number one or two or get out. Sell or restructure such weaker
  businesses, by putting them together with strong companies. Don't carry losers.*
- *Synergies are key, particularly movements of ideas and talents around GE, and transfer of knowledge that works. One must be a learning organization to find a better
  way. One must act fast and transfer relevant knowledge fast. The best ideas win.*
- *A boundaryless behaviour must exist. This should also be the basis for pay and promotion. To constantly tear down business to corporatewide knowledge-sharing is a
  key task.*
- *Not only gaining market share, but expanding the scope of the market, from sophisticated products to services through "migrating" its technology – from jet engines to
  servicing aircraft, even expanding into pilot training – will be key.*

*Most important of all, according to Jack Welch: "Balancing of top-down strategic direc-
tion and bottom-up organizational initiatives must be based on the best people – to
find them, to motivate them, and to give them voice. Everyone counts, everyone must
be involved – the best idea wins!"*

Overview

Consider a successful organization with bottom-up activities taking place. How can
an overall perspective be kept? How can it all still fit together into a common business portfolio? How can a bottom-up/top-down *balanced* perspective be developed
to provide the necessary strategic direction? In this situation the overall corporate
culture can be useful. For an internal entrepreneur in a high-growth company promoting their own business initiatives, it may be a particular challenge to also adhere
to a broad common company focus, to counterbalance what might otherwise be a
strong centrifugal focus from the many entrepreneurial initiatives that could easily
be seen as taking the firm in many directions. Having and developing common

corporate values and culture can be the key, enhancing a broader understanding of responsibility to the company as a whole, rather than only to the specific individual entrepreneurial business activity.

The ability to keep a broad, corporatewide perspective, but which also allows for supercharged individualistic growth initiatives, is therefore critical. While there are many ways to develop an organizational context – a culture with a dual focus (Abell, 1993) – to achieve this, the incentive scheme is particularly crucial. How to develop a culture that justifies a compensation scheme that both rewards world-wide individual competence and holds together the organization as a whole will be important.

The need for an overall portfolio perspective

A broad understanding of the overall business portfolio mix, such as the one given in Figure 3.1 (*see* page 30) is vital.

How do the businesses fit together? Are there potential ways to leverage the firm's available competencies by, say, pooling these across businesses? Can existing market opportunities be exploited? Creating the necessary cohesion is the responsibility of top management and this must balance with the internal entrepreneur's critical role in spearheading internally generated growth. Just as the internal entrepreneur requires space, they also need cohesion to be effective.

One way or another, therefore, an overall portfolio view must be taken to assess that there is enough pioneering, enough transformational innovation. Top management must of course do this and must spearhead the efforts to ameliorate eventual internal deficiencies in the portfolio. In this chapter we will:

- Explore the role of top management in the energized bottom-up organization.
- Discuss how to create a climate for performance (the measurement challenge).

The role of top management in the energized bottom-up organization

Key challenges for senior managers

Where is top management in the energized bottom-up organization? What is top management's role? We have already pointed out that top management plays an important role in keeping an overall view of the firm's portfolio composition. This includes building up internal pressure for pioneering and rapid expansion, counterbalancing the typical tendency of the overall portfolio to focus predominantly on the defend/dominate mode, as well as restructuring businesses. It is absolutely essential that top management has a clear view of what the portfolio mix is, as depicted in Figure 3.1, as well as a willingness and energy to focus the resources of the organization so as to rebuild the portfolio, thereby making it more balanced. As indicated, this typically means more focus from the top on supporting the pioneering activity.

How can top management approach this task? Most will realize that they themselves can typically not spearhead the internally driven growth business projects themselves. Rather, they see their roles as *catalysts* – to support their organizations to pursue growth. Management processes therefore become important, in the sense that these provide the context for interaction between top management and the rest of the organization. Figure 9.1 provides a view of the strategy process in a pioneering, bottom-up organization.

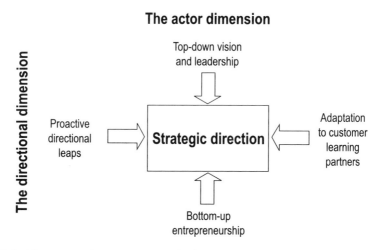

Figure 9.1: *The strategic process as a balancing process between four forces*
Adapted from Lorange, P. (at press) *Setting Strategic Direction in Academic Institutions: The Case of the Business School.*

Forming a top-down vision

If we first look at the top-down/bottom-up vertical dimension, we suggest that pioneering will be driven in the form of bottom-up initiatives by highly committed, internal entrepreneurs acting as catalysts. The pioneers provide important bottom-up input: they are essential actors in the strategic process of the pioneering firm. There must, however, also be a complementary top-down element in order to see the overall portfolio of the firm come together. There is a great need for a proactive vision in the pioneering firm, which would focus on where the firm and its parts want to go in terms of the way things *should* be, independent of the existing momentum. Such a proactive, visionary view preserves the firm's ability to avoid becoming trapped in its own history, allowing for the possibility to think new.

Furthermore, there is ideally a positive symbiosis between the CEO and the internal entrepreneur. It is important that this relationship is constructive and that the CEO in particular does not come across as a restrainer – this would be devastating. Rather, the CEO must see his or her role as one of encouraging out-of-the-box breakthrough thinking. The CEO must be a catalyst, a motivator, one who can trust his or her people in general and the internal entrepreneurs in particular. In this role it is critical that the personal energy of the CEO calls for speed, a willingness to take risks in isolation, and a robustness to deal with mistakes. Clearly, he or she needs to provide a sense of security for the internal entrepreneur. Experimenting also means forgiving; if an open-minded encouraging attitude does not exist, then risk-aversion will easily sneak in. Needless to say, the CEO needs to be a strong, balanced communicator in order to play an effective catalytic role as a growth driver. Total transparency is perhaps the most crucial part of this communication challenge.

Developing a proactive strategy

The horizontal dimension of Figure 9.1 illustrates the other important balancing element. Clearly, much of the strategy comes from adapting the customers' needs on a small scale, for instance by making present strategies even better, building on the successes of the past. In addition, top management must develop a top-down articulation of where the overall strategy needs to go. The strategy provides a balance between the bottom-up and top-down viewpoints. These complementary, proactive and historical balancing views involve looking for both visionary free spiriting, and what current and past customers want. For the CEO, the issue is to balance the proactive side with the adaptive side of the overall portfolio, so that the various elements in the portfolio add up in total.

For the internal entrepreneur, each new business growth initiative needs to have a particular balance on its own. If, for instance, a given initiative falls more into the pioneer category, it would in all likelihood be quite proactive in its balance, with relatively little adaptation. If, on the other hand, the particular growth initiative falls into the dominate/defend category, then one would expect the balance to tilt heavily towards adaptation to present customers, with relatively less proactive emphasis.

The interplay between the top-down and the bottom-up perspectives typically involves a number of iterations so that the various projects will have an appropriate balance on their own, and to ensure that the portfolio has an overall balance that makes sense from the CEO's point of view. Both the CEO and the internal entrepreneur therefore have a complementary responsibility for the entrepreneurial process. This is why we can talk about "multilevel entrepreneurship" (Chakravarthy and Lorange, at press).

The challenges of maintaining a balanced product portfolio

Let us look at these balancing challenges in some more detail. We can find that there are a number of relevant balancing dichotomies paralleling the proactive/adaptive balance, including:

- creation and destruction
- nonpermission and control
- innovation and operations/growth and productivity
- simplicity and complexity
- problem-finding and problem-solving

- passion and denial
- first-mover and waiting to learn/speed and caution
- research and focus
- timing too early and timing too late
- creating the room for new business and keeping room open for interesting business
- lead and be led
- long-term and short-term
- fluidity and definition/intuition and data.

The relevance of these factors is that both the individual growth initiative and the portfolio need to be balanced according to these dimensions. It is essential to find a point of continuum between two extremes; the trade-offs listed above can help with this. This may involve seeing schizophrenic thinking as the norm: for example, vision, creativity and similar attributes need to be in balance with discipline and budgetary focus.

The portfolio strategy task, with the CEO as the key custodian, also involves having to say no to certain bottom-up inspired strategic growth initiatives, not necessarily because the initiative might be ill conceived, but because of the lack of fit of this particular initiative into the overall corporate portfolio. The CEO will thus have to exercise decision-making power based on fit, rather than judging the project only on its own merits. Needless to say, there is a certain risk that such rejections could be seen as negative, and that the catalytic capabilities of the CEO to encourage growth might thereby be jeopardized. In this context, it may make sense for the CEO to think about creating options rather than exercising straight no's. By creating an option and holding a business initiative on a temporary basis, the CEO will have a chance to trade the option later, rather than keep it on a permanent basis in the portfolio (Pindyck and Dixit, 1995). Such options can therefore lead to a holding pattern for new business initiatives, without having to deny them the right to development, even when they may lack a direct fit with the firm's vision of its overall portfolio.

We can see strategy in the pioneering firm, therefore, as the result of four complementary forces – top-down and bottom-up; proactive and adaptive. How does this differ from what we would see in a more typical, mature firm? We would probably have less of a balanced top-down viewpoint and less of a proactive vision, thus leaving the strategy development to be driven more by adaptation to the present and past, as well as more by the bottom-up input from the present divisions in the firm. All in all, a balanced approach provides an important addition to how the pioneering firm works, in contrast with the mature firm that tends to lack internally generated growth as a key characteristic.

Creating a climate for performance: the measurement challenge

The challenge of creating a climate for performance rests to a large degree on our ability to introduce relevant measurements to monitor our progress towards the targets set, along the two dimensions with its four classes of variables given in Figure 9.1. Measurements and concrete follow-up shape performance. Dialogue among management concerning these measurements further strengthens the performance climate. What is being measured will influence the type of climate that will be created. We discuss four types of measurements, following along the two axes in our Figure 9.1.

Measurements addressing top-down vision and leadership

We will recommend three types of measurements that complement each other. While some of these measurements need to be assessed only infrequently – say, once a year – other measures might be applied at more frequent intervals.

Ratio of internal growth versus acquisition-related growth

Let us illustrate this with the example of Nestlé. Nestlé has traditionally grown extensively through heavy emphasis on acquisitions. In the early 1990s, 70% of the company's growth could thus be traced back to acquisitions, with only 30% due to internally generated growth efforts. Top management then realized that this would no longer be an appropriate balance. Acquisitions were becoming more expensive, and suitable acquisitions were harder to find – with many of the good ones having already been made. Further, the internal climate for growth might be weakened, given such great emphasis on acquisitions. A new target was set, representing a complete reversal of the past. At the start of the twenty-first century, 70% of the company's growth comes from internal sources, and only 30% from acquisitions!

Rate of sustainable growth

Both Monsanto and Hoechst have moved away from being primarily classical chemical firms, emphasizing instead the more rapidly growing bioengineering and/or pharmaceutical fields. They have thus "canned" mature, relatively slow-growing business areas, and shifted towards business areas which they consider better suited for the future. Overall, our measurement attempts to assess the portfolio strategy of the firm, and how growth is being associated with the various elements of this portfolio.

Sustainability of long-term growth versus short-term profits for the main business elements within the overall portfolio

The example of Citibank illustrates this well. Citibank used to be a strong force in retail banking in both the USA and Europe. But lack of investment in new products prevented Citibank from maintaining its market share. This was accentuated by short-term pressures on the business, with restructuring and cost-cutting. Short-term focus eventually drove the growth rate for the business down. Citibank did not want to repeat this weak showing of its retail business when it came to the emergent markets. It targeted nine key emergent markets, and decided to invest heavily in the development of new innovation initiatives, cutting across the markets, and monitored progress separately from business as usual. The result of this investment was a considerable increase in the sustainable growth of the business, with a strengthening of Citibank's market share. Top-down assessment of what would be needed to establish an acceptable longer-term basic growth rate for this key element of the overall portfolio was called for. In general, measurement of long-term growth versus short-term profits need to be established.

Measurements relating to bottom-up entrepreneurship

Strategic budget

In many instances, it is recommended to establish a "strategic budget" (Chakravarthy et al., 1991) to complement the operating budget. The strategic budget would be earmarked for the financing of strategic growth initiatives, with budget lines for the additional human resources needed to pursue the growth, as well as for strategic expenditures in marketing, research and development etc. All such expenditures would thus be related specifically to given growth projects. In summary, the strategic budget would be built around expenditures to be monitored. The strategic budget would be put together on a zero-sum basis, built up annually from the bottom, linked to each strategic initiative that is approved. To complement this, specific milestones for progress should also be monitored. The operating budget, in contrast, would relate to business as usual, with budgetary levels associated with the anticipated activity pattern that the firm would follow. The operating budget is incremental, starting out with last year's activity pattern, and adding a certain percentage along the various budgetary lines, reflecting the current activity levels which are anticipated through the anticipated growth. The operating budget would be based on costs, profits and/or revenue levels, monitored through responsibility centres such as cost, profit and/or revenue centres.

Innovation pattern

Another bottom-up measurement would be to make a periodic assessment of the number of innovations that actually come to fruition. More specifically, this assessment might be undertaken for each of the four categories for business growth that we have identified (*see* Figure 3.1). How much growth is being generated anew within the restructure, pioneer/experiment, dominate/defend, or rapid expansion categories? How is this pattern for the growth mix changing over time?

Measurement for proactive leaps

The proactive vision

As we recall, the horizontal axis of Figure 9.1 focuses on the proactive front-end visionary versus the back-end adapting to customer considerations, reaching a specific trade-off. This must be addressed both from top management and from the bottom-up side of the organization. The key is thus to come up with a tailormade balance between the proactive and adaptive considerations, as well as between the top-down and bottom-up emphasis, which would reinforce growth within each of the four categories specified in Figure 3.1. What we might consider as an appropriate balance for restructure would not be the same for pioneer/experiment, dominate/defend, or rapid expansion. We have a tailormade, tailor-focused balancing. Our measurements should thus reflect this tailormaking ambition. Figure 9.2 illustrates this. We see that a focus on a project of the rapid expansion type, for instance, would require relatively more top-down emphasis, and relatively more visionary focus. In contrast, the restructure situation would require relatively more of a bottom-up focus, as well as relatively more adaptive day-to-day emphasis.

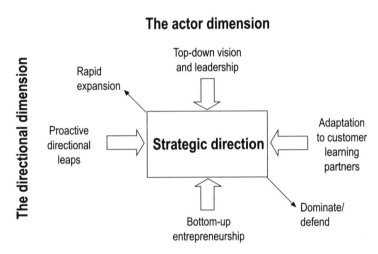

Figure 9.2: *Tailormaking of the strategic process and of measurements*

For measurement of the proactive side, one might consider monitoring the progress towards achieving one's strategic budget targets. In these cases, however, there would typically be a relatively loose link to the operating budget. The renew activities would be run as self-sufficient projects, highly linked to the strategic plan.

"Go–no go" control

In terms of follow-up monitoring of such proactive initiatives, one would typically see a heavy use of so-called "go–no go" control (Newman, 1975). Basically, this would assess whether the results from a strategic program are sufficiently promising to be pursued further, or whether the project should be abandoned. This issue of pursuance or abandonment of a strategic project is critical. One accumulates learning along the way. The "go–no go" control underscores the need to break down strategic programs in smaller entities, so as to undertake what in fact adds up to a string of small sequential experiments, to achieve prudent risk-taking and not accelerate one's resource commitment unnecessarily at too early a stage.

Let us paraphrase the way a CEO might frame this type of "go–no go" control, with the project leader being the person addressed: "I give you a free hand to pick 10 engineers from wherever you want within the organization. I will protect you from any wrath of their line managers. You will receive US$500 000 for strategic expenses. After six months, I would like a report from you indicating whether or not we have a viable business project." We see from this that specific resource commitments are being made for a strategic program, and that a clear calendar is being set, with a clear indication of whether to proceed further or not.

Cautionary control

In some strategic projects, a "contingency" control approach can also be applied (Newman, 1975). Here, the issue is to control the progress of the strategic program against a preset scenario or agenda. If the project does not measure up to this preset plan, then one would need to modify the project by switching to an alternative scenario. According to Harold Leavitt (1986), it will be a matter of "finding another footpath in the forest" – i.e. do not give up if the initial approach fails.

Measurements for monitoring adaptation

Adapting to the day-to-day focus

As noted, the development of a customer/learning partner focus would be related primarily to the restructure situation. Progress would be monitored through the operating budgets. There is a tight link between the operating budget and the project; it is indeed an extension of the operations and of business as usual. This would thus be coupled with a loose link to the strategic plan, since there would be little need to outline the project as part of the strategic plan. Protect and extend implies commonsense extensions of the already established business platform.

Steering control

"Steering" control would be critical here (Newman, 1975), establishing progress relative to budgetary standards, followed by adjustments in those parts of the operating budget that do not live up to anticipated standards. A way to consider this measurement process would be to perceive it as an analogy to steering a rocket towards a target, making frequent, but typically small, adjustments in the direction, based on an ongoing feedback mechanism of assessing real progress relative to a preset target.

The measurements are, as noted, critical in themselves. Even more important is the fact that the measurements will harness managerial behaviour. The result can be a reinforcement of the desired strategic direction. Creating a climate for performance is related closely to creating measurements that reflect appropriately the various trade-offs that need to be tailormade for each strategic situation – between top-down and bottom-up stakeholder foci, between front-end visionary and back-end adaptive foci.

SUMMARY

Bottom-up organizations that successfully pursue rapid, profitable, internally generated growth seem to do a few things differently from other firms when it comes to balancing bottom-up activities with the top-down leadership and the role of the CEO.

First, CEOs have a strong propensity for experimenting with new ideas and for allowing individuals to try out new things. The CEO provides a top-down impetus for this; key qualities needed to ensure that this works include tolerance, a tendency to forgive, and the ability to reconcile themselves (and others) to the fact that a certain experiment did not work out. In addition, capable internal entrepreneurs possessing a strong "can do" attitude and a willingness to take risks without fear of the consequences for their own career also characterizes the pioneering organization. Corporate leadership thus implies *balanced* top-down/bottom-up interaction.

Second, the CEO recognizes fully that the quality of internal entrepreneurs is an essential asset. Internal entrepreneurs will give a company a serious edge over competition in two ways: through their ability to see new business opportunities not obvious to one's competitors and – equally important – an ability to mobilize the resources needed to reap the harvest expected from these opportunities.

Internal entrepreneurs are therefore critical, and a company culture that provides them with space and support is equally essential. Network features of the organization, mainly networked teams, drive the creation of new sources of value. Management processes must be focused on driving growth, rather than on compliance with bureaucratic practices that merely take time and drain energy. The CEO must take direct responsibility for enhancing such a breakthrough performance culture.

We have, however, claimed a different critical focal point to enhance internally generated growth in this chapter – namely, the overriding importance of a proactive CEO who is able to develop a corporate portfolio dimension that strategically guides internally generated growth. Much of this growth is merely a matter of stimulating various growth initiatives. The issue of seeing such initiatives together in an overall balanced context of a corporatewide portfolio must not be overlooked. As we have seen in this chapter, truly effective internally generated growth is dependent on such an overall portfolio focus.

We have argued that three interrelated issues are especially important for the CEO to practice in order to make his or her contribution to the internally generated growth process:

1. *A readiness to balance the various growth initiatives in an overall portfolio*, dealing, where necessary, with various growth projects on a temporary basis as options. These options will then have to be managed actively, not forgotten. The CEO must have an aptitude towards reactivating the trading of such growth project options later on.
2. *Creating a climate for performance* rests to a large degree on our ability to introduce measurements to monitor our progress towards targets that relate to

growth, the strategic budget, the innovation pattern, the proactive vision, issues of control, and adaptation.

3. *Creating an effective network organization* is vital. The CEO can have a significant impact on the choice of members of his organization. Effective recruiting and promotion are essential. In addition, he can provide an organizational design which calls for openness, communication, and involving key people, rather than building on hierarchical control. Thus, network thinking and project-based management are key parts of the growth agenda.

In summary, a top-down leadership dimension is essential for creating an effective bottom-up organization driven by internally generated growth. Without such a top-down manifestation of organizational energy, it will be hard for the bottom-up organizational initiatives to thrive. However, the key is a top-down/bottom-up balance based on complementary approaches, not duplication of effort or discouragement. It must be based on a "can do" complementarity.

 **BEST PRACTICE**

Understanding how well your business is managing initiatives is a useful starting point for assessing the changes that may need to take place to strengthen your organization. In particular, it is helpful to understand:

- how well the organization is balancing top-down leadership and bottom-up organization; and
- how cohesive and dynamic the overall business portfolio is.

The following questions (drawn from concepts and issues raised in this chapter and Chapter 3) are designed to help focus thinking on your organization's current practices, and how these might change in the future.

- Are there unusual growth opportunities?
- Can existing market opportunities be exploited?
- Do we have the resources in place to take advantage of these opportunities?
- How well do the businesses fit together? Do they, for example, complement the brand, providing a strong and coherent identity? Are there synergies between businesses, and are these being exploited? (Consider how easily and successfully they are being exploited.)
- Are there businesses or products that have sprung up as a result of bottom-up initiative where, because no-one said no, they gained their own momentum, but now they simply do not fit with the overall portfolio?

- Are the proactive and adaptive sides of the organization in balance, and does the product portfolio include new and existing products in a reasonable balance, given market conditions?

It can be useful to measure businesses against the business development portfolio (outlined in Figure 3.1), assessing new and planned products and businesses in each of the four categories: pioneer/experiment, rapid expansion, dominate/defend, and restructure.

References

Abell, D. (1993) *Managing with Dual Strategies - Mastering the Present; Preempting the Future*. New York: Free Press.

Chakravarthy, B. and Lorange, P. (at press) *Nurturing Organic Growth: Multilevel Entrepreneurship*.

Chakravarthy, B. and Lorange, P. (1991) *Managing the Business Process: A Framework for a Multibusiness Firm*, Englewood Cliffs, USA: Prentice Hall.

Leavitt, H.J. (1986) *Corporate Pathfinders: Building Vision and Values into Organizations*. Homewood, USA: Dow Jones Irwin.

Newman, W. (1975) *Constructive Control*. Englewood Cliffs, USA: Prentice Hall.

Pindyck, R.S. and Dixit, A.K. (1995) The Option Approach to Capital Investment, *Harvard Business Review* **73**(3): 105–115.

10

Focusing on Breakthrough Options

To focus energy, management has to select out the most promising options created by bottom-up initiatives and nurture them into major value-creating moves. In this chapter, **Paul Strebel** presents a framework for identifying the options with breakthrough potential, based on the evolutionary and revolutionary patterns that shape an industry's lifecycle.

CASE STUDY: SONY'S USE OF STRATEGIC OPTIONS

Over its life, Sony has demonstrated a remarkable ability to make big moves. Not all of these have led to breakthroughs. But the successful moves invariably have been preceded by the development of multiple strategic options, which have provided the basis for the breakthroughs. Sony began to adopt the options approach after its development phase, once product imitation was no longer possible, because it had caught up with the competition. Top management began trying to jump-start innovation by setting targets and putting together multiple taskforces to develop new products. The introduction of prototypes into the market was managed flexibly to provide options as events unfolded for both adapting to, and leading, the market.

By the late 1980s Sony was already legendary for its ability to introduce new products from a portfolio of available options supported by a finely tuned business model. It was this capability that created Sony's breakthrough to being undisputed leader of the worldwide consumer electronics industry. More recently, Sony has applied the same approach to breaking through in the market for home video games. And it has put together another portfolio of options, with a flurry of alliances and partnerships, searching for a breakthrough in the entertainment industry.

Overview

To harness the energy and counter the centrifugal forces generated by bottom-up initiatives, the most promising opportunities have to be consciously selected out and nurtured into major value-creating moves. Top management has to make major commitments of resources, from time to time, to the one or few initiatives it believes can produce a corporate breakthrough to new levels of value creation. This chapter introduces a framework for selecting the most promising opportunities.

The opportunities for value creation generated by high-energy, bottom-up organizations include independent experiments, projects and new ventures, initiated by enterprising people on the frontline, as well as suggestions for reducing costs and managing resource constraints that are proposed by employees involved in continual improvement. In the face of an uncertain environment (Courtney et al., 1997), it makes sense to consider the opportunities generated by a bottom-up organization as possible options (Strebel, 1992; Williamson, 1999) on breaking through to new levels of value creation. This chapter looks at:

- the contrast between evolutionary and revolutionary approaches to breaking through;
- identifying strategic options with breakthrough potential; and
- deciding whether to exercise (commit major resources to fully implementing) breakthrough options.

Evolutionary and revolutionary paths to breakthrough

Which opportunities should be developed into options and whether the options should be exercised depends on the rate of change in the industry environment. Is the industry evolving incrementally enough to allow the company to develop options that build on existing competencies? If so, management can reduce the uncertainty by learning more about the environment, extending the range of competencies, while the options are being explored. Then, when the time comes to make a major commitment, it can do so with relative confidence about the potential outcome. This ideal, low-risk route to a value-creating breakthrough is an *evolutionary path*, one that builds systematically on existing competence. Management encourages competing bottom-up initiatives to show what they can do, nurtures the most promising of these, and then makes a final commitment based on the estimated value of the options when the time is ripe.

By contrast, in turbulent times the traditional methods of analysis do not apply. If the industry is changing fundamentally, options have to be developed based on entirely new competencies. Simply exploring evolutionary options cannot reduce uncertainty. The ultimate commitment of resources is very risky. To be among the industry leaders, management has to energize its people to come up with radically new initiatives and then use its judgement to make risky commitments before the window of opportunity closes. This high-risk route to a value-creating breakthrough is a *revolutionary path*, which involves moves based on new competence. Management has to deal with the risk involved and exercise its strategic judgement about the value and timing of competing initiatives.

The evolutionary and revolutionary paths to value creation, assuming an energized bottom-up organization, are depicted schematically in Figure 10.1.

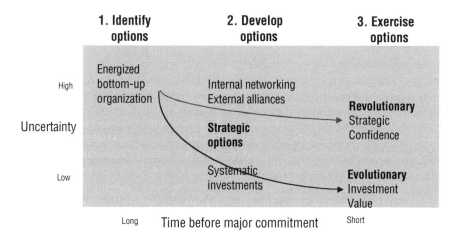

Figure 10.1: *Evolutionary and revolutionary paths to breakthrough*
Inspired by Matthews, W.H. (1990) Kissing Technological Frogs: Managing Technology as a Strategic Resource, *IMD Perspectives for Managers* **5**.

When exploration and experimentation can reduce the uncertainty (evolutionary path), it makes economic sense to capture as much of the potential value creation in options as possible, by investing systematically in wholly-owned experiments and acquisitions that provide the right to the full upside potential. On the evolutionary path, the most valuable options are typically those that leverage, or take advantage of, and extend existing competencies. The payoff to the leveraged development of competence is higher, because existing experience can be applied to the creation of value. Moreover, the cost is lower, because of the partial use of resources in place. Yet this is only true if there is some evolutionary continuity in the value of assets and competencies, as opposed to the discontinuity on the revolutionary path.

When the uncertainty cannot be reduced (the revolutionary path), it makes economic sense to invest in numerous low-cost, high-potential options, small experiments and projects based on entirely new competencies, involving alliances and other networking relationships, in which both the risk and reward is shared if necessary with other partners. This has the advantage of both exploring new competencies and conserving resources, while allowing for a possible diversification of the risk when the time comes to make major entrepreneurial commitments. Putting together an appropriate portfolio of revolutionary options requires a view on how the industry is likely to evolve.

Identifying breakthrough options

The evolutionary path

The key to breaking through on an evolutionary path is selecting options with value creating leverage (Utterback, 1994; Victor and Boynton, 1998). Leverage is based on "sticking to the knitting", building on existing core, distinctive competence. Recent research by the Corporate Strategy Board (1997), for example, suggests that the most common route to sustained profitable growth in the medium term is the rollout to new markets and customers of a single successful business model. The valuable options on this route are associated with potential new markets and customers. An example described below is the worldwide rollout of Sony's consumer electronics business.

A second route to evolutionary breakthrough is harvesting the new product offering ideas generated by a bottom-up organization, both internally and through external networking. The most valuable options here are those that fit the market and take advantage of the existing delivery systems, as illustrated by Sony's breakthrough to leadership of the consumer electronics industry with successive new product introductions.

Another evolutionary route is based on selecting the latent options with leverage that can unlock the most value creation by improving the existing business model, for example by unblocking an inefficient process, by providing access to scarce resources, or by capitalizing on hidden assets. This is what Sony did in the mid-1990s when it dropped its country organization and reorganized around product lines, in order to capitalize fully on its strong brand image.

CASE STUDY: SONY'S USE OF EVOLUTIONARY OPTIONS IN CONSUMER ELECTRONICS

During the early years when Sony was starting up, it didn't have resources to invest in a portfolio of strategic options. The question was whether to lower the risk of start-up by entering into alliances with the big Japanese trading companies, as was customary in Japan at the time. Akio Morita and his colleagues evidently decided to take the risk and higher return associated with total ownership, since the way ahead, in terms of technology at least, was more or less clearly marked by competitors, especially those in the USA. As Akio Morita recounts, they developed their own tape recorder and magnetic tape, without any help from the outside. Instead of relying on third parties for distribution, which is customary in Japan, Sony set up its own sales outlets throughout Japan.

Sony's success created valuable geographic options, which it then exercised by rolling out its successful business model, setting up its own marketing system in various countries and, later, world-scale plants.

Having caught up with the competitors, Sony also began to develop a portfolio of new product options. Management encouraged product innovation by setting up innovation targets and putting together taskforces to develop the products. Management carefully selected and challenged small taskforces, or design teams, to produce a prototype with step-by-step creative engineering. In the words of Sony managers:"We always have an image of how an ideal product would look and perform in our minds. This is not wishful thinking on our part, but a concrete plan for which exact product specifications have been drawn up, including a target price ... Once the prototypes of future models are already developed, our marketing is quite flexible.We are prepared to launch new products into the market when the need arises." (Ohsone, 1998).

Sony exercised the options of introducing new products when appropriate. It launched the first home video recorder in 1964 and solid-state condenser microphone in 1965. The Trinitron colour TV tube, which was introduced in 1968, led to a decade of explosive growth. Sony followed this, in 1979, by another blockbuster product, the Walkman personal stereo. Morita himself gave the go-ahead to the Walkman design team, overriding the objection of sales and marketing, which were not convinced that a portable tape player would sell. Competitors also held back for the same reason. After launching the Walkman, Sony exercised the option of immediately expanding the product portfolio by making improvements and introducing new variants. With 85 models on offer, sales of the Sony Walkman accounted for 40% of portable tape player sales in the USA and 50% in Japan in the late 1980s.

By the end of the 1980s, Sony's ability to put new products on the market, from a portfolio of available options supported by a finely tuned business model, had created its breakthrough to become undisputed leader of the worldwide consumer electronics industry. The American competitors had effectively retired from the race, and in Europe, Sony was number one even in the Netherlands, the home market of its major rival, Philips.

As one might expect, however, many of the new product options turned out to be worth very little, while the further development of others were big errors. For example, the huge commitment to the Betamax video recorder was unable to beat back the

challenge of the alliance supporting the VHS system, largely because of the software available for the latter. In 1990, Digital Audiotape was launched as the magnetic tape response to the compact disc, but sold only a fraction of what was planned and had to be repositioned for the professional market.

The revolutionary path

Revolutionary options mark sudden shifts in the rules of the industry game, which have a dramatic impact on the position of the players (Miller and Friesen, 1980; Strebel, 1992; Grove, 1996; Fine, 1999). To reduce the perceived uncertainty associated with revolutionary options, judgement about the industry's development is essential. Industry intelligence, then, is the key to selection of revolutionary options. Without a sense for what the next industry shifts might be, it is difficult to select an appropriate portfolio of revolutionary options. Revolutionary options emerge in two main contexts:

- Breakpoint transitions between dominant business models.
- Product/technology breakthroughs.

Breakpoint transitions between business models

Important breakpoints in the rules of the game, with the emergence of a new set of options, occur during the shifts between business models. There are two basic models: competition to offer more perceived value (periods when the product portfolios of the players diverge in the pursuit of innovative offerings), and/or competition to lower delivered costs (periods when the product portfolios of the players converge in the pursuit of efficiency). Within each of these basic model categories, different ways of offering more perceived value and lowering delivered cost can be distinguished in the life of many industries. A classic lifecycle progression of business models and the corresponding breakpoints, is shown in Figure 10.2.

The first model involves options on product innovation and offering pioneering, marked by divergence: new entrants, competitors innovating in different directions, customers willing to experiment with new and different offerings, the value chain and technology often in a state of transition. This first phase of an industry's life is usually very turbulent and uncertain. This makes it imperative for players who want a reasonable chance of survival to hedge their offering development process with options based on low-cost alliances and partnerships. For larger players that can afford it, this means options based on independent new product development initiatives.

The next phase involves high-volume standardization around a dominant offering design that a large market of customers understands and wants. The competitive game shifts to lower costs and high volumes, delivered by functionally organized companies. The new business model is based on standard procedures and systems.

A third model, characterized by options on divergent variety creation, is possible when enough explicit knowledge has accumulated to segment and serve the market with a differentiated offering. This is a business model that excels at adaptation and

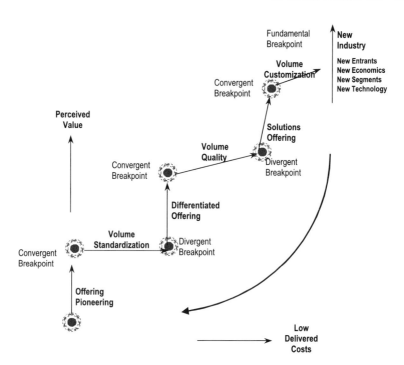

Figure 10.2: *Typical industry evolutionary patterns and breakpoints*

augmentation of the basic offering, with options based on differentiated design, functionality, image and/or quality, to develop new market segments. In consumer markets, successful brands become the key to survival. The options involve reorganization around separate divisions serving the various segments.

The fourth model involves converging offerings, when competitors start drawing on employee-driven improvement options to deliver low-cost volume with quality. The breakpoint shift is to a process organization engineered either incrementally, as in Japan with kaizen and lean management, or in radical steps, as in the USA, to deliver cost-effective, high-quality offerings.

A fifth model is associated with options on diverging offerings in the move to customer intimacy, solutions offerings based on a "high touch" approach. This provides organizational and high-net-worth customers with problem-solving and service designed specifically for their needs. The options involve a shift to a network organization capable of assembling temporary, multibusiness project teams to deliver a solution to a customer's problem. Integration across business units is the organizational challenge.

Most recently, a sixth model has emerged with options on delivery of high-volume, individually customized offerings. IT has been applied to well-designed processes to develop this volume customization. The delivery process requires the rapid, flexible assembly of cost-effective modules to respond to individual customers. Exercise of the options involves the application of information technology to well-designed value chains of activity.

The mastery of a business model leads to increasing competition, which undermines its profitability, opening the way for a new model with accompanying options. For example, while offering pioneering is still underway, the value of innovation options dominates the uncertain returns to volume delivery, until product development runs out of steam. Once the product is developed, it becomes possible to settle on a dominant design, which can be used as the basis for standardization, driving down the cost, and moving to volume delivery.

Options based on enhancement of perceived value and delivered cost go increasingly hand-in-hand as the lifecycle proceeds. In the volume-with-quality model, well-designed process organizations create improvement options on lower cost and higher quality. In the solutions model, well-designed network organizations provide options on higher value, integrated solutions to customer problems at lower cost. And in the volume-customization model, flexible modularity generates options incorporating lower cost and increased perceived value by tailoring products to customer needs at high volumes.

Apart from increasing competition, which reduces the profitability of the existing business model and related options, a sudden external shift may alter the economic balance between competing business models and sets of options. Such shifts include radical changes in political interference and/or regulation, and sudden sharp expansion or contraction in the economic cycle. Divergent innovation is often triggered by external events. New innovation options often lie dormant until something launches them into the money. The classic trigger is economic expansion, which releases savings, and increases spending power and the consumer's propensity to try new things. Economic expansion has promoted the diverging offerings evident in many US industries today. Another is sociopolitical liberalization and decentralization that opens up new markets and deregulates existing ones. Well-known examples in the last decade include the opening of geographic markets in the East and the privatization of others in the West.

The convergent pursuit of efficiency may also be triggered by external events. On the macroeconomic level, recessions force many industries into a convergent posture. The drop in demand puts pressure on processes, efficiency and costs. The long recession that followed the oil price crisis of the 1970s put an end to differentiation and made continual improvement and lean manufacturing the key to value creation in many industries. Sony made a decisive organizational move towards generating employee-driven options on continual improvement, as soon as it picked up the cost of exporting defective products. When the world recession of the seventies arrived, it adroitly exploited its cost and quality options. Later, during the long Japanese recession of the 1990s, Sony restructured quickly with a big move to install a more cost-efficient business model.

Product/technology breakthroughs

Successive product or technology breakthroughs may dominate the natural lifecycle progression of business models. Companies compete not only by extending the lifecycle with new capabilities (moving up the diagonal in Figure 10.2), but also by introducing radically new products. Options on successive new product introductions capitalize on the capabilities already in place. This is a common state of affairs in fashion, design and high-tech industries. Commodity industries, on the other hand, with very low rates of new product introduction and little scope for new capabilities, may experience breakthroughs in the delivery technology.

Attackers within the industry can create sudden product breakthroughs by identifying options on new market segments, redefining the value chain, or otherwise fundamentally changing the offering (Kim and Mauborgne, 1997). Classic examples include South West Airlines targeting people who drive long distances by car, offering them cheaper, faster air travel over the same routes. Another is IKEA, the Swedish furniture manufacturer, which turned the economics of the furniture business upside down by redefining and redesigning the core elements of the value chain, outsourcing all other activities.

Technological breakthroughs by new entrants can be especially sudden for existing players. Recent research (Christensen, 1997) has shown that the performance of new technology is often inferior to what exists for similar purposes. Yet it opens up options on a new market of customers who are at first intrigued and then satisfied with what the new technology can offer. The players and the economics of this new market may initially be quite different, off the radar screens, or scorned by the players in the older market. However, gradual improvements in the new technology progress to a point, where it suddenly provides enough value to satisfy most of the market at a cost that is much more attractive than the old technology. At this point, the whole market rapidly switches to the new, more favourable value-cost offering and the old technology is effectively dead. A classic case was the development of smaller, fuel-efficient cars by the Japanese. They were scorned at first for poor performance by Westerners, then, when the oil crisis struck, were suddenly perceived to have good quality at lower prices.

From time to time, on the technological front, massive bursts of innovation create clusters of new industries and restructure old ones, with a plethora of new options reflecting what Schumpeter called "creative destruction". These cause fundamental breakpoints that mark the transition between industry lifecycles. The first industrial breakthrough was driven by the introduction of textile machinery and water-powered factories in Great Britain in the late eighteenth century. Steel, steam and the railroad followed in the first half of the nineteenth century; autos, electricity and chemicals in the late nineteenth century; aircraft and petrochemicals in the first half of the twentieth century; and, today, the huge impact of the microprocessor, the Internet, and the emergence of genetic engineering.

Such fundamental breakpoints put enormous pressure on the players in existing industries. The microprocessor today is generating intense competition between the personal computer, consumer electronic, and telecom industries to create the standard for the personal device people use to access and process information, communicate, and engage in e-commerce. Further down the value chain of e-commerce, existing software and media companies are competing with new start-ups, like AOL, to control the portals, or gateways, to the Internet. In many other industries, there is a deluge of options in the form of alliances and a wave of acquisitions and mergers as players try to cope with fundamental breakpoints unleashed by the information revolution. A typical example is Sony's development of a flurry of new options in the media industry.

In the late 1980s, Sony made a dramatic revolutionary move, one of the biggest bets since its founding. It acquired CBS Records and Columbia Pictures Entertainment, two of America's largest media companies. With the international battle over HDTV standards looming in the background, Sony integrated forward to acquire a downstream presence in the apparent belief that these activities would dominate the future of the consumer electronics industry. Having been burned by the lack of software for the Betamax video recorder, Sony apparently was determined not to make the same mistake again.

But Sony soon found itself paying for its error in entering the media industry with big acquisition bets without trying first to lower the risk by learning the rules of the game with options based on media alliances. Unfortunately, when worldwide consumer electronics sales turned down, the media business produced a string of box-office flops. Radical restructuring of the media business was needed, before Sony Studios bounced back with some hits including "Jerry Maguire" and "Men in Black".

On the other hand, Sony established option positions in semiconductors, home video games, and laptop computers. It didn't try to get into these industries on its own, but began to make alliances. This is hardly surprising, in view of the difficulty Sony faced in managing uncertainty in these unfamiliar settings and the risk it had already taken on in the media industry. Sony manufactured Apple Computer's highly successful Power-book. Sony joined Intel to develop a line of PC desktop systems. Sony also joined with Nintendo to create a new kind of game console with the graphic capabilities of a work-station. After Nintendo pulled out, Sony went ahead on its own to introduce the PlaySta-tion in the mid-1990s. The PlayStation was hugely successful both in Japan and the USA. By the end of the 1990s, Sony was challenging Nintendo and Sega for the number one postion in game computers.

Sony's fluctuating profits in the late 1990s reflected the uncertainty created by the increasing convergence and overlap between the consumer electronics, PC, software and media industries. To deal with this uncertainty, Sony has expanded its portfolio of low-cost options in the media industry with a flurry of alliances and partnerships. In 1998, Sony Online Entertainment was created to develop the Internet business, Loew's Theatres was merged with Cineplex Odeon to form Loew's Cineplex Entertainment (51% owned by Sony), and 131 new titles were released for the PlayStation compared to Nin-tendo's 50. In addition, the first HDTV was shipped to the USA in 1998, and a deal was made with General Instrument Corp. to develop digital set-top boxes for cable TV. In early 1999, Sony announced a joint venture with Philips and Sun Microsystems to produce networked entertainment products. Sony is now evidently on a revolutionary path in search of a breakthrough option in the entertainment industry.

Deciding to exercise breakthrough options

On an evolutionary path, managers exercise those options with the highest estimated value. On a revolutionary path, they must use strategic confidence as the main crite-rion for deciding which options to exercise.

Evolutionary paths

When evaluating the exercised value of evolutionary options, the traditional methods of strategic and financial analysis can be employed. The potential value of exercised options depends on the market demand (both price and growth), and the ability of the company to implement and deliver with a cost advantage, and capture the value created in the face of competition. Since the uncertainty associated with evolutionary options is relatively low, it is usually possible to estimate the net present value of committing the resources to implement the option. The potential breakthrough options will be those with the highest estimated value.

Revolutionary paths

The uncertainty surrounding a revolutionary path is such that data-based analysis is virtually impossible. Instead, when time is available, management has to hedge its bets with a portfolio of low-cost options, as Sony is currently doing. However, as time runs out, the big question is which of these options should be exercised? Given the uncertainty, intuition is important in practice, but it should be intuition based on a developed sense of *strategic confidence*.

Strategic confidence comes from a *well-developed industry view* a sense for how the industry is progressing through its lifecycle and a related sense for the timing of available opportunities (see Best Practice below). A second component of strategic confidence is management's *ability to manage the risk* associated with revolutionary options. Contemplating a big move without managing the risk does not provide a sound basis for strategic confidence, as Sony's first big media move shows. A third component of strategic confidence is the ability to gain *access to the required new competence*. Revolutionary options, because of their rule-breaking nature, cannot leverage much off existing competencies. Access to the new competencies through acquisition, or the ongoing management of alliances and networks is essential. The gap in this regard, compared to a fourth component, the likely *response of strategically aware competitors*, is important in deciding which options to exercise.

SUMMARY

The history of Sony illustrates the critical importance of getting the emphasis right between the execution of evolutionary and revolutionary options. Evolutionary options are most appropriate when the business model is relatively stable, but are inadequate during major industry transitions. On the other hand, unprepared revolutionary moves in a highly uncertain environment can be very costly. The key to getting the emphasis right is understanding where the industry is in terms of its development.

To decide which opportunities should be converted into strategic options, and to choose the appropriate path to a potential breakthrough, managers have to continually ask themselves whether the evolutionary pattern they are in is sustainable over their strategic horizon, or whether a sudden revolutionary breakpoint might be in the offing.

Whereas the standard strategic and financial analysis is appropriate for evaluating evolutionary options, when the time comes to execute the options and make major investments, strategic confidence is needed to evaluate revolutionary options.

BEST PRACTICE

Identifying breakthrough options

To select options with the potential for breakthrough, management has to develop a sense for how the industry is likely to evolve. An effective way of doing this is to construct industry scenarios. There are several steps in the development of industry scenarios:

- Firstly, position the players. Describe the history of the business in terms of industry patterns and business models. Locate the current position of the businesses, customers and competitors in terms of the corresponding dominant business models (*see* Figure 10.2).
- Secondly, identify forces of change. List the external forces of change (trends, potential trend reversals, disequilibria and anomalies) affecting the industry. Cluster the forces favouring evolutionary paths on the one hand, and those favouring revolution on the other hand.
- Thirdly, sketch out evolutionary and revolutionary scenarios. Examine how the configurations of evolutionary and revolutionary forces will, in turn, affect the players. Develop an evolutionary scenario in which the currently dominant business model is extended incrementally. Develop a revolutionary scenario in which attackers introduce a fundamentally different business model and/or a fundamentally new product offering.
- Fourthly, select a portfolio of options for development that reflects the evolutionary and revolutionary opportunities for breakthrough in the industry.

Deciding to exercise breakthrough options

To decide whether to exercise an evolutionary option, use traditional stategic and financial analysis. By contrast, strategic confidence is needed to decide whether to exercise a revolutionary option. The components of strategic confidence point to the following guidelines for deciding on the high-risk, big moves associated with exercising a revolutionary option:

- When the industry view is uncertain and access to new competence is difficult, a big move should not be made. Where possible the option should be sold before it loses all its value.
- When the industry view is uncertain, but the required new competence can be accessed easily, the option should be kept open as long as possible to allow confidence in the option's potential to grow. A key question is whether risk management can be used to lower the uncertainty and increase management's confidence. The danger is that while this is being done, the window of opportunity on the option may close. Hence, the importance of some risk appetite in pursuing a revolutionary path.
- When confidence in the industry view is high and the competence gap is large, a big organizational move should be made to close the gap. Depending on the nature of the gap, a major organizational shift or fundamental change management will be necessary. The big question here is one of timing. Can the organization be focused quickly enough to exercise and realize the value of the option in time?
- When confidence in the industry view is high and the access gap to competence is small, management should make its revolutionary move as rapidly as possible.

References

Christensen, C.M. (1997) *The Innovator's Dilemma*. Boston: Harvard Business School Press.

Corporate Strategy Board (1997) *Unbroken Growth: Salient Insights from Inaugural Research*, report, The Advisory Board Company.

Courtney, H., Kirkland, J. and Viguerie, P. (1997) Strategy under Uncertainty, *Harvard Business Review*, November/December 1997: 67–79.

Fine, C.H. (1999) *Clock Speed*. Champaign, IL, USA: Perseus Books.

Grove, A.S. (1996) *Only the Paranoid Survive*. New York: Doubleday.

Kim, W.C. and Mauborgne, R. (1997) The Strategic Logic of High Growth, *Harvard Business Review*, January/February, 1997: 103–112.

Miller, D. and Friesen, P.H. (1980) Momentum and Revolution in Organizational Adaptation, *Academy of Management Journal*, 591–614.

Ohsone (1998) Innovations in Management: The case of the Walkman, *Sony Innovation in Management Series*, **1**: 3–21.

Strebel, P. (1992a) Developing Strategic Options, in *Breakpoints: How Managers Exploit Radical Business Change*. Boston: Harvard Business School Press.

Strebel, P. (1992b) *Breakpoints*. Boston: Harvard Business School Press.

Utterback, J. (1994) *Mastering the Dynamics of Innovation*. Boston: Harvard Business School Press.

Victor, B. and Boynton, A. (1998) *Invented Here*. Boston: Harvard Business School Press.

Williamson, P.J. (1999) Strategy as Options on the Future, *Sloan Management Review*, Spring 1999: 117–126.

11

Developing Strategy from Within

What often gets lost in a bottom-up organization is the process of strategy formation. Firms are either not planning for the future, arguing that it is too difficult in today's turbulent environment, or are outsourcing strategy to consulting firms. In this chapter, **Peter Killing** argues that this is a dangerous move, and provides practical guidelines to help managers learn how to involve their people in shaping the direction of the business, by developing successful in-house strategy.

Overview

The bottom-up organization is a much more responsive and efficient place than the organization of 10 years ago. "Doing more with less" is today's rallying cry, and that challenge becomes even more difficult when the "more" in question may need to be done on different continents. The result is that the managers who remain in today's downsized organizations are working far harder and longer than they ever have before.

However, even with the increased efficiency of modern communications and the best of intentions, two managers cannot do the work previously done by four, and in the transition from the old organization to the new, something had to give way. Surprisingly perhaps, the factor that has been lost in many companies is the strategy-making process. Many management teams are simply not spending enough time thinking about *how* and *where* they will compete in the future.

It is easy to ignore strategy. Books like Henry Mintzberg's *The Rise and Fall of Strategic Planning* (1994) argue persuasively that strategic planning, at least as practised by large corporate planning groups at head office, does more harm than good. Furthermore, there are no longer central planning groups in the superstar companies that everyone looks to these days, such as General Electric, Bertelsmann and ABB. The era of strategy created by central staff is clearly over.

What do we have instead? In some firms, nothing much. Managers are so busy grappling with today that they do not have the time and energy to devote to thinking about tomorrow. This is abdication.

Other firms have a slightly more persuasive stance. They argue that the environment is so turbulent that they cannot possibly anticipate it effectively, and if they try they will get it wrong. Their strategy, therefore, is to become faster and more flexible so that whatever happens they will be able to respond quickly. This is all very well, but there are firms that are making proactive strategic choices that are defining how business will be carried out in their industry in the future. AT&T's recent acquisitions and alliances come to mind, as do the merger between Daimler and Chrysler, and Shell's multibillion-dollar investment in Nigeria. If you decide that responsiveness is good enough you will always be late, and firms like those just mentioned may end up controlling your destiny.

A third group of firms is indeed concerned about the future and wants to do more than simply respond, but they have chosen to *outsource* much of their strategic thinking to the strategy consulting firms. This too is a mistake. The major problem is not the quality of the consultants, young and inexperienced though many of them are, but the lack of buy-in on the part of the company managers who will ultimately need to implement the strategy put forward by the consultants.

> **"A good strategy-making process results in not only a road map for the future, but a set of committed managers ready to make it happen"**

So do not ignore strategy, do not settle for responsiveness, and do not outsource strategy. Do it yourself, with your own people. This chapter provides some ideas that will help you get started, including:

- focusing on people and processes;
- understanding and actively leading the strategy-making process; and
- following the strategy-making road map.

Focusing on people and process

Most strategy books and articles focus on the tools of strategic analysis. Who has not heard of Michael Porter's five forces model, value chain analysis, or SWOT (strengths, weaknesses, opportunities, threats) analysis? Identifying useful tools is not so difficult. The trick is to create a process that makes best use of these tools and, more importantly, takes full advantage of the skills, knowledge and creativity of your people. Your own people know your business far better than a consultant ever will, and by bringing together employees who are close to your markets, customers, technology, suppliers and regulators, you can create an opportunity for penetrating analysis and creativity that cannot be equalled by any group of outsiders.

To do this, your strategy-making process needs to be inclusive and open, not a deeply guarded secret open to only a few initiates. The process needs to take place in an environment that is nonthreatening – open, fun and interesting, yet challenging. Whether you end up making major modifications to your existing strategy, or largely reaffirming your current intentions, the process of strategy-making should be the most exciting and demanding activity taking place in your business. The immediate result will be a shared commitment to a set of actions that will bring success to the business.

The longer-term result will be the creation of a group of people who have been through a significant experience together and know each other's thinking very well. When you need to make alterations in course, as you inevitably will, you should be able to do it quickly because everyone understands the broad strategic context in which the changes need to be made. You have a management team that is on the same strategic wavelength.

However, do-it-yourself strategy making does have two potential pitfalls: the possibly dangerous role of management preferences, and a potential lack of objectivity about the firm's capabilities.

Potential pitfalls in developing your own strategy

Management preferences

The people involved in your strategy-making process will have personal preferences that impact directly on the nature and intensity of the debates that will emerge at various stages in the process. These preferences, which stem from each individual's current job, work history and basic personality, may be deeply rooted and have more influence on an individual's point of view on a particular issue than any amount of rational argument. (For a fuller discussion, see Fry and Killing, 2000.)

In one recent session in England, for example, a British manager, who had had several successful assignments in the USA, argued passionately that the company's strategy should be to expand in the US market. A Japanese manager wanted to form an alliance with a prestigious Japanese firm. The R&D manager was far less concerned about geographic issues, and argued the point that the only way to build a sustainable competitive advantage was through superior technology. Such positions are not at all unusual, and the challenge for the general manager running the session was to cut through the preference-driven arguments to get to the facts supporting each case. But of course such "facts" are themselves very suspect when delivered by a manager with strong preferences.

SmithKline Beecham (SKB) spent two years in the mid-1990s creating and refining a process for allocating its R&D funds (a strategic issue in any pharmaceutical company) that would get around the problem of management preferences. At the heart of the new SKB process was a set of decision analysis routines that included problem framing, the creation of alternatives, the use of decision trees to capture risk assessments and the underlying drivers of risk, options analysis, sensitivity analysis, and agreed measures of risk-adjusted return (Sharpe and Keelin, 1998).

Equally dangerous is the situation in which your group members share many preferences. If you all have similar backgrounds (engineers of the same age and nationality, for example), and have worked together for a long time, there may be a tendency for everyone to see the world the same way. Because the future is unlikely to be like the past and new rules will probably emerge in your industry, this is potentially a serious problem. To recognize the new forces that will change your competitive landscape, and to create new solutions for the business, you need diversity in your strategy-making group.

The solution to overcoming this problem of common preferences is to ensure that you have people of different ages, backgrounds, nationalities and job function in the strategy-making group. In addition, once discussion gets under way make sure that comments from junior people, and people new to the company, are heard.

Lack of objectivity

Another problem that may emerge in a group that has worked together for some time is a lack of objectivity about the capabilities of the business. This can work in either direction: some groups are very flattering in their assessments of their own capabilities, while others are unduly pessimistic. Either extreme is dangerous, and this is one of the reasons that benchmarking has become so popular. There is nothing like a visit to a world-class manufacturing plant or distribution centre to open a few eyes. As a result, do not enter your strategy-making process with the expectation that a group of people in a room for a few days with a bunch of flip charts and overhead projectors can get the job done. It is very probable that you will need to collect new information from outside the firm as you go through the process.

Another cure for a lack of objectivity is to include people who have been hired recently from the other firms in the industry within your strategy-making group. One European business recently asked an executive who had taken early retirement from a competitor to join their strategy-making process. He added knowledge and a perspective that proved to be invaluable to the group.

Actively lead the strategy-making process

If you are the senior manager in a strategy-making process you should actively lead the process being followed. Do not delegate decisions about the overall path that will be followed, and the time to be spent on each step of the process. You should, for example, have a strong influence on questions such as:

- Are we addressing the right issues, in the right order, in the right depth?
- Are the right people involved in the discussion?
- Have we been honest – or have we just given ourselves the easy answers we wanted to hear?
- Do we have enough commitment, from the right people, to our new strategy?

Answers to such questions are critical and should not be left to chance. As the senior manager, your substantive comments will of course shape the debate – but your ability to manage the process may play an even greater role in determining overall success.

CASE STUDY: THE IMPORTANCE OF LEADING THE STRATEGY-MAKING PROCESS

In 1998 a division manager in a major European firm decided that his management team needed to go through a strategy review process. He knew that his managers believed that industry trends were working against them, and the future did not look good. Some believed that an immediate alliance was the preferred way to solve the problem. These managers were not enthusiastic about going through a full strategy-making process, as they simply wanted to debate the question of whether company X or company Y would be the preferred alliance partner. The general manager, however, was less convinced that an alliance was the best way forward, and was determined to make the process an open and honest inquiry. In the early stages, however, nothing unexpected emerged as the group went through an analysis of market trends and likely moves by competitors. In less than three years, everyone agreed, the profitability of the business was going to suffer sharply unless a pre-emptive move was made.

When it came to assessing alternatives, the general manager did something unexpected. He broke the group into teams – one representing the firm itself, and the others playing the roles of competitors. As the team playing the firm itself proposed the favoured alliances, each competitor indicated how it would respond and why. Suddenly the alliance route did not look so good. Accusations flew, and it was claimed that the competitor teams were not playing their roles realistically. But each team had done its homework thoroughly, reading everything they could find on their competitor, talking to the competitor's ex-employees, as well as its suppliers and dealers. In the end, the alliance strategy was abandoned, and at the time of writing the business was negotiating a technology licensing agreement with a small firm that had previously been ignored. The process created by the general manager had a major impact on the outcome.

Understanding and leading the strategy-making process

There are many ways to proceed with a strategy-making process and one of the first things that you should do with your group is create a road map of the process that you want to follow. However, before turning to that, let me emphasize that there is one place where you should *not* start. Do not start your strategy process with a discussion of "vision".

Don't start with "vision"

Many managers feel that they should begin the strategy-making process with a vision of where the business should be in five or ten years time. The usual argument is that if you don't know where you are going, then any road will get you there. There are, however, several good reasons why it is better to determine your destination *during* the strategy-making process rather than establishing it at the outset.

In some companies, the most senior manager has a strongly held idea about where the business should be going, and from the first moment of the first meeting wants to impose it. The purpose of the strategy-making sessions then becomes to decide how best to achieve this vision. The problems with such an approach are that:

- the vision may not be appropriate to the circumstances facing the business; and
- the imposition of the vision inhibits the creation of an open atmosphere in which ideas are assessed on their merit, not the rank of their sponsor.

At best, there will be weary resignation as people realize that they are primarily in the room to listen, and at worst, a major battle may erupt which will leave some participants bloody and bowed, and the process in ruin before it has even begun.

Alternatively, there may be no single strong vision being put forward, but if you kick off your process with a discussion of vision, a debate driven by management preferences may emerge. Thus the R&D manager dreams of a future full of new products based on breakthrough technologies (and the not so hidden implication that we need to start spending more on research); the marketing manager, on the other hand, wants the company to become much more international, and to continue to invest in Asia while opportunities abound. Such debates tend not to be grounded in analysis, and often take on a surreal air of "my dream is better than your dream". The issues raised may well be worth debating at a later stage in the process, but this is not a good place to begin.

If you already have a vision of the future, set it aside as you begin the strategy-making process. You may end up reaffirming it; you may not.

Start strategy-making with a road map

Unless you are in a crisis situation, your strategy-making process is going to require some months of work. It will involve a series of meetings of up to several days in length each, punctuated by breaks during which assigned teams may collect required information on, for example, competitors, market conditions, or a particular technology. To keep on track throughout the process you should start by creating a high-level road map of the steps that you are going to undertake (Figure 11.1). Use something like this to start a discussion of process in your first meeting, and work with your group to modify it to suit your circumstances.

As Figure 11.1 indicates, you should begin your strategy-making process with the creation of a *base case scenario*, which is a projection of how the business will fare in the years ahead if no changes are made in current strategy. If the business stays with its existing products and markets, offering the same value proposition to customers, and carrying out the same core activities (each of these elements of strategy will be explained further subsequently) will it meet its longer term goals? Is this the future we want? If the answer is yes, you simply need to ensure that you have probed deeply enough in reaching this conclusion, and that you continue to execute the strategy well. However, if the base case scenario does not yield satisfactory results, you will need to get creative and think of ways in which you could move beyond your current strategy by thinking "outside the box". This might mean looking at entering

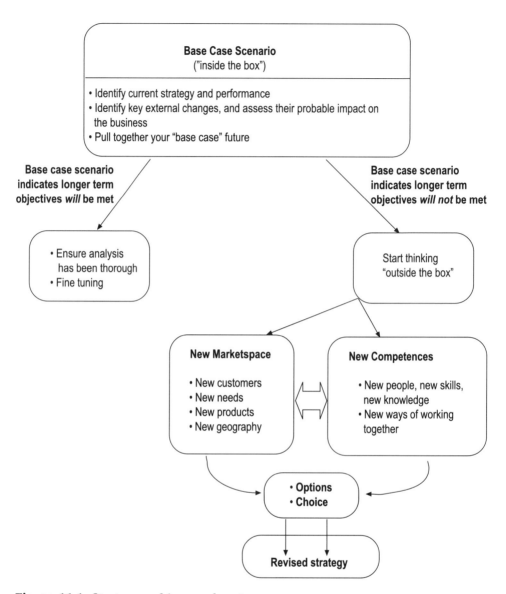

Figure 11.1: *Strategy-making road map*

new markets, serving new customer needs, adding or shedding core activities, and so on. Thus the comparison of the base case scenario results with your goals for the business lets you know whether or not change is required, how soon it will be needed, and how major is the required change.

Following the strategy road map

Creating the base case scenario

To build a base case scenario you need to do four things:

1. Identify the current strategy.
2. Review your current performance.
3. Identify the major trends that will affect the business in the years ahead and their probable impact.
4. Assess the probable future performance of the business.

You should begin with an identification of your current strategy and current performance because this will help you frame and focus the analytical work that is to come. If, for example, you judge the business performance to be poor, your timeframe for analysis will be relatively short, as you focus on how to turn the business around. If current performance is excellent, your attention is likely to be on the longer term. Your description of your current strategy will become a touchstone as you go through the steps outlined in the road map. When you are assessing the likely impact of trends on the business or creating new strategic options, for example, your reference point will be the current strategy.

Identify your current strategy

Your current strategy comprises four elements:

1. product market focus
2. value proposition
3. core activities
4. short-term goals.

Product market focus

Your product market focus statement spells out the nature of the products or services you offer and the characteristics of the markets you serve. You may find it useful to map out your product market focus with the use of several diagrams. The first is usually the value chain, stretching from basic raw materials to final consumer. This provides a framework for thinking about relationships up and down the chain, and generates questions such as who has the power in the chain and why? Later in the analysis, you will consider how the value chain, and the existing relationships, might change in coming years. Are you in the right place in the chain?

The second useful diagram is a product–market segmentation matrix, with product categories along one axis and markets on the other. Indicate the importance of each segment to your business, and your results in the segment. A later stage is to assess which segments have attractive growth and profit prospects, and which do not.

Value proposition

Your value proposition is a statement of the fundamental benefits that you have chosen to offer to the market. These benefits need to be considered from the customers' point of view. Customers don't particularly care, for example, that a business is seeking to be the industry's lowest-cost producer. This is only important if the low costs get translated into low relative prices or other benefits. The aim therefore should be to express value propositions in terms of fundamental customer benefits such as price, features and service. Later you will assess whether or not the value proposition that you offer will continue to be important to the markets that you are serving.

Core activities

Your core activities are the primary value-adding activities that you chose to perform. Do you, for example, carry out your own manufacturing, or do you choose to outsource it, focusing instead on design and marketing? Such choices have a fundamental impact on your cost structure, capabilities and flexibility. As you look ahead, you may decide that you have to add, or perhaps eliminate, some core activities.

Short-term goals

At any point in time you will have a set of short-term goals that are driving the business forward. You may be trying to maximize profitability this year, or maybe, like Amazon.com, you are trying to maximize revenue growth hoping that profits will come later. GEC, the British defence conglomerate, decided that it had to sell its Marconi defence business to one of the major European aerospace companies quickly, before the planned rationalization of the industry occurred. GEC wanted to sell while there were still enough bidders to create an auction, and not be left with only one potential buyer. Such short-term goals are an important part of your strategy and must be examined along with the other three components.

Review current performance

Don't let your discussion of performance be dominated by your financial people. Of course the financial aspects of performance must not be ignored, but make sure that your discussion includes employees who are, for example, close to your customers, close to your new developments, and close to your day-to-day operations. They may

> **"When reviewing current performance, financial figures are often a lagging indicator of performance"**

know of things that are going well, or not well, that have not yet shown up in the financial statements.

To get a discussion of current performance underway you can use a diagram like that shown in Figure 11.2, and ask everyone to plot the performance of the business three years ago, today, and their best guess as to three years in the future. They will,

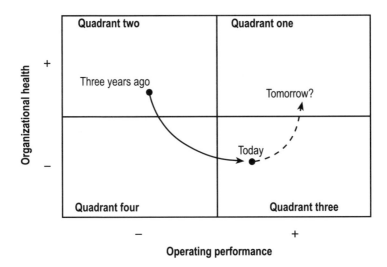

Figure 11.2: *The performance matrix*

of course, want clarity as to what each axis represents, and this is a discussion that you need to have. In general terms, *operating performance* includes the measures that businesses usually use to assess their performance, such as profitability, financial strength, growth, changes in market share, and various measures of productivity. Measures of *organizational health* are softer than those of operating performance, including such things as management and worker enthusiasm for what they are doing, whether or not people are "burning out" (an increasingly common problem), willingness to learn and to work across boundaries when required and so on. However, for each business the appropriate measures will be different, and before getting too far into your strategy-making process, you need to decide which are important. You will, for example, need to decide later if your base case scenario is good enough. It helps if you have discussed in advance which elements of performance are critical for the business, and it is on these measures that you can make such a judgement.

Building and assessing the base case

As a result of the work that you have done thus far, you may be able to see a clear enough future for the business if it continues with its existing strategy and to build a set of projections that reflect this. There is no use being overly detailed, because you are bound to be wrong in some aspects of your thinking. But, broadly, have you painted a satisfactory future? Will the shareholders be pleased? The management team? Other important stakeholders? This is also the time to discuss vision. If there is a strong vision for the business, will the base case achieve it? If so, great. If not, it may be time to rethink the vision, or to engage in some "outside-the-box" thinking to see if there are ways of achieving the vision at acceptable levels of risk.

> **CASE STUDY: ASSESSING THE BASE CASE AND THINKING "OUTSIDE THE BOX"**
>
> *ICI of the UK is a classic example of a company whose base case scenario in the mid-1990s did not satisfy either top management or shareholders. The company had been performing poorly for years and the outlook was for more of the same. Under Charles Miller Smith, the new CEO, a bold strategic plan was created, which reinvented ICI as a speciality chemical company, by purchasing four businesses from Unilever and selling major ICI heavy chemical businesses. Given ICI's long history as a heavy chemical company, this was definitely an "outside-the-box" solution – its ultimate success is still unclear.*

Your base case assessment will be more complex if you cannot clearly project the future of your business if it continues with its existing strategy. You may, for example, face known discontinuities, but be unable to predict the result. Say you are an oil company, trying to assess whether or not Exxon will be allowed to purchase Mobil. You can assess the impact on you if it happens, but you cannot know whether or not it will happen. In such a case you may want to build scenarios and test your strategy under each possible outcome. On the other hand, the problem may not be assessing the outcome of a discreet event, but you may face a whole range of equally probable futures. Perhaps you are introducing a new product to a new market, and simply do not know if your market share will be 10% or 30%. Again, your best solution may be to create several scenarios and test each against your objectives. (For further discussion, see Chapter 10, as well as Courtney et al., 1997.)

Moving "outside the box"

If your base case scenario is not going to produce the results that you want, you are going to need a change in strategy. By this point, your strategy-making group will probably have ideas for change that were generated as they looked at the external forces that will impact on the business. There may be calls for entering new markets, cutting or adding core activities, offering new features to customers and so on. On the other hand, you may find that you have a dispirited group who cannot see any way out of the unsatisfactory future that they see for the business. In either case, as you look for "outside-the-box" options, you may want to try some unconventional approaches to generating new ideas, such as "serious play" (Roos and Victor, 1998). You may find it useful to revisit the four elements of strategy that you identified earlier, this time looking for aspects that you could change.

Changing your product market focus

If your existing products and markets are not going to bring you the growth and profitability that you need, then expanding up or down the value chain or moving into new markets may make sense. You already know your customers, and they know you. What else could you sell them? How far will your brand name stretch? A very bold move in this regard has been Mercedes' introduction of the A-class and the Smart car, products that take the company well beyond its traditional tightly defined market focus. On the other hand, you may improve results by *reducing* your product market focus, and doing a better job on fewer targets. Maybe you are trying to do too much.

Altering the value proposition

If your customers find your product or service offering unattractive, you may simply need to do a better job of delivering it. On the other hand, you may need a new value proposition. Yesterday's market leader becomes today's also-ran. Whoever would have believed that the Japanese automotive companies would have lost their luster by the end of the 1990s? What was once a superior combination of features and cost became decidedly ordinary looking. When you are making such judgements about your own product line, do not rely on your own views: ask your customers, and watch for bias in the process. It is usually best if the question is posed as a comparison between your products and others, and the customer does not know who is asking.

Adding or eliminating core activities

You may be carrying out activities that an outside supplier could perform more efficiently at lower cost. For example, Nike does not make its own shoes. Should you be doing your own manufacturing? What about IT? Many US banks have outsourced most of their IT departments. The opportunity is both to save costs and, at least as important, to allow you to focus on what you are really good at, the things that bring you success in the marketplace.

There is also a possibility that you need to take over an activity that is currently being done by a supplier. Perhaps the supplier is vulnerable to takeover or increasingly unable to keep up with your growth rate. An interesting case in point occurred when Barnes and Noble, the largest bookseller in the USA, bought the wholesaler that was supplying books to Amazon.com. Such moves can quickly alter the balance of power in an industry.

Setting new short-term goals

Your base case scenario may have convinced you that your short-term goals are inappropriate. It may be that they are too ambitious and will take the business into challenges for which it is not ready. Alternatively, perhaps they are not ambitious enough, given the longer-term objectives that you are trying to reach. The challenge for many businesses is to set targets that stretch, but are not simply dismissed as unrealistic by those who have key roles to play if they are to be achieved.

Options, choice and commitment

If you have time, do not rush the process of examining the strategic options that you have generated. If they are indeed "outside the box", then people will probably feel uncomfortable with them. Do we really need to do this? It looks too risky? We do not have the required competencies. Both to ensure that you make the best choice and to build commitment, let the naysayers express their views, debate the issues openly, collect more data, and look for similar moves made by companies in other industries. Refer back constantly to your unsatisfactory base case scenario saying "you may not like this option, but is it better than continuing as we are?" Do whatever you can to get the key people behind the choice you make, because their commitment will be vital to your ultimate success.

 # SUMMARY

In spite of the increasing demands made on your managers' time and the rapid changes taking place in today's world, you and your key employees must take the time to think hard about the future of your business. It is important to work intensely together in a strategy-making process. Whatever strategy you develop will sooner or later need modification but, and this is the key point, if you use your strategy-making process to build strong relationships among the people at all levels who are key to the future of your business, the relationships themselves will be your enduring competitive advantage. Treat strategy-making as both a social and an analytical process, for this is the ultimate advantage of doing it yourself.

 # BEST PRACTICE

Unless you are in a crisis situation, your strategy-making process will require some months of work. It will involve a series of meetings of up to several days in length each, punctuated by breaks during which assigned teams may collect required information on, for example, competitors, market conditions, or a particular technology. To keep on track throughout the process you should start by creating a high-level road map of the steps that you are going to undertake (Figure 11.1). Use something like this to start a discussion of process in your first meeting, and work with your group to modify it to suit your circumstances.

As Figure 11.1 indicates, you should begin your strategy-making process with the creation of a *base case scenario*, which is a projection of how the business will fare in the years ahead if no changes are made in current strategy.

To construct the base case scenario:

- Identify current strategy and performance.
- Identify key external changes – and assess their probable impact on the business.
- Pull together your base case future.

If the base case scenario indicates longer-term objectives will be met, then check anaysis and fine tune. If the bases case scenario indicates longer-term objectives will not be met, then start thinking "outside the box". This involves considering new competences and new marketspace. New competences include:

- new people, new skills, new knowledge
- new ways of working together.

New marketspace includes:

- new customers
- new needs
- new products
- new geography.

This analysis should generate a series of options. The strategic choice made then forms the basis of the revised strategy.

If the business stays with its existing products and markets, offering the same value proposition to customers, and carrying out the same core activities, will it meet its longer term goals? Is this the future we want? If the answer is yes, you simply need to ensure that you have probed deeply enough in reaching this conclusion, and ensure that you continue to execute the strategy well. However, if the base case scenario does not yield satisfactory results, you will need to get creative and think of ways in which you could move beyond your current strategy by thinking "outside the box". This might mean looking at entering new markets, serving new customer needs, adding or shedding core activities, and so on. Thus the comparison of the base case scenario results with your goals for the business lets you know whether or not change is required, how soon it will be needed, and how major is the required change.

References

Courtney, H., Kirkland, J. and Viguerie, P. (1997) Strategy Under Uncertainty, *Harvard Business Review*, November/December, 1997.

Fry, J.N. and Killing, J.P. (2000) *Strategic Analysis and Action*, 4th edn. Prentice Hall.

Mintzberg, H. (1994) *The Rise and Fall of Strategic Planning*. New York: The Free Press.

Roos, J. and Victor, B. (1998) In Search of Original Strategies: How About some serious play? *IMD Perspectives*, December, 1998. Available on **www.imd.ch**.

Sharpe, P. and Keelin, T. (1998) How SmithKline Beecham Makes Better Resource Allocation Decisions, *Harvard Business Review*, March/April, 1998.

Wetlaufer, S. (1999) Driving Change: An Interview with Ford Motor Company's Jacques Nasser, *Harvard Business Review*, March/April, 1999.

12

Using Collective Learning to Focus the Energized Organization

Exploiting the strategic flexibility of an energized organization is not possible with the traditional methods of alignment and control. In this chapter, **Xavier Gilbert** explains how companies can create a create a dynamic context for continually adapting their direction and focusing their energy. The key is collective learning that exploits the tension between frontline energy and corporate integration.

> ### CASE STUDY: NOKIA
>
> *Looking at the way Nokia has been able to navigate the rapids of changing technology and market response since 1995, four attributes stand out: firstly, a remarkable openness to information, even when it is disturbing, e.g. information from the market place about products that are not doing as well as expected, customers who are dissatisfied, energized employees who want to move faster. Secondly, this openness is accompanied by a willingness to continually update the strategic agenda and explore its implications with employees. When senior executives appear at management development programs, they don't just make the same presentation everyone has seen before, they come to listen, solicit information, and get feedback; they leave with questions to be discussed with others.*
>
> *Thirdly, management has been very effective at encouraging bottom-up initiatives, energizing the organization with some of the approaches discussed in Part Two of this book, tolerating a dose of chaos on the frontline, and relying on networks of knowledge workers and mechanisms for sharing competence. But they have not stopped there. Fourthly, management pays special attention to debriefing, trying to identify the factors that have led to success or failure in product launches or in bidding processes, so that they can better select the options that might make the next breakthrough. Put together this amounts to effective orchestration of activity with collective learning, accompanied by enormous growth in sales, profits and market capitalization.*

Overview

There is a lot of evidence that centralized systems perform poorly in chaotic, fast-changing environments or under crisis, yet corporations seem slow in accepting this evidence. But let's face it; if you want renewal, or more simply responsiveness, you need initiative, frontline leadership, learning, smart experimenting, and divergence. Many executives say they want a learning organization, but they get nervous at the idea of experimenting. They praise the merits of empowerment, but don't like it when they are no longer asked for the "right responses". Many executives want leaders or entrepreneurs, but get nervous when they spot one within their own ranks.

The energized organization is always likely to be a somewhat untidy one compared to the traditional centralized system. By its nature, a bottom-up organization is divergent and difficult to control from the top. This chapter looks at how companies can create a context for focusing their energy with collective learning.

Dilemmas of the energized organization

The energized organization is like a two-pole magnetic field: one pole is the energy at the frontline, anticipating trends and breakpoints, proactively making the market, creating opportunities, initiative and entrepreneurship. This energy source creates divergent tensions within the organization. The other pole is the corporate integrative energy, leveraging the potential advantages of coherence and of economies of scale and scope. This energy source creates convergent tensions.

Both energy poles provide clear benefits in a chaotic context; they cannot exchange their roles. They seem to be mutually exclusive. Allowing for more frontline initiative would necessarily be at the expense of corporate integration and vice versa. To use an analogy, the assumption is that to be effective the orchestra conductor must stifle the individual musicians. This, as we will see, is not the case. But there is a tension.

This tension is generally resolved by letting one of the two poles take the upper hand. The most common approach is to centralize decisions and trade-offs, by design or by default, because all the tough ones end up being delegated upwards. Sony's "thinking globally and acting locally", for example, could be interpreted in that manner. Attenuating the tension by distancing conceptualization from action will require alignment and control mechanisms that destroy the proactive energy, rather than fostering it. Proactive energy requires rapid hand-to-brain interaction, allowing action feedback to be interpreted and redeployed immediately into action.

Another approach to remove this tension is to make the organization a loose federation of kingdoms that constantly challenge the centre to demonstrate that it adds value. This may mobilize the frontline energy poles, but it deprives them from the opportunity to benefit from size and synergy advantages and leverage each other's energy.

In fact, both energy poles are critical to the effective energized organization and the ability to make them complementary is one of its core competencies. Without frontline initiative, the organization cannot navigate proactively in a chaotic environment; without corporate integration, it cannot do so efficiently and competitively. The challenge for the energized organization is thus to leave room for both divergence and convergence and to blend the benefits from each.

This chapter explains how organization learning performs exactly that role: it blends divergent openness and convergent synthesis to develop to new knowledge that eventually supports corporate renewal. This chapter investigates:

- how collective learning captures the energy from the divergence–convergence tension by transforming it into renewal;
- how the two foundation processes, strategic thinking and operating coordination, can capture this energy by being seen as learning processes; and
- the leadership roles that support these learning processes.

Organization learning is a divergent–convergent process

Divergent information openness

At first, learning is divergent. It is triggered by the gap between aspirations and reality, by new information that does not fit with expectations. This need to understand, explain and find meaning opens new questions and leads to the search for more information. It creates a willingness to move out of comfort zones and accept disturbing information. It acknowledges unknown territories and the urge to discover them.

This *information openness* supports divergence, particularly at the frontline level where it is most likely to be triggered, albeit with a relatively narrow perspective. This is where information that is most likely to challenge the corporate road map, to question corporate assumptions and beliefs, and to point to new directions, will surface. Information openness is centrifugal. But this is how new opportunities can be spotted, how new markets will be made (rather than old markets followed), and how frontline initiative and entrepreneurship will develop.

CASE STUDY: THE INFORMATION-AGE LEARNING APPROACH TO NEW PRODUCTS

Information-age players are market-makers who are remarkably flexible about what will work next: since consumers do not know yet what they need, how could anyone else know? How do we find out? There is one principle beyond a starting idea: the foot in the door to get volume as fast as possible, which in turn provides the necessary space to learn rapidly from the consumers about the functionalities they want. Perfection is not an early requirement. Occupying the terrain is, even through unorthodox economics like low, and even zero, entry price. Future revenue streams will then leverage the occupied land through information-rich functionalities.

But what is critical here is the learning mindset that supports this approach: the willingness to be receptive to any piece of information provided by the consumers, to put it on the map, to experiment, and the urge to learn and redeploy the learning fast.

One example of this is Linux. This server-based operating system is one of the serious challengers to Microsoft's dominance – it is already used on more than seven million computers around the world and SAP, Intel, HP, IBM and Oracle have announced their intention to support it. Indeed, there is no licence fee: its Finnish developer, Linus Torvalds gave it away for free "because at the beginning it wasn't good enough to charge for it and because distribution is too much trouble" (Seulamo, 1999). But every user was keen to improve it – which happened incredibly fast. And now it makes money, with upgrades, add-on software and services, through those companies that are keen to distribute it with their own products. And Torvalds got shares from the Initial Public Offerings (IPOs) that leveraged his baby.

Information openness needs to be supported by organization processes that also encourage divergence, in particular, processes that allow information to flow easily and rapidly between different parts of the organization, closing the distance between the different parts. Lowering organization distance accelerates the circulation of information and increases its transparency. This additional information richness will trigger more questioning, more experimenting, more trial and error, and more learning. Information redistribution processes, the ease of accessing what others know, incentives to disseminate what is known, eclectic recruitment, diverse career paths, exposure to and acceptance of the "not invented here", are many processes that feed divergent, rich learning.

But information openness is only marginally helpful if it is not supported by robust road maps – visions, intents, business ideas, name them as you like – of where it might all lead to and how it might all work.

Convergent road-mapping

After the stage of divergent information openness, learning needs to be supported by convergence mechanisms. Road maps play this role by hosting the new, unexpected, disturbing pieces of information. With road maps, there is a common reference for assessing the significance of new information, whether it confirms prior hypotheses, or points to new directions. Without road maps, "shooting from the hip" is the most likely response to new information.

Road-mapping is supported by discussions, and confrontation of viewpoints that lead to coherence. Scenario-building, raising "what if" questions, stretching hypotheses, and challenging the existing models to the extent that they involve many different circles at different levels and in different parts of the organization, will lead to a common understanding of, and commitment to, the route to be followed.

The road map resulting from this collective learning will provide a shelter from chaos and complexity, allowing the organization to focus flexibly on the priorities it points to. It also allows it to push decisions on the frontline whenever this is where the most relevant information resides. By the same token, it allows frontline units to co-ordinate among themselves within the framework it provides to resolve tensions and contradictions, without resorting to corporate arbitration. It is a frame of reference that will be continuously improved, sometimes corrected, with the addition of new information. It consolidates the learning enough to put it to work.

Road-mapping is mostly moderated at the corporate level through several processes that provide convergence. In chaotic environments, it is a key attribute of leadership, providing the overview, a sense of direction and priorities to the team. It is supported by strong communications; best practice tells us about evangelist senior managers who keep reinforcing the same clear (but rarely simplistic) business ideas, resulting key success factors, and operational priorities.

CASE STUDY: COMMITTING TO GSM

Between 1992 and 1997, the most critical years in the transformation of Nokia from a collapsing conglomerate into a winner in the mobile telecommunications sector, Matti Alahuhta, CEO of Nokia Telecommunications, made sure he talked with the participants at every single management development initiative that took place in his unit. Every time, he was presenting the same road map: this is our business idea, this is our window of opportunity, this is how we will get there. Every time, his message was enriched with the latest successes and failures, the latest competitors' moves, and the next opportunities.

Road mapping is also supported by career management processes that rotate future executives across the corporations technologies, products and markets, providing them with an overview of the most critical issues and tensions. It is supported by decision processes that visibly take into account the different perspectives that pull the organization and bring them together, rather than allowing them to result in "consensual procrastination".

The road map keeps being tested through action; it guides action but is also validated through it. Implementing the road map is not just getting things done according to plan; it is also the source of critical learning that is meant to confirm, adjust or redirect the road map. But this action-learning implies some degree of divergence. This is a difficult idea to accept for the adepts of disciplined implementation, as prescribed by management textbooks. Yet, in a chaotic, unpredictable environment, well-rehearsed acts are of limited value. The frontline initiative, ability to anticipate, and imagination do make a competitive difference.

Divergent action-learning

This divergent action-learning requires room for experimenting, for trying out new approaches to local market-making and local responsiveness. The purpose is not maverick entrepreneurship, but learning, which implies smart experimenting – experimenting that identifies independent and dependent variables to test hypotheses and generate explicit learning.

In every part of the organization, on every front, the road map is constantly challenged. These challenges provide a broad range of learning opportunities provided they are treated as such, rather than given the "try harder" response. These inputs allow the road map to be more adaptive, agile and contingent. Across the organization, they provide a wealth of proprietary learning that will eventually be the ferment of corporate renewal.

Organization processes may inhibit or support action-learning. For example, processes may be in place to support frontline initiatives, by allowing them to access the necessary know-how and resources or by hosting them where these are available. Job definitions may be narrow or broad when individuals are expected to take it upon themselves to make sure that nothing falls in between. Organization cultures may imply that one needs to get as many blessings as possible before any single move, or may discourage such self-censorship. Career paths may inculcate headquarters' political correctness or provide sink-or-swim frontline responsibilities as early as possible.

CASE STUDY: NURTURING INITIATIVE AT 3M

At 3M, new business initiatives are able to borrow part-time or on-loan resources from other business units. These resources may consist of experts in specific technologies needed to make the initiative viable, marketing expertise, trial production capacity, piggy-backing on existing channels etc. At the same time, the window of opportunity for a new initiative to prove itself is limited; eventually, it will have to demonstrate its value-creation.

The convergent forces of corporate integration can also do a lot to moderate their intervention and support frontline learning. Encouraging risk-taking and allowing mistakes, taking delegation seriously, and throwing the ball back when the frontline is tempted to delegate difficult matters upward, are examples. Best practice shows that in the fast-learning organizations, procrastination is the worst offence, while making mistakes as a result of an honest try is part of learning.

Convergent debriefing and reflection

Action without debriefing is merely activism. Reflecting on what has happened to draw lessons that help think about the future secures a learning step. It helps the organization reconverge before moving on. This reflection must first address the reasons for success and failure. These are areas that most organizations would rather not revisit. Failures are obviously embarrassing and it is tempting to forget about them as soon as possible, after the witnesses have been suppressed. Interestingly, successes are equally poorly understood and remain the subject of misleading fantasies.

Debriefing implies nondefensiveness; its purpose is not finger-pointing but identifying the parameters that have led to success or failure. This reflective process allows us to reuse these parameters in future road maps with an understanding of the contextual variables that make them effective. They can be customized for new future contexts. Debriefing and reflection also imply a learning and improvement willingness that is absent from some companies. The low tolerance for bad news and feedback, defensiveness at senior levels, and justification of the past, soon discourage the search for improvements at frontline levels.

Without debriefing the completed tasks, and without reflecting on some key lessons that can be redeployed in the future, not only will the same errors be repeated, but the corporation loses the opportunity to refocus its energy and to identify new actionable parameters of its competitiveness. Debriefing thus helps the organization energy converge.

CASE STUDY: LEARNING REDEPLOYMENT AT LAFARGE

Over the years, this global construction materials company has invested in ready-mixed concrete and aggregates to complement its cement activities. Time had come to review the economic justification for these integration strategies. A senior line manager was appointed to head a unit in charge of drawing the lessons from all cases worldwide where integrated positions existed in the company. All performance parameters were analysed and the learning was consolidated in a set of strategic guidelines meant to help decide when integration made economic sense and manage it when it did.

These guidelines were packaged to provide learning material to be used in a series of workshops – cases, exercises and role plays – reviewing different aspects of integration. These workshops were then conducted worldwide, always with the involvement of corporate line management.

But this is only one example; the same process is followed in all the company's activities. Says one of the senior executives: "The ability to leverage best practice across units and activities is a major justification for our size and global presence."

Debriefing and reflection are supported by several organization processes. For example, processes can provide the discipline to make debriefing the normal closure to any activity. Measurement processes focused on key operational parameters will also help organization units to benchmark themselves against similar ones and seek to improve their performance. Similarly, organization cultures encourage providing and receiving constructive criticism, encourage personal development, and foster renewal.

The convergent forces of corporate integration can play an important role in supporting debriefing and reflection, by ensuring that the lessons learned are circulated and redeployed. This is the opposite to storing them into repositories. What is needed is to intensify their circulation through internal publicity, encouraging personal networks, facilitating the internal mobility of brains, bringing together knowledge demand and supply.

CASE STUDY: SKANDIA'S PROTOTYPING

In the early 1990s, Skandia was able to develop an entire new life insurance product, comprising product development, a unique utilization of investment opportunities, a new distribution approach, and a series of supporting back-room and administrative processes, and to deploy it at minimum cost through a large number of countries, in spite of the important required localization. This was achieved starting from a prototype flexible enough to be adapted to the very different conditions in different countries, together with the systematic accumulation and redeployment of the know-how acquired each time it was implemented anywhere.

With this continuously enriched know-how, small units could handle this complex product with the sophistication of a large professional staff, yet with the flexibility of a small entrepreneurial unit.

Organization learning is a spiral through divergent information openness, convergent road-mapping, divergent action learning, and convergent debriefing and reflection. Information openness has its sensors at the frontline level. Road-mapping requires corporate overview and synthesis capabilities. Action learning rests on frontline entrepreneurship and initiative. Debriefing and reflection is fostered by corporate knowledge brokerage. Organization learning blends the energies of frontline initiative and of corporate integration to provide superior competitiveness.

Strategic thinking as a learning process

In chaotic competitive environments, strategic thinking is an continuous process; there is never one completed and final strategic plan. The strategic process is more like the development of a navigation plan that sets a clear destination, but keeps integrating new information from the weather forecasts, observation of the sea, and the experience of the skipper, to decide on which course to follow. In short, it is a learning process.

The divergent energy at the frontline level provides a large proportion of the information needed to feed strategic thinking. All too often, this information reaches the top strategists through surprises and crises while it has been available, albeit in a fragmented manner, at the frontline level for a while. The observation of competition and market readiness to adopt new technologies or, as is most often the case, to cherry-pick functionalities from new technologies, starts from the frontline. The frontline information openness, when it exists, is encouraged and is used, places sensors in all markets.

Learning organizations are quite effective at circulating this information internally so as to facilitate its synthesis. In particular, their senior managers spend a lot of time questioning the frontline on what they see, what works and what doesn't, and discussing with them the possible meaning of this information. For example, this can be observed when senior executives appear at the management development programs organized for their troops. Some arrive with the strategy presentation everyone has already seen many times, deliver it, and go away after a few polite questions. They see this exercise as one of the duties of top management. Others come mostly to listen and discuss; they seek feedback, ask for opinions, solicit information, and leave with more questions to be discussed with the other organization levels. They see these encounters as valuable learning opportunities that, when all put together, end up shaping the corporate strategic thinking.

These discussions are an integral part of convergent road-mapping. In the context of strategic thinking, they provide a road map that the frontline can easily relate to. Parts of it have been discussed several times already; available options have benefited from the frontline inputs and feedback. It provides a common sense of direction, a common sailing plan. It is not necessary to insist on how important this is when navigating in a chaotic context. The fact that, to a certain extent, and under the integrative leadership of corporate levels, the sailing plan has been established collectively, mobilizes the frontline energy towards the common destination.

CASE STUDIES: ROAD-MAPPING AS COLLECTIVE LEARNING

Bertrand Collomb, CEO of Lafarge, explains:"If the captain is the only one who knows or understands the objective or the stakes, the capacity of his crew to react will be very limited. In other words, it is no longer possible for the head of a company to have a solitary and isolated view of its stakes, challenges and objectives. A vision can only come into being through a dynamic movement involving the many different circles within a company."

Similarly, Göran Lindahl, CEO of ABB, believes that "the strategy process must involve all levels, be widely communicated, and remain constantly open to challenge."

In chaotic competitive environments, implementing the road map retains a tentative dimension. Fast learning to confirm or adjust the course is thus critical. This implies smart experimenting, and managing options. Action-learning divergence at the frontline level is necessary to generate the information needed to validate the road map and to build the best practice. This collective learning results from the frontline entrepreneurial energy and is integrated at the corporate level into more robust strategic road maps.

This integration is supported by debriefing and reflection, systematically analysing what can be learned from implementation. It ensures that this dispersed learning is consolidated and redistributed as an input into strategic thinking. Again, the debriefing and reflection phase of the learning spiral takes advantage of the divergent and convergent energies in the organization

Strategic thinking thus needs to be thought of as a learning process where both the frontline level and the corporate level make inputs. In that manner, strategic thinking blends, and gets the best of, the divergent and convergent forces that energize the organization.

Operating co-ordination as a learning process

Co-ordinating operations in a manner that supports organization learning provides an opportunity to focus energy around key issues. Take a real-life example: a company is selling a professional communications product to large and small organizations, allowing them, for example, to manage fleets of vehicles, or service personnel in the field. The country team in a Latin American country identifies a great opportunity to sell to the military a localized version of the product. This deal would help enter the country, demonstrating the company's dedication to the local needs. It would be a strong foot in the door to enter further large local enterprises and government accounts.

At corporate level, the product people are not convinced. They do not believe that this opportunity is large enough to justify the time and money needed to customize the product to the local specification; there are many other more visible and larger opportunities also competing for development time. The development investment and the production disturbance would be too costly.

This is the information-openness phase in the learning process that the frontline local team and the corporate product people are about to enter jointly. The learning could go two ways: ask for top-management arbitration – there, we would have winner and a loser and the learning would be minimal – or co-ordinate a course of action that would meet both perspectives.

Both sides, frontline and corporate, choose to talk more and agree to challenge the road map. Additional questions are raised, in particular:

- Are there more similar opportunities in other markets?
- Is there a gap in our strategy, an opportunity missed?
- Are our current priorities, at frontline and at corporate product level, robust enough?

This debate provides an opportunity to challenge the strategic road map from different angles. It will come out of this process either more robust or improved. Again, this is collective learning.

In our example, both parties agree not to go ahead with the opportunity. Discussions with other markets indicate that there are none where the required development investment could be leveraged. Cost, in this case, turns out not to be the most important issue. More important, all agree, would be the loss of focus that would put at risk other products that all markets need even more. Again, the learning from testing the idea further goes beyond the issue at hand. Perspectives are broadened and the road map comes out of it more robust.

As it turns out, the debriefing phase in this collective learning process helped it to go further. Through the discussions across the markets and with the corporate product team, some other common needs have emerged pointing at some gaps in the offer. This constitutes more learning that will strengthen not only the road map itself, but also the operational co-ordination capabilities that come out of this situation now even more capable of generating future learning.

Operational co-ordination, across frontline units and between the frontline and corporate levels, should also be viewed and managed as a learning process, by going explicitly through its four phases

- information openness
- road-mapping
- action
- reflection.

Again, this process will blend the energy from frontline entrepreneurship and corporate integration; it will mobilize the best of both and energize the organization.

Learning leadership relies on new managerial roles

Steering the learning process within the organization is of such importance for focusing the energized organization by blending frontline entrepreneurship and corporate integration, that it needs to be supported by specific leadership attributes. Managers at all levels, in different capacities, have learning leadership responsibilities.

The frontline is a place of intensive information openness and action-learning. The frontline leader must first make sure that some of the energy is applied to information openness, curiosity, accessing various information sources, and exchanging this information. It is often surprising to see how uninformed frontline levels are regarding the ongoing developments in their sector. With the Internet age, when it is so easy to get selected news pushed for free on your computer screen, this is almost unforgivable. Frontline leaders are responsible for ensuring that the divergent energy of their team is applied to bringing back the competitive and market information they necessarily come across.

The frontline learning leadership is also responsible for local entrepreneurship: seeking new opportunities, shaping business ideas for the local markets, and pushing up new successful ideas. Without this energy to experiment and to design localized solutions, there is no raw material for organization learning. Breakthrough knowledge starts, by definition, with fragmented, dispersed activities. The knowledge generated in these activities is leveraged by circulating it and making it usable across the organization.

Intermediary and corporate levels are responsible for integrative road-mapping and debriefing. They provide the synthesis perspective necessary to bring together front-line information and experience into new road maps and learning. They are responsible for generating the convergent energy, but through a learning process that also leverages the divergent frontline energy. Their leadership focuses on developing proprietary knowledge from dispersed inputs, proposing integrative road maps, and ensuring the circulation of knowledge across the organization to ensure its cross fertilization.

Executive levels are in charge of the overall maintenance of the learning context. They provide a vision of the competitive map, and closure at strategic crossroads, and they ensure that within this overall sailing direction there is a vivid learning context. These responsibilities are critical facets of learning leadership. In particular, through the organization culture they shape, the role models they provide, and the processes and infrastructure they put in place, they can foster organization learning.

CASE STUDY: LEARNING LEADERSHIP AT LAFARGE

The senior management of Lafarge has put in place in its various activities "performance" units that are responsible for analysing the various performance parameters at the operational and strategic levels in these activities. They represent a considerable investment in learning and senior managers make their commitment very clear. In addition, a number of processes – the "Lafarge way" – are instigated by top management to stimulate a learning mindset throughout the corporation; these processes are concerned with making information transparent, providing clear road maps, ensuring that decisions are made at optimal levels, and making sure that the lessons are learnt.

These units are headed by senior line managers, and the assignments are part of a normal curriculum between different line positions. They are considered as effective ways to develop strategic thinking capabilities of managers. Their responsibility is to ensure not only that the knowledge is developed, but that it is disseminated as fast and effectively as possible through the organization, via workshops (the development of which is aided by substantial investments).

During these workshops, frontline managers are asked to contribute to this evolving body of knowledge, for example through additional cases, by adding observations gathered from their own experience, by challenging and putting in perspective some of the proposed conclusions. As a result, this body of knowledge keeps evolving as a synthesis between the corporate integrative energy to disseminate best practice, and the frontline energy that keeps generating more first-hand experience and feedback.

It should be noted that Lafarge also practices job rotation between activity units and corporate functions, as an affective learning leadership development device.

SUMMARY

Organization energy comes from two poles: frontline entrepreneurship and corporate integration. Both are necessary in their own rights, but they are also complementary: one without the other would suboptimize the energy level that the organization can generate. Organization learning blends these two sources of energy by relying on specific divergent and convergent learning phases where each pole of organization energy can contribute its best and be leveraged by the other:

- Information openness is enriched by divergent frontline curiosity.
- Road-mapping requires corporate perspectives.
- Action-learning implies frontline divergent experimenting.
- Debriefing and reflection are activated through corporate integration and knowledge brokerage.

Two critical organization systems, strategic thinking and operating co-ordination, will, if designed and applied as collective learning processes, help blend divergent and convergent organization energy from the frontline and corporate levels.

The role of leadership in maintaining and steering organization learning thus appear as critical. Learning leadership, at all organization levels, is the glue that ensures that the organizational energy, divergent and convergent, is optimally mobilized.

BEST PRACTICE

The "compass model" (Figure 12.1) allows us to assess the divergence–convergence capabilities or learning capabilities of an organization along four critical dimensions: *culture*, *leadership*, *processes* and *infrastructure*. Like the metabolism of the human body, these four dimensions shape the organization's ability to evolve, develop itself, and compete.

How is *divergent information openness* supported by the organization metabolism? Information openness relies on:

- *Curiosity* – being receptive to new information;
- *Openness* – not filtering out new information easily;
- *Access* – seeking new information;
- *Transparency* – being open about what one knows and doesn't know;
- *Exchange* – volunteering information to those who may need it.

Table 12.1 explains this further.

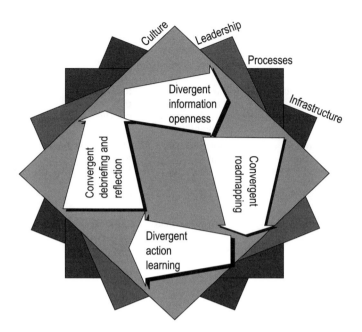

Figure 12.1: *The compass model*
Note: A measurement instrument is available to assess the divergent–convergent capabilities of the organization along the four dimensions of the compass model. This instrument can be customized to address the specific vision of a company.

How is *convergent roadmapping* supported by the organization metabolism? Roadmapping relies on:

- *Flexibility of perspectives* – being able to look at an issue from different perspectives;
- *Overview capabilities* – being able to see the whole picture and to sort out important from the secondary;
- *Synthesis initiative* – being able to shape convincing road maps;
- *Providing focus* – being able to fix priorities and help others focus;
- *Enriching the map* – being ale to reshape the road map to take into account new relevant information.

Table 12.2 explains this further.

How is *divergent action-learning* supported by the organization metabolism? Action learning relies on:

- *Action orientation* – having a preference for hands-on activities;
- *Initiative* – being a self-starter;
- *Responsibility taking* – believing that one is the master of one's own fate;

Table 12.1: *Divergent information openness*

	Culture	Leadership	Processes	Infrastructure
Curiosity	People are generally interested in what others know	Senior managers ask a lot of questions from all levels	Critical external trends are monitored systematically	Subscriptions to online information are widely available
Openness	Good new ideas are well accepted	Senior managers ask for feedback from collaborators and subordinates	Recruitment processes are eclectic	"Push" information is used for nonroutine issues
Access	Going to the information source wherever it is in the organization is normal	Senior managers gather a lot of outside information	There are processes to monitor information on suppliers, customers *etc.*	Internet access is a normal working tool
Transparency	Admitting one's ignorance on a subject is not necessarily seen as a weakness	Management seeks diverse opinions on key issues	Organization units regularly share information of common interest	The organization structure is very flat
Exchange	Volunteering information to those who may need it is the norm	Senior managers share what they know openly	Performance assessment includes information-sharing attitudes	Information technology is on every desktop

Table 12.2: *Convergent road-mapping*

	Culture	Leadership	Processes	Infrastructure
Flexibility of perspectives	Looking outside functional boundaries is natural	Management bases its decisions on many perspectives	Co-ordination taskforces are used very frequently	The facilities have areas where people can meet cross-organizationally
Overview capabilities	People have a good sense of the most critical issues	Management communicates the strategy often	Career planning ensures that people develop a good overview	There are convenient and effective meeting rooms available to all
Synthesis initiative	People have to make tradeoffs and resolve tensions at their level	Management involves different people in discussing new information	Decisions are made where the needed information is available	Technology facilitates a broad contribution to decisions
Providing focus	Keeping clear priorities is the norm	Management can simplify complex issues into clear directions	Processes reinforce a coherent sense of direction	There is one common information infrastructure
Enriching the map	Strategies can be challenged when justified	Management can spot and interpret the discontinuities in our business	Career paths expose people through many perspectives	Practical approaches are provided to bring discussions to closure

- *Trying things out* - being willing to get off the beaten path, to take risk;
- *Action-learning* - believing that any activity can yield learning.

Table 12.3 explains this further.

How is convergent debriefing and reflection supported by the organization metabolism? Debriefing and reflection rely on:

- Debriefing - being able to revisit what was completed to draw learning points;
- Nondefensiveness - being able to give and take constructive criticism;
- Thinking - being able to review one's own personal behaviour and to project it into the future;
- Learning - being willing to learn and establish one's own learning agenda;
- Improving - believing that improvements are always possible.

Table 12.4 explains this further.

Table 12.3: *Divergent action-learning*

	Culture	Leadership	Processes	Infrastructure
Action orientation	People tend to focus on what can be done, rather on what cannot be done	Management encourages well-calculated risks	There are processes to nurture and support new initiatives	Through information technology, new initiatives can be quite transparent
Initiative	People are discouraged from seeking everybody's permission for everything	Management takes delegation seriously	Performance assessment emphasizes taking initiatives	New initiatives can be decided at fairly low organization levels
Responsibility taking	People willing to take responsibility for fixing problems	Managers throw the ball back at those who try to use them as referees	Career paths include early frontline responsibilities	The information infrastructure supports frontline decision-making
Trying things out	People are expected to get off the beaten path	Management encourages people to question things	Management-development emphasizes action-learning	Organization units can take initiatives outside of their boundaries
Action-learning	People look at failures as opportunities to learn	Management provides people with stretch and challenges	Career paths are designed to provide learning opportunities	New initiatives are hosted where the relevant knowledge is available

Table 12.4: *Convergent debriefing and reflection*

	Culture	Leadership	Processes	Infrastructure
Debriefing	Debriefing projects, meetings etc. is considered normal practice	Management always insists on ending up with key learning points	Processes for effective debriefing are widely disseminated	Information technology is used to gather feedback more widely
Nondefensiveness	Constructive criticism is accepted well	Managers admit it openly when they do not have the answers	Sources of poor performance are analysed carefully and openly	Information technology is used to provide full transparency of results
Thinking	Being able to reflect on one's own behaviour is considered important	Managers typically ask for feedback from their team	Performance assessment includes the ability to learn from experience	The facilities have special areas for more reflective activities
Learning	People are expected to invest in their own development	Managers feel responsible for their team's learning	The company's knowledge base is reviewed and assessed regularly	There are internal "yellow pages" detailing who knows what
Improving	Reflecting on possible improvements is part of the culture	Management typically focuses on what to do next to improve	Career-planning facilitates knowledge transfer across the organization	Information technology is used to collect and disseminate best practice

Reference

Seulamo, M. (1999) *Finns in Business*, (international issue of *Talouselämä*) July 1999.

13

Using Information to Channel Human Energy

The effective use of shared information is key to orchestrating activity and converting frontline energy into high performance. In this chapter, **Don Marchand** presents seven key principles that managers must use if they want to orchestrate activity and develop the information capabilities needed to improve business performance and create a successful e-business. Critical to this is their personal conduct, behaviour and mindset.

CASE STUDY: BANCO BILBAO VISCAYA

In the mid-1990s, the senior managers of Banco Bilbao Viscaya (BBV), Spain's fastest growing and most profitable retail bank, made bold efforts over the next five years to transform their company's business approach with new information capabilities (IC). There are three reasons for their success.

1. *Their senior managers understood that their growth strategy required a determined effort to implement new IC to achieve business success. There was to be no compromise on the journey to systematic improvement.*
2. *These managers did not believe that their traditional way of doing business could be combined with new IC-based methods. Instead, they sought to redefine their existing approaches in order to maximize their information capabilities and integrate new e-business models. For BBV, this meant fully integrating their branches with direct ways of doing business, including Internet and call-centre banking.*
3. *The managers and their people believed that superior execution of their information capabilities each day was the source of their company's competitive advantage.*

Overview

How managers focus and channel human energy today with information and IT impacts directly on business performance. In today's fast-paced, information-rich new economy, information is power. Business leaders know this. They have invested in IT, expecting to develop their ability to exploit that power and achieve better business performance.

Often, a company's IT investment has been a cost with no clear payback. The power of information has benefited consumers, resulting in pressure on companies to offer more products and services at ever lower prices. This has increased the intensity of competition with no clear winners. Most companies haven't found a way to use information and IT to achieve a strategic competitive advantage.

Now e-commerce is exploding on the scene. Some business leaders are concerned that they face a new round of investment, again without any certainty that the result will benefit the bottom line. Others are optimistic about the coming changes, confident that now they can find a way to use information to competitive advantage. They see themselves on the threshold of a new era when the ability to gather and use information opens up exciting possibilities.

This chapter considers two key questions:

- What will it take for an energized bottom-up organization to realize the potential of the information age?
- How can information be used for strategic advantage and impact on the bottom line?

The power of information capabilities

Information results in better bottom-line performance for those bottom-up organizations that can integrate and manage three distinct capabilities that encompass not just information systems but also the actions of people using those systems. Winning companies have executive teams who understand, value and develop each of those capabilities so that they work together. These three ICs are:

1. *Information behaviours and values* – the way a company's managers and employees use and share information to execute their work.
2. *Information management practices* – the way a company senses, collects, organizes, processes and maintains information.
3. *Information technology practices* – the way a company deploys its investment in IT, such as hardware, software and networks for supporting operations, business processes, management decision-making and innovation in new products and services.

Measuring and managing information capabilities

How can a company develop its IC? It is a truth in business that something must be measured before it can be managed. Until now managers have not been able to track how well information is being used within their company. Information orientation (IO) is a new business performance metric that captures the extent to which all three ICs are developed in a company. It is the interaction of the three capabilities that lead a company to achieving high IO. When a company is high on IO, they will be high on business performance.

These findings were discovered during a comprehensive two-year research project conducted at IMD and sponsored by Andersen Consulting involving over 1300 senior managers from 103 companies in 37 countries and 26 industries (Marchand et al., 2000).

Becoming an effective information orientation leader

Another key research finding was that achieving high IO begins with you as a manager – your mindset, behaviours and practices that are connected to effective information use in your business. How managers focus and channel human energy today with information and IT impacts on business performance directly. Managers do not fail because they lack intelligence or motivation. They fail because they cannot face the reality about events, products and people. They cannot hear bad news. Or they cannot seek new ideas and information, especially if they are unsettling to today's successful ways of working.

If "managing" means controlling people, information, resources and processes, most managers, because they are controllers, think that they are succeeding. But managers who cannot be candid and truthful, and who cannot face their mistakes and learn from them, will fail. To lead, managers need to know how to use information. Leading means sensing new knowledge and focusing on the right information to run the business today and to change it tomorrow. Most of all, it means inspiring people in the business to use information and knowledge effectively.

This chapter presents seven key principles that managers can follow to improve the IC of their business unit or company through their personal conduct and behaviours. Managers need to:

- personally set standards and values for effective information use;
- know and communicate the role of IT in the business;
- know personally how to manage information effectively;
- influence mindsets of others;
- understand what good IC means, not just advocate it;
- anticipate the future of the business by disrupting the current business model; and
- realize that good IC today is a crucial step towards creating the successful e-business for tomorrow.

In companies with high IO, the senior managers lead by knowing what information creates value for them, their people and their business. They are aware, even obsessed, with sensing and using the right information. They continuously challenge their own information management practices, information behaviours and values, and IT practices. They have a keen sense of urgency about "what we don't know." They worry about how to use information more effectively to:

- sense the reality of the outside world; and
- change their business practices to exploit that emerging reality.

Managers in these companies focus on facing reality by being open to new ideas, treating bad news as good news, and instilling and celebrating the right information behaviours, information management, and IT practices in themselves, their people, and their companies. These managers gain credibility among their people by practising the behaviours and values of effective information use that they fully expect others to practice as well.

In companies with poor IC and low IO, however, the senior managers talk about good behaviours and values as well as information management and IT practices, but focus on managing by controlling people, events, processes and resources. Their behaviours and values seem disconnected from their words about personal integrity, information-sharing, and being open to bad news or frankness – even when the truth hurts. In these companies, managers speak about the positive business benefits of using information or IT effectively, but do not practise what they preach at work.

Moreover, they often treat information as a political weapon to compete with other managers, rather than as an asset that the company can use to improve business results. They speak about IT's key role in making the business more competitive, but do not use the technology themselves. Or they believe that the Internet and e-business are for others, not for them. They urge their subordinates to be open and candid with them, but employ information selectively to control other people's decisions and actions. In conversations with managers in these companies, there is an air of unreality, since they speak about information, people and IT as important for competitive survival, but act each day in ways that contradict or undermine the achievement of good information capabilities.

Therefore, the way managers face their business reality each day and the way they talk about, and behave with, information to achieve better business performance either builds or diminishes IC in their company. The seven principles that follow should help managers lead an energized organization to high IO and superior business performance.

Principle 1: personally set standards and values for effective information use

Managers must personally set the standards for information behaviours and values in their company and business unit to orchestrate the activity of the organization. Integrity, transparency, sharing information, and a positive view of control all depend on the mindset and personal example of managers. If they do not practise these behaviours and values, their people will not have sufficient trust and confidence that managers will use information and behave consistently. Acting on these behaviours and values also enhances the manager's personal credibility in making changes that can lead to improved information behaviours and values in their people. In sum, managers should not expect their people to be proactive with information-seeking and new ideas unless they are too.

CASE STUDY: RECOGNIZING THE ROLE OF LEADERS IN ORCHESTRATING ACTIVITY AT GENERAL ELECTRIC

Jack Welch, the CEO of General Electric Company (GE), captures the essence of why high integrity, a constructive view of control, transparency, and sharing are vital to people's behaviours and values at GE. For Welch, the key to being a good business leader is to "engender enthusiasm" in people to enable them to have more freedom and more responsibility: "What we are looking for . . . is leaders who can energize, excite, and control rather than enervate, depress, and control," (Slater, 1999). Welch believes that managers must be team members and coaches, who must facilitate idea generation and information sharing rather than "controlling". This implies that managers must develop personal integrity in themselves and their people. They must also manage their people to inspire them to contribute their knowledge and share ideas. "To be blunt, the two quickest ways to part company with GE are, one, to commit an integrity violation, or, two, to be a controlling, turf-defending, oppressive manager who can't change and who saps and squeezes people rather than excites and draws out their energy and creativity."

Thus, for Welch, not compromising on integrity is critical to building an atmosphere of trust and confidence. It encourages the sharing of ideas and information and promotes responsibility, rather than control in a negative sense: "I dislike the traits that have come to be associated with 'managing' - controlling, stifling people, keeping them in the dark, wasting their time on trivia and reports, breathing down their necks. You can't manage self-confidence into people."

> *In addition, Welch believes that integrity enhances the ability to face reality and act quickly and decisively on it. Moreover, facing reality means learning from mistakes, since most managerial mistakes come from not facing and dealing with reality. Thus Welch sees a direct connection between integrity and transparency as well as the link between integrity, control, and sharing by building trust and confidence in people.*
>
> *Welch also places enormous emphasis on "keeping business simple" by not complicating decisions unnecessarily and by being clear about what performance criteria and measures count for employees and managers: "Numbers aren't the vision – the numbers are the product. We always say that if you had three measurements to live by, they'd be employee satisfaction, customer satisfaction, and cashflow. If you've got cash in the till at the end, the rest is all going to work, because if you've got high customer satisfaction, you're going to get a share. If you've got high employee satisfaction, you're going to get productivity. And if you've got cash, you know it's all working."*
>
> *With straightforward and understandable measures, managers and employees can focus on what is important in a business and how to generate ideas and information that create business value. For Welch, the secret to innovation is to always assume that there are better ideas on the outside of the company that must be proactively sensed and shared wherever in the company they can make a difference:*
>
> *"The operative assumption today is that someone, somewhere, has a better idea; and the operative compulsion is to find out who has that better idea, learn it, and put it into action – fast ... The quality of an idea does not depend on its altitude in the organization ... An idea can come from any source. So we will search the globe for ideas. We will share what we know with others to get what they know. We have a constant quest to raise the bar, and we get there by constantly talking to others."*

Principle 2: know and communicate the role of information technology in the business

Managers must not only know how to use IT, but must also understand and communicate to their people what the appropriate role of IT is in their business. Without a basic understanding of what IT can do, managers have the possibility of either overestimating its value, by relying on the knowledge of others, or underestimating its value, by not applying their own managerial judgement appropriately. Percy Barnevik, the former CEO of the ABB Group, characterized his managers in the early 1990s as "BCs" or "ACs", depending on whether they were born before or after the personal computer (PC). He suggested that this demarcation signalled a dramatic shift in managerial attitudes toward using IT. Those born before the PC, BCs, were unlikely to experience and think naturally about the transformational impact of IT on their business and their life as a manager. Those born after the PC, ACs, were more likely to view IT as a natural tool in their professional life and also appreciate its transformational role in the business. While this distinction may be viewed as old hat today in the Internet era, it nevertheless captured the view that using IT was vital to understanding it in the business. No future managers can afford not to view IT as an essential tool for doing the business and changing the business at the same time.

This is particularly important in the era of e-business, when managers must be able to imagine the many ways to use IT and the Internet to transform their business. If managers neither care about, nor understand, the Internet and miss the potential for e-business in their industry, they probably cannot see – and therefore will not support – the actions their company must take if it is to win in the new economy.

There are distinct differences between low-IO and high-IO companies in the managerial mindset toward IT and its use.

In companies with low IO, senior managers perceive IT in two very different ways. Inside the company, IT is treated as a cost and a support function for basic operations and business process support. Managers tend to view the IT function and the chief information officer (CIO) as somehow disconnected from the real business. There is a constant need for the IT function to justify its existence, separate from the business units and the more established functions of the company such as human resources and finance.

These same managers, however, naively view the Internet and e-business as potential sources of competitive advantage for their company, even though the company is unlikely to have the IC to support alternative models of e-business. Since the managers are new to the Internet and e-business, both personally and professionally, they do not realize that a large part of Internet and e-business is, generally speaking, already a competitive necessity in their industry, as opposed to a mere competitive advantage. In many of these companies an IO credibility gap exists, since their current ICs are unlikely to sustain their future expectations about competing in their industry.

In contrast, in companies with high IO, senior managers understand that IT practices are vital to achieving superior performance, but remain realistic about treating IT as a necessary, but not the only, source of competitive advantage in their company. They know that without the right information behaviours and values and information management practices, IT alone will not make the difference between achieving competitive necessity and competitive advantage.

These managers also have realistic expectations about e-business and the Internet in their industries. They understand that the companies that will win in the e-business economy will be those that exploit e-business opportunities today in their existing business and prepare for the disruptive effects of e-commerce in their market in the future.

For example, in 1998, Jack Welch was among the first CEOs of a major global company to establish an e-business unit within every major business division of his company (GE). The mandate for these e-business units was "to Dell or be Delled" in their respective industries, i.e. to explore ways to disrupt their industries with e-commerce business strategies before competitors and new entrants could.

Companies with high IO expect to use IT, including the Internet, to compete. However, to get ready for tomorrow's disruptive e-business competition, they are also targeting business investments in information technology. Senior managers in these companies do not view IT as separate from the business, but as part of leading a successful company in the e-business era. Since they have good personal and company experiences with IT, they are in a position to improve systematically their companies' information capabilities, and they are ready for industry leadership challenges. They seek to exploit realistically the business potential of IT and e-business for top business performance. Their mindsets, experiences and attitudes toward IT and e-business are in line with their expectations for IT in building IC that enable their companies to stay ahead in their industries.

Principle 3: know personally how to manage information effectively

Managers must know how to use information effectively, not just how the company uses information to create business value. Since the 1980s, companies have used IT widely for operations and business processes. The IT industry has also pushed the personal use of IT with PCs, cell phones, pagers and other digital appliances.

Historically, however, information management in business has focused largely on accounting and finance, marketing and sales, manufacturing and logistics. There has been little effort to improve personal information management – how managers and knowledge workers sense, collect, organize, process and maintain information. Companies have given managers and knowledge workers more power to make important business decisions and take on added responsibility, but few understand how well these people use and manage information in their everyday working lives.

This development is the information paradox. On the one hand, personal information management in a company is an important part of organizational and individual success. Management guru Peter Drucker (1999) has concluded: "For the knowledge worker in general, and especially for executives, information is the key resource. Information increasingly creates the link to their fellow workers and to the organization, and their 'network'. It is information, in other words, that enables knowledge workers to do their job."

On the other hand, managers spend little time or attention improving how they and all their people – not just knowledge workers – use information to network with each other more effectively. Managers have either relied on administrative staff and IT specialists to understand what information they needed about the business, or they have abdicated their information responsibilities in favour of decisions based on gut feeling and intuition. Lack of information about problems and situations, they claim, can be a virtue.

To break out of this information paradox, managers must take responsibility for the information that they use and share to create business value. Managers cannot expect their company to be good at using information if they do not take personal information responsibility themselves. In companies with high IO, managers create value by taking responsibility for their use of information. They do not expect – nor do they want – administrative staff or IT specialists to make decisions about what information managers need to understand. Since a good deal of information needed by managers is located outside and is relatively informal and ill-defined, they have to take personal responsibility for sensing, processing, and sharing the information with other managers and employees.

Further, to evaluate the personal information practices and effectiveness of other managers and knowledge workers, managers must develop their own good personal information practices. Since knowledge work is done by individuals in teams and projects, managers cannot talk about good information practices without demonstrating them. Since a good deal of a manager's work is public and shared, behaviours and values of individual managers are under constant scrutiny. So fellow managers and workers can see first-hand how well a manager senses outside intelligence and shares it with others while he or she performs, rather than seeing it simply in the decisions the manager says are based on his or her information activities.

Peter Drucker (1999) has suggested that managers must ask two questions of themselves regarding their personal information responsibilities:

- What information do I owe to the people with whom I work and on whom I depend? In what form? In what time frame?
- What information do I need myself? From whom? In what form? In what time frame?

By answering these two sets of questions periodically, managers can become more aware of their information responsibilities to others and of others' to them. They can be in a better position to understand what types of information they require to manage their business and to create business value. This focus on knowing what you want, and knowing how to share and use it, is also important to enable people in the company to understand how they share and use information and what information is most significant for executing their responsibilities. This principle of reciprocity, carried out each day at the individual level, creates the climate for understanding what information and information practices are critical to running and changing the business.

For example, the principle of reciprocal information responsibility means that managers and employees must take the lead in the design and implementation of new information practices and IT systems for the business. Managers cannot abdicate this responsibility to administrative staff and IT specialists, only to complain later that they did not deliver. Managers must recognize that they are in the best position to know what they want; ultimately, it is they who must take personal and organizational responsibility to see that they get it.

To escape the information paradox – and ensure that personal information awareness and use can translate into information effectiveness companywide – managers have to assume their information responsibilities if they expect their employees to do the same.

Principle 4: influence the mindsets of others

Managers must create the right expectations for their people in changing business strategies and the mix of business capabilities. Managing involves influencing the mindsets of people in a company and the people with whom the company does business – customers, suppliers, partners and the competitors.

Mindsets are the distinctive viewpoints, needs, agendas and expectations that influence directly how individuals perceive their role and engage in work. In shaping their people's viewpoints and expectations about the business, managers can act in two ways. On the one hand, they can work toward understanding the mindsets of others and candidly exchange views and expectations about what a business should do and how. On the other hand, they can act before they understand other people's viewpoints and expectations. In this case, management becomes (negative) control, and to achieve their priorities and implement change, managers are forced to engage in explicit acts of persuasion and power plays.

While you may believe that managing in the real world involves both types of behaviours, it is clear that companies with high IO emphasize the first one. As a manager, you cannot foster the right information behaviours, follow the right strategies, and get the right mix of business capabilities without first understanding the viewpoints of others before and as you act.

For example, a business improvement program at a large European retail bank aims at developing a clear understanding among all managers and employees of the link between having the right mix of business capabilities – including IC – and focusing successfully on customers for cross-selling financial products and services. All employees are aware of the links between building the right business capabilities and achieving superior business performance. A basic responsibility of senior managers is to manage the mindsets of their people in terms of how the bank operates to achieve growth and customer value. This includes what the employees are expected to do in their work, how the bank uses product and customer information in selling to and serving customers, and how it rewards individual, team and company performance.

This persistence of managers in promoting inclusive understanding of the core business strategies for growth and the mix of business capabilities required to achieve these strategies over a period of years is a distinctive element of the company with high IO.

In contrast, companies with low IO exhibit one or both of the following tendencies. They may emphasize a narrow and manipulative view of control. In this setting, managers speak about the traditional mindsets of their people and the need to overcome reactive behaviours and ways of doing business. Managers often recognize the mindset issues in their company, but press for more control over their people as a way of managing change. Managers are not candid with their people and take decisions behind the scenes, since the climate for mutual understanding and frank dialogue is low or nonexistent.

The second tendency of companies with low IO is to create a credibility gap between their business strategies and the business capabilities to execute these strategies over time. These are companies that promise customers a lot in services and products, but for a variety of reasons are not in a position to deliver fully, since they have diluted or failed to build the right mix of business capabilities. For example, if a company pursuing a cost-cutting strategy persists with this strategy over several years, the company will seriously dilute or erode its IC, especially information behaviours and values, among its people. Senior managers in the company may suddenly announce that customer delight and creating business opportunities are the critical strategic priorities. However, following several years of redundancies and delayering, the IC to deliver their new, intended strategy will be seriously lacking. If senior managers persist in these objectives without recognizing rapidly the need to build appropriate information capabilities, their employees may view their strategy statements as either unrealistic (we can't deliver on the promises), or, at worst, highly cynical (how can we deliver on our promises to customers without the right business capabilities?).

Another manifestation of the credibility gap, as the case study below shows, occurs when a company effectively sells its IC to customers over time, but for whatever reason cannot implement them effectively.

CASE STUDY: GLOBAL FREIGHT-FORWARDING COMPANY

A leading, global freight-forwarding company has, over the last 12 years, been unable to implement an integrated freight-forwarding IT system on a worldwide basis. In the late 1980s, the company outsourced the project to a consultancy but, over seven years, was unable to achieve any results. In the mid-1990s, the company organized an internal team to implement the same IT system. After four years, the company was ready to implement two pilot sites for the global system – still a long way from a global approach.

In the mean time, the senior managers had succeeded in repositioning their company in the minds of their best and global customers. To delight customers and work effectively with other companies on multinational accounts, the company sold its integrated global freight-forwarding system and Internet capabilities to customers around the world. The customer response was favourable. Multinational customers had long clamoured for real-time monitoring of their shipments globally and direct interfaces with the company's Internet site for other services.

The company's managers succeeded in selling IC that they really did not have in place to large customers and now are compelled to deliver on these capabilities any way they can. The company's new CEO has drawn one moral from this story: "If you promise high IO, you had better have the information capabilities to deliver it!"

Principle 5: understand what good information capability means, don't just advocate it

Managers must not just be advocates of good IC in their business: they must understand the conditions for implementing IC in their business. If you want to improve IC in your business, there is no room for wishful thinking. Senior managers can advocate stretch targets for enhancing information capabilities, but they must figure out if the conditions in their business give their people a realistic chance of gaining substantial improvements. Our research identified four types of cases in which senior managers advocate improvements in IC, but may or may not fully appreciate the conditions in their company to make such improvements happen.

Type A: ambitious and highly focused on building information capabilities

Companies with high IO did not always possess high IC. They grew them. Two of the high-IO companies in the research study planted the seeds for their IC before the 1990s. In both companies, the arrival of a new CEO in the mid-1990s, coupled with an urgent and intense focus on building IC to meet ambitious growth targets, led to five years of consistent improvements in each IC.

At the beginning of their journeys, the companies identified stretch targets for both business performance improvement and changes in IC. At the time, an external observer might have concluded, correctly, that their goals were not in line with their business capabilities. However, senior managers set their goals very high knowing that even if they fell short of the stretch target, they would exceed the accepted rates of improvement in their industries. "Stretch" meant that as these business leaders raised their business targets each year, they aggressively pursued improvements in IC. Although on the face of it the goals of these companies might have seemed ambitious, they were in fact realistic, given senior managers' understanding of the business conditions of their companies. Thus, over five years, both companies made remarkable improvements in its information capabilities and business performance.

Type B: ambitious, but missing key information capabilities

In some cases, senior managers take a strong stand on some ICs, such as information behaviours and values, but do not understand their company's deficiencies in others, such as IT practices. This was the case with one European retailer of eyeglass lenses and frames, which started in the 1980s as a small French company with a very customer-centred service approach. Information practices and behaviours were highly localized in the store, yet transparent and proactive; the focus of the business was on store management and operations.

In 1997, when the company acquired a large UK competitor, the number of employees doubled to about 8000, while the number of stores more than tripled to 700 across 17 countries. The CEO, who had believed previously that "IT was not in the genes of his company," had to face the prospect of significantly improving IT practices for operations and business process support. This meant expanding information management practices from store operations to regional supply chain processes and shifting the localized information values and behaviours to a broad-based, 700-store retail operation.

In this case, the CEO became aware that business performance could be significantly improved by aggressively attacking deficiencies in IT practices and information management practices across the company. In the light of its service focus, winning brands, people culture, and entrepreneurial growth, this company could close the gap between advocating ambitious business improvements and creating the business conditions for high IO.

Type C: urgent information capabilities turn-around required, but conditions are poor

Managers are very keen to improve their information capabilities, but either do not understand what actions to take with their people, or focus on the wrong ICs from the start. Changing information behaviours and values can take years to improve significantly in established companies. Many companies have a long history of poor information behaviours and values. These may be caused by senior managers' approach to command and control, vertical and highly fragmented approaches to IT and information management practices, and people cultures that breed suspicion, lack of information-sharing, and use of information as a political weapon.

Prior to the mid-1990s, for example, a major US financial services company had experienced poor information behaviours and values on the part of several CEOs over many years. One CEO in particular had behaved autocratically towards managers and had been dismissed for falsifying performance information given to the board of directors. Because of the low levels of information integrity, transparency, and sharing displayed by several CEOs over more than a decade, efforts by the company's CEO at the time of writing to improve information behaviours and values have met with mixed success. While he and members of his senior management team would like to improve IC in the company rapidly, and have personally taken steps to change their behaviours and values, lower-level managers and employees regard their efforts at change with doubt and suspicion. In this case, good intentions alone will not lead to major improvements in information capabilities.

Type D: changing business expectations, but low information capabilities – the danger of wishful thinking

Companies with low IO clearly face the greatest challenges in linking managerial expectations about business performance or information capabilities improvements with the reality of conditions in their business. A company that has performed poorly over the last five years and has low IO, coupled with a business strategy that emphasizes cost reduction, faces a major credibility gap with its employees and its customers.

If the senior managers advocate a growth strategy and begin talking about customer delight and new business opportunities, they must at the same time be sure to outline the specific steps to substantially improve the three ICs concurrently. Without decisive and well-executed steps to improve their own and their people's information behaviours and values, coupled with clear changes in IT and information management practices, these managers run the greatest danger – wishful thinking. They announce changes in business strategy, but underestimate the weakness of the company's ICs and the steps they must take in order to correct them aggressively to improve the bottom line.

Principle 6: anticipate the future of the business by disrupting the current business model

Managers need to have the courage and foresight to disrupt a successful business model in order to capitalize on future potential – they cannot wait to see what the future holds. The decision to grow a company by exploiting new business opportunities and delighting customers requires senior managers to anticipate the future and build business capabilities that fit the future view of the business, not necessarily the current one. Inventing a new business approach while running an existing business challenges the mindsets of managers in two ways:

- First, they must decide to disrupt their existing business model for an uncertain future one – their attachment to the existing business model damages the chances of successfully adopting the new model over time. "Creative destruction" sounds good until your management team tries it.
- Second, they and their people are reaping the benefits of the existing model while taking actions to undermine them for unclear and risky new ones. This situation places people who run the existing business in a difficult position. After all, why put today's benefits at risk when the threat of future competition is unclear? In this case, senior managers in established companies face a dilemma. If they wait until the future threats become known, they lose time and the opportunity to make the first move for early advantage. If they act when the potential threats are not yet clearly perceived, they risk taking the wrong steps in building business capabilities that may not be appropriate.

A business strategy that focuses on growth makes companies leverage information capabilities for their current and future business success. Today, in the era of e-business, the decision to augment or transform IC involves rethinking current business approaches or inventing entirely new ones. Managers must take advantage of using IC to enhance or save on other business capabilities such as processes, people, organizational structure, and/or external relationships. To do so, senior managers are faced with three major options for designing new business approaches and coping with existing ways of doing business.

Approach A: exploit information capabilities fully in a start-up

A senior management team that starts exploiting IC in a start-up operation separate from its traditional business is unencumbered by a legacy of organizational structures, processes, people and low IO.

CASE STUDY: SKANDIABANKEN

When senior managers of the Skandia Group decided to launch a new direct bank in the 1990s in the Swedish banking market, they were able to invent a pure model: direct banking, cross-selling products, and attracting customers with higher interest rates on savings and responsive, flexible services. SkandiaBanken, through its affiliation with the Skandia Group, was able to gain immediate brand recognition. Yet the new direct business model leveraged IC wherever possible to substitute for unnecessary management layers, overly complex business processes, vertical reporting structures, and an extensive system of physical branches.

> *In addition, the direct model exploited weaknesses in the more established banks in the Swedish market by positioning itself as a low-cost, but highly customer-focused bank in which customers were treated as individuals, not accounts. Moreover, early on SkandiaBanken advertised its customer and service integrity and its competitive savings rates as a direct response to the image of low customer and product integrity of established banks. A series of bank "bail outs" in the early and mid-1990s, and lower returns on customer accounts, provided SkandiaBanken with a market window to exploit its direct business model and its unique information capabilities in the Swedish marketplace.*

For an established company, designing a start-up operation offers the advantages of a pure model for exploiting IC fully. However, while the new enterprise may succeed, the existing business units of the established company may not benefit from synergies between the pure business model and the current ways of doing business.

Approach B: add new information capabilities to the existing business

Many senior managers in established companies today believe that they can have their cake and eat it. They think that they can leverage new direct business models and IC without changing their existing business approach. These managers think that they can have the best of both worlds, but they risk getting the worst. In such cases, it is difficult for managers and their people, having grown up with, and benefited from, the traditional way of doing business, to fully support a new IC-based business model that may threaten or disrupt the way they currently do businesss.

CASE STUDY: THE PC MARKET

During the 1990s, Dell Computers successfully exploited a direct business model for selling desktop and portable PCs and servers against companies such as Compaq, IBM and H-P, who sold through wholesaler, distributor and retailer networks. Dell's "pure" model, using a direct sales force, call centres and the Internet, has allowed Dell to gain important market share against its larger rivals. In each case, the established companies have aimed at preserving their traditional external relationships with wholesalers, distributors and retailers but at the same time adopting direct ways of doing business through call centres and the Internet.

However, these attempts to straddle intermediary and direct channels have met with mixed success (Porter, 1999). Compaq has consistently lost market share to Dell over the last five years. IBM has had major difficulties in making its PC division profitable. H-P has been slow to adopt direct ways of doing business and engaging in direct sales of its PC products over the Internet (Kalish, 1999). With one foot planted firmly in their traditional ways of doing business through retail channels, these companies have found it very difficult to sustain the benefits of their existing business model and to capture the benefits of the new direct business approach. Their managers have been reluctant to disrupt their accepted ways of doing business with powerful retail partners for an uncertain future in the direct way of doing business.

Approach C: transform your business model with new information capabilities

The most challenging position for managers is to transform a traditional business into a company competing with new IC. These companies require multiyear journeys and major changes in people, structures, processes and external relationships.

While many company managers may aspire to growth strategies, the best companies believe that competitive advantage is a product of both good strategy and superior execution each and every day. Their pursuit of operational excellence with IC stimulates managers and people to always make good better and permits the companies to fight today's competitive battles successfully and prepare for future success. Contrary to management teams in many established companies, these managers are always seeking information and ideas in the outside world to achieve superior performance.

Principle 7: realize that good information capability today is a crucial step towards creating the successful e-business for tomorrow

Managers who lead their company toward high IO are in the best position to implement the virtual, bottom-up organization in the new e-business economy. There were many predictions of the virtual organization during the 1990s (e.g. Davidow and Malone, 1992; Tapscott, 1996). At the beginning of the twenty-first century, however, it is impossible to predict the many forms the virtual organization will take. How will the Internet and e-business evolve? Will they require new forms of organization based on knowledge and information, rather than physical things? Will the virtual organization be an organization at all? Or will it perhaps be temporary aggregations of knowledge workers delivering business value by continuously realigning themselves in projects, deals and relationships through global networks (Malone and Laubacher, 1998)?

What we do know is that whatever shape the virtual organization takes in the e-business economy, a company's ability to achieve superior business performance will be based on the right mix of business strategies and capabilities leading to high IO. The reasons for this are threefold. Virtual organizations will be growers. They will have to survive by growing, not cutting. These companies will focus on two key strategies. First, they will need to reinvent their products and services continuously to create business value. Virtual organizations will be aggressive learning organizations because they have to be. Their managers and people will need to be proactive in generating and using new ideas and information faster and better than competitors. Second, virtual organizations will need to delight each and every customer they have – real-time and online. Customizing individual products, sensing customer needs, and responding one-to-one will require these companies to design their business processes with the utmost flexibility. Customer relationships and services will be customized and unique because they have to be.

Virtual organizations will use their IC as a competitive weapon to enhance or save on the traditional levers of strategic change such as people, organizational structure, processes and external relationships. These companies will substitute information and digital processes for physical processes wherever feasible. They will minimize organizational structures that block appropriate information- and knowledge-sharing across functions, processes and organizational boundaries. They will save on people by cutting activities, tasks and responsibilities that add no value and by leveraging people's willingness to make their knowledge explicit and usable, to benefit the company and themselves. Finally, to exploit the full business value of new forms of network-based competition, co-operation, and co-option (Tapscott, 1996), they will seek to "Internetwork" people in companies with partners, customers and even competitors. In short, virtual organizations will succeed by inventing new ways of fully leveraging their IC in their business models.

Virtual organizations will require high IO to stay ahead of the pack. There is no guarantee that going virtual or direct in the future will help a company to achieve competitive advantage. Despite what many academics, consultants and managers have claimed in the 1990s, new entrants and established companies in diverse industries will adopt many or all of the elements of this organizational model. So being a virtual organization in the future will be more of a competitive necessity than a competitive advantage. The leading companies in an industry will be compelled to react and respond to the business capabilities that their competitors or new entrants adopt. Like leading marathon-runners, these companies will be forced to run faster and harder as part of the lead pack in their industry. They will have to execute the business capabilities of the virtual organization and e-business just to stay in the lead pack.

The few companies that attain competitive advantage in and across industries will be those that exploit their growth strategies and use IC to achieve high IO and superior business performance. Only these managers and companies will be able to stay ahead of the lead pack in their industry. Which characteristics of the virtual organization they adapt or invent will depend directly on their journey to continuously improve their IO. These will be the companies whose managers have built the information capabilities in the past and who expect to sustain their industry leadership in competing with information in the future.

 # SUMMARY

ICs have been invisible previously to business managers. By making them visible, this chapter offers companies, especially those with energized organizations, the key to attaining superior business performance. The management path to leveraging IC involves seven principles identified in a major two-year international study examining how senior managers in a global sample of companies lead their people to use information and IT to improve business results.

Leading a bottom-up organization on a journey to achieve high IO and attain superior business performance takes hard work, persistence and personal commitment.

Knowing this, the intention in this chapter was not to start a new management fad or offer a quick-fix solution. To undertake the journey you will have to develop the right mindset about effective information use in your business. Lead and inspire people along the way – your company will be better for it.

BEST PRACTICE

A manager's effective use of shared information converts the centrifugal forces created by energy on the frontline of the company into high performance. To "lead" is to sense new knowledge, focus on the right information to run the business today, find the right information to change it tomorrow and, most of all, inspire people to use information and knowledge effectively in the business.

Are you an information orientation leader?

IO begins at the top. It takes more than authorizing an IT investment and training staff to use information. It calls for different behaviours, values and practices. Whenever an organization asks people to think and act differently, the leader has to model and be a symbol of new behaviours.

Your people will look at what you do, not what you say. Are you prepared to "walk the talk" on information orientation?

- *Do you set the standard for the behaviours and practices you want your people to adopt?* Do you share sensitive information? Do you actively seek out information and new ideas? Do you accept, even welcome, bad news? Do you learn from your mistakes, and share that learning with others?
- *Do you understand the possibilities and limitations of IT in your business?* Do you use technology (computers, the Internet) in your daily life? Do you see the IT function and the CIO as part of your business? Do you understand that the Internet and e-business are already a competitive necessity and potentially sources of competitive advantage?
- *Do you know how to use information effectively?* Do you ask yourself the questions that management guru Peter Drucker poses for information leaders? "What information do I need myself?" "From whom?" "In what form?" "In what timeframe?" "What information do I owe to the people with whom I work and on whom I depend?" "In what form?" "In what timeframe?"

- *Do you create the right expectations for your people?* Do you try to understand the mindsets – the distinctive viewpoints, needs, agendas and expectations – that influence your employees, customers, suppliers, partners and competitors? Do you use this insight to promote an inclusive understanding of your core business strategies for growth and the mix of business capabilities required? Do you give your employees and managers clear criteria and measures to guide them when they make decisions?
- *Do you understand the conditions under which your company must improve its IC?* Are you working from a reliable assessment of the scope of your company's challenge and the precise source of its weaknesses? Have you set challenging targets for your people to reach?

References

Davidow, W.H. and Malone, M.S. (1992) *The Virtual Corporation*. New York: Harper Business.

Drucker, P.F. (1999) *Management Challenges for the 21st Century*. Oxford, UK: Butterworth Heinemann.

Kalish, D.S. (1999) Dell Shakes up US Industry with Sales Efficiency Model, *Wall St. Journal Asia*, June 23, 1999.

Malone, T.W. and Laubacher, R.J. (1998) The Dawn of the E-Lance Economy, *Harvard Business Review*, Sept/Oct, 1998: 145–152.

Marchand, D.A., Kettinger, W.J. and Rollins, J.D. (2000) *Information Orientation: The Link To Business Performance*. Oxford: Oxford University Press.

Porter, M.F. (1999) *On Competition*, p. 57. Boston: Harvard Business School Press.

Slater, R. (1999) *Jack Welch and the GE Way*, pp. 28, 37, 90, 97. New York: McGraw-Hill.

Tapscott, D. (1996) *The Digital Economy*. New York: McGraw-Hill.

14

Focusing People around Processes

Organizational complexity can soak up an incredible amount of energy in bottom-up organizations. This is especially true as companies grow, diversify and internationalize. In this chapter, **Jean-Philippe Deschamps** explains the essential role of processes in orchestrating activity and how they can be harmonized to channel energy.

CASE STUDY: FOCUSING ON THE INNOVATION PROCESS AT TETRA PAK

As we all know, many of today's large and successful companies were born out of the vision and dogged determination of an enterprising innovator. But how can such companies maintain the innovative spirit of their founders as they grow, diversify and prosper, and new generations of managers come to the forefront?

This question was on the mind of the CEO of Tetra Pak, the highly successful liquid-packaging company, when he and his top aides decided to re-energize the company around its innovation process, and go for growth through new products. For years, Tetra Pak had been immensely successful at spreading its initial innovation worldwide. Thanks to its ubiquitous aseptic milk and fruit juice packages – "bricks" as they were known – dairy farmers, fruit juice bottlers and many other food and beverage packers around the globe had converted their consumers to the habit of storing perishable liquid food in an "ambient package". This had led to considerable savings throughout the distribution chain and to a significant increase in convenience for all: packers, distribution, retailers and consumers.

The challenge for Tetra Pak's management was to mobilize the organization to meet a new set of challenges: how to go from an incremental approach to product line extensions and renewal, to more ambitious and radical innovations in packaging; and how to maintain the founders' entrepreneurial spirit, while at the same time "professionalizing" the new product-creation process and making it sustainable, as required in a multibillion-dollar global company. Tetra Pak's top management team was convinced that the innovation process had to be singled out as one of the company's core processes – together with its vitally important order-to-delivery process. Both would contribute equally to the company's recently launched customer satisfaction initiative.

A small innovation process team was set up to mobilize the senior management group and get things started. Very quickly, however, management realized that its highly operationally oriented corporate management group would have neither the time nor the resources to support efforts on such a scale. The innovation process required dedicated managers and new capabilities that did not exist in the line organization. Two senior managers were therefore empowered with this responsibility at the executive committee level – a vice president for strategic business development, and a chief technology officer. Together, management announced that they would orchestrate the innovation process and all its components, from market and competitor intelligence, idea generation and technology development, to strategy and planning, project management and market launch.

Appointing dedicated champions helped put the innovation process at the top of the management agenda, but there was a need to involve the key product division directors directly in the process improvement efforts. This was achieved by instituting an innovation process board and asking them to participate. So at Tetra Pak today, innovation is explicitly managed as a core process. The process has two joint "owners" – the chief technology officer and the strategic business development director. The process is supervised by a high-level, multidivisional coaching mechanism: the innovation process board, chaired by the chief technology officer. The various processes within innovation have been identified, mapped and allocated to owners and process improvement teams. The company has an infrastructure in place to manage the multiple initiatives which it has created. The innovation process is now firmly on people's minds.

Overview

To run a bottom-up organization effectively, senior managers need to deploy and orchestrate an ever-expanding set of technologies, product lines, geographical markets and global key accounts, without forgetting external suppliers and partners. It often becomes so complex and time-consuming that there is hardly any time left for management to anticipate and implement profound strategic changes. All the company's energy is focused on orchestrating activity across multidimensional matrices, regardless of whether these are recognized and formalized or not.

This growing complexity is forcing management teams across the world to rethink their organization. Everyone is searching for new, more effective ways to capture and channel the energy of employees, vendors and partners. The common objective is to capture new market opportunities, and address rapidly changing customer needs and wants to create more value.

For years, the simplest approach to meet that challenge has been to split the company into a number of independently managed business units. The underlying philosophy is well known: to keep it simple and manageable, keep it small. In companies like Hewlett Packard (HP) or Philips, it has become a way of life. When a business grows too large, as was the case with printers at HP, management will typically split it into several distinct lines of businesses, each focusing on a particular product or market segment. Large, multibusiness companies around the world are increasingly following this principle. By doing so, they gain in focus. Energy gets channelled into a specific and manageable set of products and customers. However, running the corporation as a federation of highly independent lines of business makes it more difficult for management to play the role of business architect and to cope with converging markets and fast-expanding horizontal technologies. For example, the pervasive growth of digital technology and the convergence of business and consumer electronics, IT and telecommunications, is demanding integrated responses, which highly decentralized organizations cannot always provide.

An alternative approach exists, however, which enables management to reap the benefits of bottom-up business decentralization, yet provides integration. It consists of orchestrating activity and channelling energy around the organization's business processes. This means refocusing people on the company's critical, value-creating chains of activities, rather than on their specialized skills or organizational boundaries.

Although very promising, process management has not been implemented widely in large companies. Despite the hype consultants created about process re-engineering and the broad media coverage it received, few companies have actually extended their process management system to all their key processes. Typically, only a few basic operational processes – product development, order fulfilment, and customer service – have been redesigned. Even fewer companies have gone the whole way and reorganized themselves around their business processes.

The limited number of companies having implemented a process-centred organization is probably caused by three factors: a certain lack of appreciation for the far-reaching benefits of that approach (what will it give us that we cannot achieve with our current organization?); a perceived dearth of management mechanisms to manage such organizations (how do we manage processes, as distinct from functions, products or markets?); and a fear of adding another element of complexity (aren't we going to create chaos by superimposing yet another layer to our already multidimensional matrices?).

To offset these legitimate fears, it seems appropriate to reflect on the main challenges and benefits of process-centred organizations. This chapter looks at how to harmonize processes by:

- building a process management system and infrastructure;
- setting up the mechanisms needed to sustain the processes over time (these are the concrete tools that will allow management to tap and channel peoples' energy towards the creation of more value); and
- mobilizing and motivating people around the company's core processes, top-down and bottom-up.

Building a process management system

Managers typically learn first to manage functions. Then, when promoted, they learn how to manage business units or divisions, hence how to integrate functions to achieve their goals. In most cases, the model under which they practise and learn is a hierarchical one. During most of their career, they will have been entrusted with a direct line authority over those people operating with and under them. Unlike in Japan, where project management is highly valued, few senior managers reach the top of Western companies by having managed increasingly large and successful projects. Even fewer have managed cross-functional processes without having the corresponding hierarchical authority.

Yet, value creation and performance improvements result from a conscious attempt to recognize and optimize the company's business processes. Managers therefore need to learn how to manage processes, and that means channelling the company's energy across functions and departments, hence across hierarchical lines.

Managing through processes has strong organizational and cultural implications. Organizational, since the company's core processes need to be identified across functional lines, process owners empowered, and new organizational mechanisms set up. Cultural implications because management skills and styles need to gear up to the challenge of managing multifunctional interfaces, getting things done through people one does not control, and resolving conflicts. As we all know today, the ultimate form of leadership is directing people one does not command.

Every manager today is familiar with the notion of process, i.e. the series of interconnected activities that cut across functional or departmental lines to create value. We know well, for example, that new product development and order fulfilment – two of the most widely recognized business processes – involve many more functions than R&D and/or manufacturing.

Most managers have been exposed – often through the total quality management (TQM) wave – to the key steps in working through, mapping and improving processes. But for many, the exposure will not have gone much further than a short TQM briefing, followed by practical re-engineering exercises. It is useful, therefore, to outline the concrete steps through which one builds a process management system and infrastructure:

1. Unbundle and map the company's processes.
2. Select the most critical ones – the core processes.
3. Allocate clear process ownership and coaching responsibilities.
4. Define various modes of intervention and roles with regard to processes.
5. Address the deficiencies of each core process and their subprocesses.

Unbundling and mapping the company's processes

Processes can be classified into three groups or levels, according to their nature and tangibility, or according to the type of value they create:

- operational or Level 1 processes
- managerial or Level 2 processes
- leadership or Level 3 processes.

At the lowest level are the *operational processes*. They create an immediate and tangible value for the company's stakeholders (e.g. customers, employees and owners/shareholders). Table 14.1 gives a few representative examples of these operational processes. Customer-oriented processes are generally the ones that have attracted most re-engineering efforts.

Table 14.1: *Examples of operational (Level 1) processes*

Processes creating value for customers	Processes creating value for employees	Processes creating value for owners
New product development	Recruitment	New business creation
Order fulfilment	Management development	Investor relations
Customer management	Performance evaluation	Reporting
Customer service	Compensation and rewards	Dividend setting

At a higher level are the *managerial processes*. They typically create the input, framework and context for operational processes. They deal with such things as performance-target setting, strategy formulation, information-infrastructure building, resource building, co-ordination and integration, and planning and budgeting. Some of these processes are supporting a specific category of stakeholders (Table 14.2). Others, for example those dealing with policies, infrastructure or systems, support the company's operations more generally. With the exception of information systems planning, these processes have typically attracted much less re-engineering effort than operational processes.

Table 14.2: *Examples of managerial (Level 2) processes*

Supporting customer–oriented Level 1 processes	Supporting employee-oriented Level 1 processes	Supporting owner-oriented Level 1 processes
Product strategy and planning	Staff resource planning	Financing
R&D strategy and planning	Career planning	Budgeting
Manufacturing strategy and planning	HR policy setting	Capital investment planning
Supplier base building	Performance target setting	Auditing

At the highest level are the *leadership processes*. They provide the input, context and framework for the business management processes. They deal with such things as vision building, values and goal setting, organizational mobilization and company transformation. Despite their importance, few companies view them or treat them as manageable processes, essentially because they remain highly intangible. Strong and visionary CEOs will typically focus on the outcome – they will develop new sets of values and a vision on their own – rather than on the process by which these will emerge. Weaker CEOs, on the other hand, will tend to ignore that there are, indeed, processes that could help them develop a vision or build a momentum for change.

Processes can be also be classified into three groups based on their mode of execution. Some will typically occur in the course of management-imposed cycles, at regular intervals and along a predetermined routine. They are recurring processes. The most common recurring processes are planning and budgeting. Others typically take place on a continuous basis, without any particular starting or finishing point, nor specific cycle pattern. They are on-going processes. Business intelligence or management development fall into this category.

Finally, certain processes are initiated explicitly at a certain point in time and for a particular objective, and they end when the objective has been met. They are ad hoc processes. Most of the company's projects – be it for R&D, product development or some change efforts – fall into this group.

When combined, these two dimensions determine nine process types with very different management requirements. Unbundling and mapping a process implies, therefore, to segment, recognize and characterize its constituting elements (subprocesses) along these dimensions. The unbundling of the innovation process into its subprocesses illustrates how to apply and use this typology (Table 14.3).

Focusing on core processes

In most cases, management knows intuitively what its core business processes are, i.e. those that condition its basic competitive performance, hence determine its long-term growth and profit potential. Core processes vary significantly from industry to industry, both at the process and subprocess level. They may also vary somewhat among companies within the same industry, reflecting different choices as to the

Table 14.3: *Unbundling the innovation process*

Process types	Ongoing processes	Recurring processes	Ad hoc processes
Operational (Level 1) processes	Idea collection and generation	Idea selection and evaluation	Program management Product lifecycle management
Managerial (Level 2) processes	Market, competitor and technology intelligence	Product and technology strategy and planning	Program and project review and control
Leadership (level 3) processes	Innovation climate improvement	Innovation visioning and priority area selection	New technological competency building

chosen way to compete within one's industry, and/or a different segment focus.

For example, innovation – the ability to win at new products – is undoubtedly a core process in pharmaceuticals, consumer electronics or performance chemicals, but much less so in basic process industries like newsprint paper, metals or bulk chemicals, which are much more sensitive to capacity management and operational effectiveness. But even within the same industry – say pharmaceuticals – competitors may value various subprocesses differently. Some will focus on internal research and drug discovery, while others will emphasize external drug hunting through a proactive search and licensing of new molecules or genes for clinical development and marketing.

Management attention frequently focuses on operational (Level 1) processes, and most of the core processes earmarked for re-engineering will typically be found in that category. Given the importance of the other processes, however, it is highly advisable to identify core processes from the other groups as well. A balanced core process portfolio should include at least a couple of critical managerial (Level 2) processes, and one leadership (Level 3) process to shape the future. Similarly, it is a good practice to select at least one core process that serves each stakeholder category. People will be more motivated to deliver superior customer attention and service if, in turn, they feel management is sparing no effort to create a work environment that they value. Attention to employee-oriented processes, e.g. training and management development, career planning, communications, and performance appraisal and rewards, is a potent way to create such a climate.

Allocating clear process ownership and coaching responsibilities

Processes exist, whether they have been recognized formally or not. Some are more clearly identifiable with a given function, hence will be part of that function's responsibilities. Management development, for example, will generally be entrusted to the human resources function, while customer acquisition is clearly in the realm of marketing. But many other cross-functional processes may not be managed in an optimum fashion, simply because no one feels responsible for them. Managing through processes, therefore, means entrusting each one of the company's core processes to an individual manager or to a group of managers who will be collectively accountable for its optimization and execution.

The process management literature – and actual company practice – highlights that two types of roles and responsibilities are needed for effective process management: a process *ownership* role, and a process *coaching* role.

Process owners are empowered by management to improve and manage a process across functional and organizational boundaries. To do this, they are expected to mobilize a process management team – including representatives from all the relevant functions and departments – and to lead that team in redesigning the process. Once the re-engineering has been completed, process owners are responsible for co-ordinating and managing the process in a continuous improvement mode.

Process coaches – typically members of senior management – select and empower the various process owners, and guide them in their re-engineering efforts. One of their prime missions is to help solve cross-functional conflicts, which could interfere with the successful completion of the process redesign activities, and to oversee the process once re-engineered.

Companies that have adopted a process-based organization will typically allocate these two types of process management mandates either to specific individuals, or to teams or committees. Process owners are often individual managers chosen from the function that plays a leading role in the process. But ownership can also be entrusted to a team that has been assembled to manage a process collectively, and empowered as a team. Similarly, coaching responsibilities can be entrusted either to a senior manager, or to a cross-functional steering mechanism, typically gathering the heads of the functions that will be most involved in the process.

Four different types of collective mechanisms can be found for the management of cross-functional processes:

- Cross-functional or cross-disciplinary bodies with a decision-making mandate and an executive empowerment – we will call them *boards* (in a broad sense).
- Cross-functional or cross-disciplinary bodies with an advisory role to management, but no executive authority – we will call them *councils*.
- Functional co-ordination mechanisms, typically involving the same function heads across different organizational units – we will call them *functional committees*.
- Formal or informal networks of managers/employees (from the same or different functions), sharing a common interest or mandate – we will call them *networks*.

Defining modes of process intervention

There are basically six different types of things one can do with a process:

- *Audit* the process, to identify its status and opportunities for improvement or redesign.

- *Fix* the process if it is broken, and/or improve it if it is sound but not optimized.
- *Redesign* the process (or re-engineer it) if it is not delivering value, time- and cost-effectively.
- *Invent* a new process altogether, if there was not one in place to start with.
- *Intervene* in the process, to remove obstacles and address conflicts that may arise in the course of its redesign or execution.
- *Execute* the various tasks, workflows and activities involved in making the process function.

Practice shows that the first step – simple in appearance – is actually quite complex and very critical. Processes are the real activity-building blocks of the corporation, and they criss-cross the organization. The challenge is to define the company's processes exhaustively, while maintaining an appropriate level of resolution. The traps are in defining the processes either too broadly – hence making them unmanageable – or too narrowly, hence getting lost in too many details. Four guidelines should be observed when identifying and unbundling processes.

Firstly, management ought to think of processes in a broad sense. The processes to be considered are not just the business and operational workflows. Business management and leadership processes need to be included as well. They are, indeed, the ones that will ultimately support the company's ongoing adaptation to its market and competitive environment and, at times, lead to its transformation.

Secondly, it is important to take a broad view of value creation, the raison d'être of most operational, business management and leadership processes. Through their processes, companies create value, not just to their owners or shareholders, but also to their customers, their employees and, ultimately, to all their stakeholders. Unbundling the company's processes means recognizing all those processes that create value to each category of stakeholders.

Thirdly, processes can be segmented at different levels of detail. Unbundling and mapping the company's processes means selecting different resolution levels for different purposes. The company's core processes need to be considered in their wholeness for re-engineering purposes, but ought to be managed at the subprocess level on an ongoing basis. For example, a company may want to rethink its total innovation process – a core process – but will need also to look at the way it manages individual programs and projects – subprocesses.

Fourthly, processes differ from each other in many ways, and each factor has a considerable influence over the type of re-engineering that will be effective, and the organizational mechanisms needed to manage it. One does not handle a creative process like innovation in the same way as the more mechanistic supply or demand chain management.

Processes differ from each other in terms of:

- *Nature and tangibility* – some processes deal with concrete business activities and work steps; others relate to more intangible managerial endeavours.
- *Mode of execution* – some processes are occurring on a permanent basis; others occasionally or cyclically.

- *Complexity* – some processes involve many hierarchical layers, functions, departments and sites; others imply only a few of them.
- *Uncertainty level* – some processes require a high degree of speculation and creativity; others consist only of fairly predictable activities.
- *Interdependence* – some processes are interconnected with other processes; others are relatively independent of the rest of the company's activities.

The first two dimensions – process nature and tangibility, and mode of execution – are probably the most important when it comes to deciding which management mechanism to set up. It is therefore useful to delve further into these categories to build a kind of process typology.

Companies that manage through processes need to sort out precisely the respective roles of each category of actors – process coaches, process owners, process management teams, and line managers. This is not so much a matter of writing long job descriptions, but rather of ensuring that every one is sharing the same understanding as to what makes the process work optimally. Clearly a lot depends on the level of support provided by line management. This is why it is advisable to involve the heads of key functional departments and business units in the process coaching mechanisms (e.g. the steering groups) that will be set up to guide process owners. Table 14.4 highlights a typical allocation of responsibilities.

Table 14.4: *Typical process management modes*

Who does what?	Audit	Fix/ improve	Redesign	Invent	Intervene	Execute
Process coach	Initiates	Supports	Initiates	Initiates	Intervenes	Oversees
Process owner	Leads	Initiates	Leads	Leads	Initiates	Leads
Process team	Executes	Executes	Executes	Executes		Executes
Line management	Contributes	Contributes	Contributes	Contributes	Supports	Supports

Addressing the deficiencies of each core process and their subprocesses

The first task of any newly appointed process management team is to conduct an audit of the process allocated to its responsibility. The objective of such audit is to assess the current status of the process, and identify opportunities for improvements or, more drastically, for re-engineering. Some companies have established a set of process indicators to characterize their process development stages. Philips, for example, has adapted the Humphries software maturity indicators to classify its

Table 14.5: *Process maturity stages*

Criteria/stages	Missing	Chaotic	Described	Controlled	Managed	Optimized
Process awareness shared widely	No	Yes	Yes	Yes	Yes	Yes
Process mapped and well-understood	No	Partly	Yes	Yes	Yes	Yes
Process owner and coach in place	No	Partly	Yes	Yes	Yes	Yes
Resources (people/ funds) available	No	Partly	Partly	Yes	Yes	Yes
Competencies and tools available	No	No	Partly	Yes	Yes	Yes
Process performance measured	No	No	Partly	Partly	Yes	Yes
Problem anticipation/ solving in place	No	No	No	No	Partly	Yes
Problem prevention in place	No	No	No	No	No	Yes

Adapted from Humphries' software maturity stages.

product creation process in six stages. It provides a common vocabulary, and allows management to have an overview of the status of each of its processes (Table 14.5).

Process audits have been covered widely, notably in the TQM literature. Audits should assess a process from three complementary perspectives:

- *Quality of the input to the process*: do we have adequate information? the right people involved? sufficient resources to make the process work?
- *Quality of the process itself*: are all the activities necessary? sequenced correctly? performed effectively?
- *Quality of the output of the process*: is the process delivering what it is supposed to deliver in terms of quality? timing? cost?

Creating mechanisms to sustain the processes over time

Once process owners and coaches are in place, they will be confronted with an organizational and management challenge. How do we make people from different functions work together constructively on the process? How do we manage the process in practice? In some instances, it may just be a matter of mobilizing and aligning people, for example on a project. In other cases, process owners and coaches will need to set up special organizational mechanisms to muster support for, and run, the process.

Management mechanisms will be different for each type of process. Reverting to our earlier classification, the mechanisms needed to support a recurring process will often be different from those required to manage ad hoc or ongoing processes. We will look at:

- extending mechanisms to handle recurring processes;
- empowering current mechanisms to handle ad hoc processes; and
- inventing new mechanisms to handle ongoing processes.

Extending existing mechanisms to handle recurring processes

Most companies are reasonably well equipped to handle recurring processes, at least from a cycle management point of view. Consider the budgeting, strategic review, product- or technology-planning processes, some of the most common examples of recurring processes. Ownership is usually entrusted to the head of the leading function in charge of the cycle – the chief financial officer or the controller for budgeting; the strategic or corporate planner for strategy reviews; the marketing manager or senior product manager for product planning; the chief technology officer or head of R&D for technology planning. Critical recurring processes will usually be coached by a subset of the top management team: a budget committee, a strategic review committee, a product committee, or a technology or R&D committee. Problems will be encountered in two areas, though.

The first problem will occur when a recurring process has not been formally recognized, nor managed, so far, as such. This happens often with processes like idea evaluation and selection. Generally, these processes do not belong specifically to any particular function, hence the difficulty in appointing a natural process owner.

The solution generally consists of entrusting the processes to a cross-functional body, established specifically for that purpose. Certain companies, for example, have set up an innovation council or an innovation office to manage the processes linked with idea generation, evaluation and selection. Innovation council members – who could include people from outside the organization, for example lead customers – should be selected not on the basis of their function or status, but rather for their entrepreneurial personality and drive. "Serial idea killers", who sometimes thrive in conventional organizations, should be systematically excluded from such idea management bodies. In that respect, process management mechanisms like innovation councils are fundamentally different from conventional line management committees. They are in charge of proactively managing a process on behalf of top management and that should determine their staffing and level of empowerment. The second problem is more arduous: how do we avoid recurring processes turning into administrative game-playing exercises for a limited number of managers doing business with themselves? How do we ensure that these processes tap the creativity, insights and energy of all the staff concerned throughout the corporation?

To address this challenge, management can organize critical recurring processes in such a way as to allow a maximum number of people to participate actively. For example, the strategy review process can be handled in many ways. Some managers may consider it their personal duty. They will lock themselves in their office to do their homework and prepare the report, which they will personally present to top management. They will often do so in order to shield their staff from yet another administrative burden. They may also consider strategy as the privileged domain of the business unit leader. Other managers – and this is probably the most frequent case – will do the job together with their top management team as part of a senior management retreat. Yet others might see in that process a unique opportunity to get a dialogue going on strategy throughout the organization. They will conduct strategy reviews as a real process involving a wide range of people in a top-down, bottom-up sequence.

Certain companies have institutionalized a number of get-together events to support recurring processes like technology-planning or long-term product strategy formulation. These events, which formally belong to the process cycle, may have different names – "technology forum", "innovation meeting", "planning scrum" – but their purpose is generally the same. They offer concrete opportunities to involve people down the line in the process, to take advantage of their insights and get their buy-in, while providing them with a learning opportunity.

Empowering current mechanisms to handle ad hoc processes

Every company tends to have a long experience of ad hoc processes, since most projects fall in that category. Mechanisms to manage projects are well known. Process ownership is in the hands of the project or team leader. Process coaching is generally entrusted to a project steering group, usually consisting of senior functional managers whose staff is involved in the project or concerned by its outcome. They are the internal customers of the project. Three problems need to be overcome with these types of processes, which are, by nature, temporary and cross-functional, thus cannot be associated easily with a given function.

The first and most critical problem is one of empowerment. What degree of authority and accountability should we entrust to the project or team leader, and to the steering group as a collective body, vis-à-vis the individual heads of functions or departments? This issue raises a perennial question: how do we redefine and balance the respective roles of the horizontal project organization vis-à-vis the vertical line structure? Ultimately, the solution adopted will reflect the company's management philosophy. Management teams with a good tolerance for ambiguity – a requirement for operating in a process-centred organization – will not fear adding empowered horizontal lines of command across the vertical organization.

Conventional management teams, however, will feel more comfortable staying with clear, vertical accountability. Consequently, they will tend to deprive project leaders from a real authority over their project team members, thus limiting their role to project co-ordination. Surprisingly, and despite the unanimous support for heavyweight project managers in the management literature (e.g. Wheelwright and Clark, 1992), many companies are still part of the second category. They hesitate to enforce the project empowerment principle, at a considerable penalty in terms of project effectiveness.

The second problem is caused by the resistance of line managers to the proliferation of enterprise projects, which they may see as disrupting the normal functioning of their organization. In process-centred companies, indeed, projects often lose their exceptional and temporary nature to become a permanent, parallel form of organization. Willingly or not, projects encroach into the line organization's domain. This happens, for example, when people get allocated more or less permanently to a long-lasting project, or when they go from project to project as part of the same team. The project structure then becomes the real home of all those project-dedicated people. Certain line managers who see it as diluting their own responsibilities resent this. It happens also when a project team is turned into a "venture team", and is asked to manage the new business it has developed as a project, and to do it outside the current line organization.

As for the issue of empowerment, the understanding and co-operation of line managers will not be obtained without a strong advocacy by the CEO in favour of that new form of management. The belief that real work gets done within one's functions and departments – as opposed to collective groups like project and process teams – is so engrained in some line managers, that turning it around requires a profound educational program.

The third problem is linked with the difficulty of ensuring that a project team does not turn itself into an isolated, self-centred organization, but taps into the insights and resources of the broader corporation. Again, this may require beefing up the coaching mechanism, or – better – extending them with additional advisory bodies, representing other relevant parts of the organization one wants to involve in the process.

For example, as part of their innovation process mechanisms, large companies will often set up two advisory bodies to provide input and guidance to their project teams. A design review team comprised of the most experienced engineers of the corporation, can help on the technical side by challenging and advising the team. Similarly, a market advisory council can be established to allow the leading market managers to bring the voice of the market to the team and, again, to challenge and advise the team.

Inventing new mechanisms to handle ongoing processes

A real difficulty exists with ongoing processes. How can we mobilize people from across the organization on processes that are supposed to proceed continuously, across functions and departments? The typical example in innovation is the intelligence process. Searching for unarticulated customer needs; scrutinizing competitor developments to anticipate their next moves; monitoring new technologies for opportunities and threats – all these activities are manageable processes, even though they are rarely formalized as such. To be effective, they need to be conducted on a continuous basis, and to build on the skills, contacts and energy of a wide range of people throughout the organization, not just from a given function.

One of the many possible organizational responses to such a challenge is a rather novel form of mechanism. We will call it the "energized or managed network". It belongs to the range of mechanisms that management must still invent – although some already exist at least in partial forms – in order to tap, mobilize and channel the incredibly potent energy of employees, vendors and partners across the organization.

The very concept of a managed network may be perceived as an oxymoron. The word "network" conjures up something rather spontaneous and informal, not something that is managed formally. Within companies, networking has multiple purposes: deepening one's professional discipline, building contacts and relationships, and forging influence and support circles. When it enhances professional development, or leads to an informal co-ordination across departments or countries, networking is beneficial to the company.

But despite their advantages, networks are seldom initiated, organized or managed as such. They tend to be left to the individual's initiative. At best – for example in the case of professional discipline networks – they may be encouraged by management.

A managed network should remain configured as a network, i.e. a relatively loose group of people sharing a common interest and building on each other's skills, ideas or contacts. It should remain relatively informal and fluid in terms of internal organization, and it will not appear on the company's formal organization chart. However, it will be managed in the sense that:

- its creation will be the result of a management initiative;
- it will be recognized as such – its members will be acknowledged as being part of it, and they will accept certain obligations in the same way as club members are recognized and adhere to club rules; and
- it will be entrusted to one or several network animators chosen by management to maintain an adequate level of creative tension between the members (the network nodes) and/or perform the mission expected from them.

Managed networks exist in certain companies, but they are uncommon and limited in scope. A common example of such networks is typically found in the R&D area with technology gatekeepers or competency networks. These are groupings of scientists and engineers sharing a common interest and know-how, typically a scientific or technological discipline. Gatekeeper's networks are externally focused. They provide a permanent monitoring of new technology developments of relevance to the company. Competency networks tend to have an internal focus: sharing know-how and experience across R&D centers.

The potential benefit of managed networks would be maximum in the field of market, customer and competitor intelligence, as well as for idea generation. Management should, indeed, organize networks of market sniffers or competitor scouts. The idea behind such networks is always the same: tap the knowledge, contacts and insights from people throughout the organization. Market-sniffer networks may be focusing on a given type of customer, on a key account or on a critical market issue. The important thing is that they should be open to people from various locations and functions, not just marketing and sales. Competitor scouting networks should be organized for each of the company's leading competitors. Idea generation networks could be organized by product category, and again be open to people from various functions, not just marketing and R&D.

To bear fruits and be sustainable, networks need to be energized and managed. Like all other processes, they should be entrusted to a process owner, and be supported by a process coach. The owner of market intelligence networks, for example, could be the head of advanced or strategic marketing. If a market advisory council has been established to gather the heads of the leading market companies, it would be a natural coaching group for all these market networks.

Similarly, competitor scouting networks, could be entrusted to the competitor intelligence officer. Gatekeepers and competency networks are generally put under the responsibility of the chief technology officer.

Animating and managing a process-focused network is a rich and complex management task involving:

- establishing a network charter and rules for membership and functioning;
- phasing in/out members (who should always be highly motivated voluntaries);
- ensuring the support of the network members' department heads;
- appointing and supporting network and subnetwork nodes and animators;
- building an intranet-based information and communication platform;
- organizing information-sharing events with the relevant functions concerned;
- arranging for adequate recognition and rewards for well-performing networks;
- ensuring a continuous rejuvenation and refocusing of the networks as needed.

Mobilizing people around processes

The concept of process management may be intuitively compelling and its benefits appealing. Nevertheless, its application is far from straightforward. Obstacles on the road that leads to a process-centred organization abound, not least being the resistance of the line hierarchy, which may feel threatened, as illustrated in the case study below.

CASE STUDY: HOW A MAJOR ELECTRONIC COMPANY ABORTED ITS OVERAMBITIOUS PLAN TO REORGANIZE AROUND PROCESSES

A multibillion-dollar division of a global Fortune 100 company undertook, a few years ago, to rethink its organization. The division operated four relatively independent regional businesses in the USA, Europe, Asia-Pacific and "overseas" (meaning the rest of the world). Its CEO was convinced that the technology-intensive and fast-cycle industry in which his division was operating made it imperative to further decentralize operational responsibilities. Local site managers, who controlled all product development and manufacturing activities for a given product line within their region, needed to be empowered more fully by their regional headquarters. Simultaneously, certain strategic activities, like technology development and long-term product planning, partly decentralized in the regions, needed to be integrated better at the division level. In short, the business, he felt, needed to redefine the roles and missions of its divisional, regional and local site organizations. The objective of this change would be to achieve a more appropriate balance between strategic functions that needed to be consolidated and integrated and operational responsibilities that ought to be decentralized further.

The CEO appointed one of his staff aides – in charge of organizational matters – to set up and lead a task force that would make concrete recommendations to his management team. The staff assistant – fully aware of the latest management thinking – had grasped immediately the extent to which process management concepts could help address his company's challenge. The taskforce, comprised of a few internal staff assistants and an external advisor, took on its mission with passion and started outlining a completely new process management architecture.

The core processes of the business were quickly identified and segmented into 80 or so subprocesses. Proposals were made for allocating each process to the most natural owners, and for maintaining the line organization into the driving seat through a carefully balanced allocation of process coaching responsibilities. The roles of divisional and regional headquarters were redefined on the basis of the specific processes that needed to be managed at these two levels. Management jobs, ultimately, would be redefined around the processes they entailed, whether at the owner, coach or participant level. Certain functions, presently handled at the divisional or regional levels, would be eliminated as unnecessary and pushed down at the regional or site levels. Others, performed at the regional level, would be consolidated at the division level. The guiding principles were simple: processes – not boxes on a chart – should form the basis of the new organizational architecture. Processes define jobs, and not the reverse. The taskforce had convincingly re-engineered the whole division's organization.

The presentation of the taskforce recommendations to the entire top management team came as a shock. The CEO, who had launched and supported the effort, was astonished by the far-reaching changes that were implied. He had never thought that process management would be both so compelling and so threatening. The other members of the top management team remained resolutely silent. Obviously everyone was trying to figure out how much power and influence he or she would gain or lose under the new organization. And the challenge of explaining the purpose and benefits of the new scheme to subordinates was on everyone's mind.

After the initial surprise and a lot of internal discussions, the senior managers rapidly raised many objections against the new process-centred organization. The main concerns were the risk of dilution of individual accountability – when too many people are involved in a process, who is ultimately going to be in charge and accountable? – and the risk of chaos during the transition phase. The CEO – who had not been at the root of the new concept – was unable to overcome such objections, and after numerous debates, the scheme was abandoned as "too complex and risky". The company patched its ill-functioning organization, and plodded along without really addressing its challenge.

Clearly the taskforce had done a very thoughtful conception job. They had avoided the two main traps, which have doomed the fate of process management concepts, when they are applied too dogmatically:

- *Going too far and eliminating the functional organization altogether, which in most cases is unrealistic.*
- *Making two organizations – functional and process – coexist with different sets of managers, which is the surest way to multiply conflicts.*

The taskforce had simply redefined functions and jobs along various forms of process management or execution responsibilities.

However, the process chosen for devising and implementing the change had been totally deficient. (In retrospect, four lessons can be drawn from this story: These are explained in the section on Best practice below.)

SUMMARY

Channelling the organization's energy around its core business processes means refocusing people on the company's critical, value-creating chains of activities, rather than on their specialized skills or organizational boundaries. Although very promising, process management has not been implemented widely in large companies. Despite the hype consultants created about process re-engineering and the broad media coverage it received, few companies have actually extended their process management system to all their key processes. Typically, only a few basic operational processes, e.g. product development, order fulfilment, and customer service, have been redesigned. Even fewer companies have gone the full way and reorganized themselves around their business processes. Yet this offers a key to creating focused energy in a bottom-up organization.

BEST PRACTICE

Lesson 1: the CEO's personal commitment and involvement must be the driving force of the change

Of all the changes companies make, none is more politically sensitive than a reshaping of organizational roles and responsibilities, particularly when it affects people's jobs on a grand scale. Consequently, the implementation of process-management concepts has to be viewed as a major change process in itself. Actually, it falls perfectly into the leadership process (Level 3) category defined earlier, and should be managed as a process. The owner of such a transformation process has to be the CEO or – in the case of our example – the group vice president in charge of the division; the coach will be the board of directors. The CEO must be intimately convinced of the content and benefits of the approach, in order to be able to convince others and face the unavoidable fears and objections of his or her staff.

In the case study above, the CEO had delegated that responsibility to a staff assistant, and did not have much prior insight on the concept of process-centred organizations. In short, he had handled the process rather casually, which explains why he couldn't sell it to his management colleagues. This contrasts heavily with the commitment towards managing through processes demonstrated by the CEOs of Xerox, SmithKline Beecham, Pepsi Cola–North America and USAA, as reported by Professor David Garvin (1995) in a recent round-table interview.

Lesson 2: the change to a process-centred organization cannot be done in one go: it should be introduced gradually

The example cited earlier illustrates how a change taskforce – particularly if it consists of staffers – can be carried away by an attractive concept, and how it can lose a sense of proportion and realism regarding what can be implemented and how fast. The CEO's concerns about his organizational deficiencies were real, but he focused mostly on issues related to the management of its technologies and new products. By extending its process management concepts to most, if not all the division's processes, the task force was begging to see its proposal rejected as too extreme.

Change management practitioners often debate (and disagree) on whether it is preferable to introduce a major change in one go – the "diving in" approach – or gradually. When the issue is the introduction of a process-centred organization, practice shows that the most effective changes are introduced progressively. Companies should focus on re-engineering their key processes first, then make the organizational changes necessary to handle them as processes. As managers get used to the idea that a horizontal, process-based organization is a useful complement to the vertical line structure they know, the benefits should be sufficiently visible to offset the fears and objections.

Lesson 3: although well-known in theory, process management raises a lot of management issues that need to be sorted out

The change from a functional organization to a divisionalized organization around business units, which most companies have undertaken since the 1980s, was less radical than the proposed change to a process-centred organization. In the first case, the boxes on the organization chart changed, but people stayed in boxes. Hierarchical reporting lines remained the rule. With a process-centred organization, we are changing the nature of people's jobs. Horizontal lines, cross-functional teams and networks become more important than vertical lines of command.

Such a change puts many management systems into question, not least the issue of performance measurement and rewards. Some of the most frequent objections – and their answers – are outlined below:

- *How can we measure the performance of a process owner?*
  On the basis of process performance targets, which should be based on a number of indicators to be developed for each process.
- *How are process management team members evaluated and by whom?*
  Jointly, by their process owner (or project leader) and their functional or departmental supervisor.
- *How can we motivate people to join and animate the new managed networks?*
  By managing them as clubs, with certain privileges, some emulation, and a lot of recognition and career progression prospects for talented animators.
- *How can we make line managers support the new system?*
  By introducing qualitative and quantitative process management and coaching criteria in their balanced score card.

Lesson 4: managing within a process-centred organization changes the nature and mental models people have about their work; this requires retraining

The process management philosophy and system proposed in this chapter challenges a number of beliefs and assumptions people intuitively make about their work and what makes organizations effective:

- *Process management goes against individual accountability, the only dependable way of managing a large organization.*
  Process management does not eliminate individual accountability. Actually, it makes people (process owners and coaches) accountable for things (cross-functional processes) that were rarely accounted for before. But it adds another important element of success: team accountability. A process team should feel as accountable for its redesign mission and the effectiveness of its process, once re-engineered, as a football team feels collectively responsible for the victory of its matches.
- *Managers cannot be made accountable for the performance of people that are not under their line of command and control.*
  This belief has always been negated by the very application of project management principles. Actually, process management is an extension of project management, and many practitioners consider it as a unique testing site for, and school of, leadership. By developing managers' ability to integrate cross-functional inputs and motivate people they do not control, process ownership forms future general managers and leaders. Process coaching, on the other hand, forces senior managers to move away from a role of direction and control to one of guidance and supervision, essential if empowerment is to become effective.
- *Nothing gets achieved through committees; real work gets done within one's functions and departments.*

Committees have a bad reputation because their focus is generally unclear (executive? advisory? co-ordination?); their accountability is vague (no-one feels responsible for their output); and their membership tends to be fixed by statutory rules (belonging to a committee generally goes with a job). Process management does not create new committees. It generates collective process coaching mechanisms with a defined scope (a particular process), a clear mandate (boards with an executive authority, councils with an advisory mission), and an unambiguous accountability, since they should be judged on the basis of preselected process performance indicators.

- *Process management misuses people's sharp-edged skills, and teamwork dilutes the quality of functional work, leading to collective mediocrity.* Functional experts who object to seeing project managers empowered, and feel dispossessed, sometimes make this comment. Actually, a number of process management mechanisms are created to tap the unique skills of functional specialists. This is the case with design review teams or market advisory councils, which have been mentioned in this chapter as an interesting source of input on the innovation process. So are the get-together events – such as technology forums – which ensure that the company's expertise is put to good use and process management teams get challenged by specialists.

Despite its compelling advantages and a few convincing implementation examples, process management has clearly not achieved the success it deserves. Few companies have gone far beyond re-engineering a few of their key processes. And without a proper process management system, the benefits of re-engineering may be short-lived. Processes are organic, living things that require constant attention and frequent rethinking by dedicated people. The process philosophy and system described in this chapter will not be naturally accepted, understood and adopted by organizations that have thrived for years under a vertical, hierarchical structure. As with many new and revolutionary concepts, people need to unlearn traditional forms of organization, before they learn how to manage through processes. The magnitude of this educational and change process, from top to bottom, should not be underestimated, but its prospects justify the effort.

Acknowledgements

Many of the ideas in this chapter have been developed jointly with P. Ranganeth Nayak, while working on the concept of the "High Performance Business" at Arthur D. Little. Others have been influenced by the work of Professor David Garvin from the Harvard Business School.

References

Garvin, D.A. (1995) *Leveraging Processes for Strategic Advantages, Harvard Business Review*, Sept/Oct 1995, pp. 77–90.

Wheelwright, S.C. and Clark, K.B. (1992) *Revolutionizing Product Development – Quantum Leaps in Speed, Efficiency and Quality*. New York: Free Press.

15

Co-ordinating Laterally

The three-dimensional matrix structure has proved difficult for most companies to master. Yet it is little more than a warm-up for the challenge that faces the bottom-up organizations of the future. In this chapter, **Jay Galbraith** outlines how different types of lateral co-ordination provide a key to orchestrating activity in multidimensional organizations.

> **CASE STUDY: CITIBANK'S USE OF MULTIPLE CO-ORDINATING MECHANISMS**
>
> *In the mid-1980s, Citibank's commercial banking operation was organized around country profit centres as the primary dimension, with functions influenced by cross-country co-ordinators. Some global products were co-ordinated across countries by teams, while other products and customers were handled across coountries on a voluntary basis by networks of people working on the same issue in the different countries.*
>
> *Since 1985, banking has been transformed by a range of factors. These include deregulation and consolidation; convergence and competition with insurance, investment banks and non-banks (including GE Capital); the rise in foreign direct investment (FDI); and digital technology. The first response of Citibank was to consolidate products like foreign exchange on a regional basis. Some activities were left in countries but were put in a matrix with regional co-ordinator. The rise of FDI meant more customers were investing in more different countries. Citibank focused on this growing customer segment, and created the World Corporation Group (WCG). It also created customer teams for selected customers to service them around the world. Within Europe the priorities were now countries first, products second, customers third and functions fourth.*
>
> *Then in the early 1990s, Citibank began to receive pressure from its largest customers. It undertook a strategy review and saw that FDI was the driving force behind globalization. More companies and customers had presence in more countries. Citibank recognized that it was present as a bank (took deposits and made loans in local currency) in twice as many countries as its nearest competitor. In 1995, it refocused priorities again, making the global customer the top priority.*
>
> *In this way Citibank shifted the order of its priorities from countries, functions, products and customers in 1985, to customers, products, countries and functions by the late 1990s. It matched its strategic priorities by changing the types of co-ordination forms it was using to manage the four dimensions. It has matched the level of lateral co-ordination form with its strategic priorities.*

Overview

One of the keys to mastering bottom-up organizations is lateral co-ordination capabilities. Traditionally companies created a line organization based on decentralized profit centres. If the profit centres were business units, as at Hewlett-Packard, the company co-ordinated laterally across these businesses to focus on country subsidiary concerns and shared functions like finance and human resources. If the profit centres were country subsidiaries, as at Nestlé, the company co-ordinated laterally across the countries to get a business focus and to share the same functions.

Most companies still struggle with these three-dimensional matrix-type structures. But it now appears that co-ordinating the three dimensions was merely a warm-up to the challenge of orchestrating activity in highly energized organizations. In addition to the usual trio, customers are demanding to be served by global account teams and opportunity teams for putting together products and services into global solutions. Industry convergence is requiring new configurations of business units. A proliferation of channels, business processes, communities of interest, commodity purchasing teams etc. all require more lateral co-ordination capabilities. Today we need to master these capabilities and create the multidimensional multinational.

This chapter describes three of the steps necessary to master lateral co-ordination:

- To match the different types of lateral co-ordination with the strategic priority of the dimension like the global customer.
- To build the lateral co-ordination capability.
- To create a leadership management process that can decide on the strategic priorities on a timely basis.

Types of lateral co-ordination

Lateral co-ordination is an information and decision process for co-ordinating activities where different portions of that activity are executed in different line organizational units. For example, the line organization could be a geographical structure based on country subsidiaries as shown in Figure 15.1. Then each subsidiary with information about – and a stake in – an activity, such as serving the same customer, contributes a representative for communicating and co-ordinating that activity. It is through lateral co-ordination processes like this one that companies co-ordinate businesses, functions, customers, channels and processes across countries. Within a country subsidiary, managers responsible for businesses, functions and customers form networks with their counterparts in other subsidiaries to co-ordinate their common interests. These lateral networks decentralize decisions about businesses, functions and customers. They have the advantage of increasing the organization's capacity to make more decisions, more often, about more issues. The company can

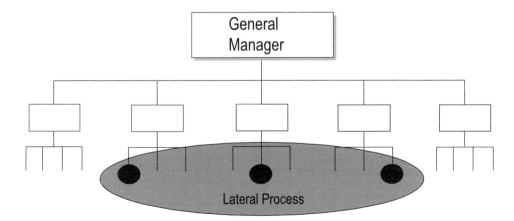

Figure 15.1: *Lateral processes across departments*

then respond to more dimensions in its business environment. These lateral networks represent the main tool for managing the new complexity.

In order to master the use of these lateral networks, the company must be able to distinguish different types of lateral co-ordination and to match the type with the strategic priority of the dimension. The company also needs to build the lateral co-ordination capability. Not many organizations have the capability today to master multiple dimensions. The first companies to become the multidimensional multi-nationals will have a decided advantage. Let us look at these two requirements for mastery.

The different types of lateral coordination are portrayed in Figure 15.2. The task of the organization designer is to match the types and amounts of lateral co-ordination that are commensurate with the strategic priority of the dimension. The reason for the matching is that lateral co-ordination comes at a cost. The lateral co-ordination requires an investment of time in communicating, deciding and resolving conflicts. The matching is facilitated by the existence of different types of lateral co-ordination networks. These different types involve different amounts of co-ordination time, different amounts of power and control over resources and different amounts of difficulty and conflict. These issues are represented in Figure 15.2. The figure shows that the first type, voluntary co-ordination, is the simplest and easiest to use. It is also the least expensive. The further up the steps that the organization proceeds, the more difficult and more expensive the forms of lateral co-ordination become. Therefore, the organization designer should proceed up the steps, adding more lateral co-ordination only to the point where the costs of co-ordination match the benefits of co-ordinating across units. That point will be determined by the strategic priority of the dimension being co-ordinated. We will describe briefly each of these forms of lateral co-ordination.

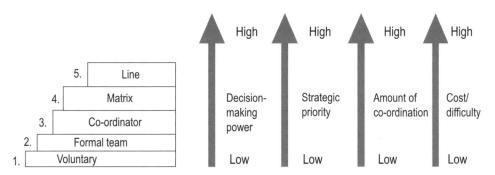

Figure 15.2: *Types and amounts of lateral co-ordination*

Voluntary co-ordination

This is a process of informal or formal communication followed by the participants choosing voluntarily to co-ordinate and in what way. It is often called self-organization because it is formed at the initiation of those comprising it. The managers perceive a situation and communicate spontaneously among themselves to respond or resolve the issue. The response is improvised by those with direct contact with the customer or issue at hand. It is a desirable form because it is fast and responsive. However, in order to work effectively, people need to know each other, have common interests, and control the resources needed for a response to the issue.

In order to deal with the first issue companies are stressing networks and networking. Mentors share their networks with newcomers. Formal meetings are called for all people who form an interest group or community of interest, e.g. technical people working on digital signal processing technologies. These people will continue contacts throughout the year and share ideas and know-how.

Many issues can be co-ordinated in this voluntary, self-organizing manner. The more issues that can be dealt with in this informal way, the faster the organization responds and the more people that are engaged in responding to more issues. Xerox is actually creating software to facilitate this "hallway" type of interaction when people are separated by time and distance. But there are occasions when the voluntary approach needs more formalization and more resources applied to it.

Formal teams or groups

These are a way to devote more co-ordination effort along a dimension. In order to co-ordinate new product development efforts for example, companies create product teams across functions and countries by dedicating people to the effort. It is more formal because there is usually a product plan to which team members commit and are held accountable for accomplishing the plan. Resources are prioritized and made available to the team members. Thus, they are more likely to reach agreements when co-ordinating across borders.

These cross-border teams can be simple or complex. Many companies form simple cross-border product teams to speed products to market. But some companies are also under pressure to reduce prices and costs. These companies have created commodity or component teams to co-ordinate across their product teams. The idea is to get all product teams to adopt the same component from the same supplier. The larger volume from the single supplier can allow volume discounts, decreased inventory and decreased administration. But such co-ordination across product groups is controversial. Will common components compromise product performance? In order to deal with the conflict, these companies have also created a steering committee for rapidly escalating and resolving disputes. So these teams are multidimensional, -product and -component, hierarchical and steering. The reason for the complexity is the increased co-ordination to meet simultaneously lower cost and faster time-to-market goals. This strategy requires more cross-unit co-ordination and more decision-making power to be focused on timely product decisions (Galbraith, 1994).

As a result, this form of lateral co-ordination is more costly but creates more value through the co-ordination. It is also more costly because it is used in addition to, not in place of the voluntary form. The use of lateral forms, as indicated by the steps in Figure 15.2, is a cumulative process. As more complicated forms are added, the simpler forms are not abandoned: they are still needed but are insufficient by themselves to achieve outcomes like time-to-market goals for new products. Both the voluntary and formal forms are needed. In general, the organization adds more complicated forms until the desired co-ordination is needed. To use less complicated forms would be to fall short of accomplishing the strategy. To use more complicated forms would be to incur unnecessary costs.

Co-ordinators

One step up are co-ordinators. For example, a full-time product manager may be added to chair the product teams and aid in resolving cross-country conflicts. These co-ordinators have titles like product manager, project manager, brand manager, world-wide business manager, and process owner. These roles are added to give full-time attention to cross-border co-ordination of a strategically important dimension.

The common features of the co-ordinator role is that they are "little general managers" and have no formal authority. They are extensions of the general manager's role, which is divided and delegated to the co-ordinators. If a product management unit is added to the European managing director's office, the unit acts as an extension of the managing director but exclusively for cross-border products. Then the people executing the product management role must influence the countries through persuasion because they have no formal authority. These people are selected on the basis of their ability to exercise this influence. If more power is needed, the organization can add features such as budget control to enhance the role. Part of mastering the lateral forms is the understanding of different types of power and the matching of people to co-ordinating roles.

The implementation of the co-ordinating role is more expensive than the previous lateral forms of organization, because it involves hiring a group of people whose sole task is to integrate the work of other people. When extensive information is needed, there may even be co-ordinating departments created. This cost is incurred in addition to the cost of voluntary and formal groups of various types. It is an investment in management. This investment is to achieve time-to-market, global integration or leveraged buying. These strategic goals cannot be achieved by the country hierarchy acting alone; the investment gives the organization the capability of acting multidimensionally.

The co-ordination role is difficult to execute because of the conflicts it generates. The organization consists of managers from two or more dimensions. In the international company, people represent businesses, functions and geographies. Each will see the situations differently, and conflicts will result. Top management needs to adopt a conflict-resolution process that resolves these inevitable conflicts on a timely basis and in the interests of the company. This type of cross-border decision process is the subject of the latter part of this chapter.

Matrix organization

This results when authority is given to the co-ordinator resulting in two line organizations. For example, product managers in the countries would report to their country managers and to the European product manager. The logic is that the strategic priorities for products and countries are equal and require a balance of power among the managers responsible for them. The matrix achieves the balance but at a cost of more conflict. A definition of roles and responsibilities for each dimension is very useful here. This matrix form is one that many companies have abandoned after struggling with it for a long time. One way to prepare for the matrix is to move up the steps in Figure 15.2, adding one more complex form after another and building the lateral capabilities along the way. This evolution will be described in the next section.

Line organizations

Finally, line organizations can be created by giving sole authority to the dimension. In the example used so far, the product lines could become the profit centre and the country managers could become the co-ordinators. In this way the company could have evolved from voluntary co-ordination for products to cross-country product teams, to product co-ordinators to a product–country matrix to product profit centres. Shorter and shorter product life and development cycles have driven companies like ABB and HP to evolve their structures in exactly this manner.

We have described the different types of lateral co-ordination forms, with reference to how companies like HP change to more complicated and powerful types as dimensions change in strategic priority. We will now take a closer look at Citibank's commercial banking unit mentioned earlier (Malknight and Yoshino, 1992).

CASE STUDY: CITIBANK

In about 1985, commercial banking was organized by country profit centres as the primary dimension. Second were functions such as finance, credit and information technology. These functions had co-ordinators that influenced the activities within countries. Inside the countries were product profit centres, e.g. syndicated loans, foreign exchange, mergers and acquisitions, project finance. These were often co-ordinated across countries on a voluntary basis or occasionally with a team for some global products like foreign exchange. In large countries, there were customer-focused units organized by industry, such as financial services and oil and gas. For large clients, these customer units would create networks and voluntarily co-ordinate services delivered to Exxon.

Banking since 1985 has been transformed by deregulation and consolidation, convergence and competition with insurance, investment banks and non-banks (GE Capital), the rise in FDI and digital technology. The first response of Citibank was to consolidate products like foreign exchange on a regional basis. Some activities were left in countries but were put in a matrix with a regional co-ordinator. So products moved up to level four or five on the scale in Figure 15.2. The rise of FDI meant more customers were investing in more different countries. Citibank focused on this and created the World Corporation Group (WCG). They also created customer teams for selected customers to service them around the world. Thus the customer dimension was escalated to levels two and three. Within Europe, the priorities were now countries first, products second, customers third and functions fourth (with some exceptions).

Citibank began to receive pressure from its largest customers in the early 1990s. They undertook a strategy review and saw that FDI was the driving force behind globalization. More companies and customers had presence in more countries. Citibank recognized that it was present as a bank (took deposits and made loans in local currency) in twice as many countries as its nearest competitor. In 1995, it chose to focus on the global customer. It would not compete in Germany for Daimler-Benz's business. But around the world it would compete for Daimler's business in cash management, foreign exchange and loans in local currencies. Citibank would become a cross-border bank. Global customers were first priority, second were global products (foreign exchange) for these global customers; countries were third, and were no longer profit centres; functions were fourth.

Organizationally, the change was to move to a customer profit-and-loss structure. Customers (1300) were grouped into industries and moved from level three to level five on the scale. Products moved to level five but were second priority to customers. The global customer was served first, so product profit centres could seek additional volume elsewhere. Countries were moved from level five to level three where they were joined by the functions. Some functions, such as operations, which were at level one, moved to level two to share best practices and increase global networking.

In this way Citibank shifted the order of its priorities from countries, functions, products and customers first to countries, products, customers and functions and then to customers, products, countries and functions. It matched its strategic priorities by changing the types of co-ordination forms it was using to manage the four dimensions. It has matched the level of lateral co-ordination form with its strategic priorities.

Citibank's changes took place over 10 years and it built its lateral capability, like customer accounting systems, as it went. Most companies experience the need to co-ordinate multiple dimensions but have not developed the capability. Let us now examine how we can build the necessary lateral capabilities to enable these types of lateral forms.

Building lateral co-ordination capability

Having established the need for lateral co-ordination as a prerequisite for orchestrating activity, the question is how can companies achieve it? In order to execute the lateral forms and co-ordinate multiple dimensions, companies need to build the capabilities that support cross-border, cross-functional and cross-business co-ordination. This capability consists of personal networks, teamwork across cultures, management of conflict, multidimensional accounting systems, and internationally experienced managers. The importance of building networks was addressed above. It should be emphasized again that the networking feature is the foundation of all the other lateral forms. Without networks and effective relationships across the organization, there will be no effective lateral co-ordination.

The other requirements for lateral co-ordination can be built by following a sequence of changes of adding the more complex lateral forms to the simpler ones. At each step, two things happen. One is that work gets co-ordinated across units to create some value. That is the primary purpose of the change. But the organization is also learning and building the capability to execute more and more complex forms of lateral co-ordination. The key is that management assumes the responsibility for capability-building and captures the learning and development that is created. Let us take an example of adding a fourth dimension, a customer dimension, to a firm organized by business units, countries and functions. This dimension is usually added when customers request a simplification of their multibusiness, multicountry relationship with a vendor.

The first response of a vendor is to weigh the strategic importance of the global customer. Some, like Citibank, P&G, and IBM, have focused on this customer as a growth opportunity. Others, like Nestlé and Unilever, have not. For those companies for whom the global customer is important, a lateral co-ordination capability is needed in order to serve this customer. Let us assume that the company has a good level of personal networking experience and skills. It can then take a series of steps to build the customer co-ordination capability.

Form a few customer teams

Teams can be created for the five or six customers who most want to be treated on an integrated global basis. The global account team is chaired by the account manager serving the customer in the home country. Then, in every country where the customer wants integrated service, account representatives are made part of the team. Representatives from the eight or ten largest countries and businesses serving the customer become the core team. Working with all members they put together a customer strategy and a plan to execute it. Typically the team members and certainly the core team members are convened for a week's workshop consisting of all five or six teams. This workshop is devoted to addressing the needs of the global customer. The plans and ideas are shared across the teams and the bonds are established within the teams.

The primary purpose of the change is to provide integrated service and create a satisfied customer. But in addition some 250 to 300 people (about 50 on each team) have participated in the change effort. There are 300 people who now understand the needs of the global customer. There are now 300 people who have been trained in formulating strategies to serve the global customer. There are 300 people who have added to their cross-border networks and personal contacts. This knowledge and network is the beginning of a capability to serve global customers through lateral co-ordination.

These 300 people will themselves have had different experiences. If there was some selection and self-selection, most of the experiences should be positive. Some will have negative experiences and opt out in the future. The experience provides a useful learning and sorting function. The leadership should actively follow and assist those who have had a positive experience and want more. The experience is also an audition in which many will demonstrate a superior performance on cross-border, cross-business teams. Management can observe them in action and can solicit inputs from the participants to identify them. The key is for the leadership to see their task as one of identifying and building new leadership and capability on this new dimension of the global customer and to use the teams as an opportunity to do so.

The experience also provides an opportunity to learn about the process of providing integrated service to customers. By collecting team members' and customers' observations and ideas, the process itself can be improved next around.

In this manner, each step up the stairs of Figure 15.2 creates two outcomes. The first is to co-ordinate some dimension across the organization. This outcome remains as the intended purpose. But a second outcome is the opportunity for management to engage outsiders like customers, to change the mindsets of the doubters, to train agents of change, to build personal networks, to select and develop new leaders, to build knowledge and experience, and to improve the process. For those managements that capture this opportunity, they can use each change to build the organization's lateral co-ordination capability.

More customer teams

The next step would be to expand from a few to a dozen and then to 50 or 60 teams for customers who want the global account service. Previous team members can help recruit and select the newcomers. The assignments can be made attractive. Often the global customer is the most advanced customer. People looking for growth and development will be attracted to learn from them. The most effective and most enthusiastic account managers can teach the workshop to the newcomers. Again the workshops can generate ideas across teams and bonding within teams. More networks are created. In fact now there are several thousand people participating, learning about the global customer, creating customer strategies and building networks across borders. Management get more opportunity to see more people working in cross border teams. They can begin to identify the most effective leaders, the best managers of cross-cultural conflicts, the most effective at influencing without authority, and those that establish the best rapport with the global customer.

Global accounts co-ordinator

The next step is to create a position on the management team to co-ordinate the company's efforts to serve the global customer. At a minimum this change creates a voice or a champion on the management team for the global customer. Someone of higher status can now appeal to recalcitrant country managers. The co-ordinator will probably expand the number of teams again. But perhaps most importantly, this role can fund and build a customer-focused infrastructure.

One task is to create a common process for building global customer plans and strategies. Initially some experimenting by customer teams is useful. But soon the countries get overwhelmed with 15 different planning formats. The co-ordinator can collect best practices from the various teams, initiate a taskforce staffed with veterans of global teams and create common guidelines forms and processes and put them on the intranet. The common process makes it easier for customer teams and country and business management to work together.

The next step is the design and building of customer-based information and accounting systems. The question always arises: *Are we making any money serving these global customers?* With country- and business-based accounting systems and profit centres, it is usually impossible to tell. Depending on whether the countries and business have compatible systems, this change can be a major effort requiring central funding and leadership from the global account co-ordinator. In the end, the customer teams have information with which to measure their progress, compare their performance with other teams and demonstrate global profitability.

The two steps can then be combined by generating revenue and profit targets for customers in the planning process. The teams can have revenue and profit goals for their global customers. The teams can also have goals for revenue and profit in each country. Perhaps more importantly, the goals can be added up in each country. Then each country manager can have revenue and profit goals for local clients and global accounts. The country manager can get credit for, and be held accountable for, targets for global customers in their country. The accounting system is important because the costs and revenues from the global customer are rarely connected. For example, an account team in the London office of one of the Big Five worked for a year to win the global audit of a big UK firm. They were successful but most of the work for the next few years would be in the North American subsidiary and in a recent acquisition in Australia. That means that the work was done and the costs incurred in the UK, while the revenues were booked in North America and Australia. With customer profit accounting, the UK can identify the revenues and costs and receive credit. The targets can be adjusted for these disconnects. Thus, in addition to being a champion for the customer, the global accounts co-ordinator can create the processes and information systems to manage the global customer as well as continue to develop and identify talent and leadership on the teams.

Some companies, like ABB, can stop at this point. The level of co-ordination matches the benefits that the company receives. For other companies, particularly service companies, more customer co-ordination is needed. Some service firms focus on hundreds of global accounts. As the number of global accounts and teams exceeds several hundred, the global accounts co-ordinator role can be expanded into a department or a group. In part for ease of supervision, the customers and teams are grouped into broadly defined industry categories, such as consumer products, financial services, oil and gas, pharmaceuticals and life sciences, and multimedia. But the main reason is customer satisfaction. Customers want auditors and consultants who understand their business. Bankers do not want to teach their auditors about derivatives. Pharmaceutical companies assume their consultants know what the Human Genome Project is all about. So the global accounts activity can be expanded and specialized by customer segment.

The global accounts leadership usually leads an effort to establish a common segmentation scheme across the company. In some countries like Germany, the UK and Japan, customer segments were probably already in use. What is important is to have compatible schemes across the countries. Then a one-to-one interface can be established to facilitate communication between countries and within an industry.

The global accounts group is usually expanded by adding global industry co-ordination. A global industry co-ordinator is selected for each industry that is common across the countries. For many companies the need for global co-ordinating roles is experienced but there are few people who are qualified to fill the roles. But if a company has followed the advice presented in this chapter, and used the opportunity created by the initial customer team implementations, then the company should have grown its own talent by now. An audit firm can serve as an example.

CASE STUDY: DEVELOPING THE GLOBAL CO-ORDINATOR

A young Swiss auditor was identified as a talented performer on audits of banks in Zurich. When a global team was created for Citibank, the auditor, who had experience in audits of Citibank's subsidiary, became the Swiss representative on the Citibank team. Based on good performance, the auditor agreed to an assignment in the UK. The move gave the auditor the opportunity to work in the London financial centre. While in London, the auditor served as the UK representative on the Credit Swiss global team. The next assignment was to lead an in-depth audit of the Credit Swiss–First Boston investment bank in the USA. The auditor was then made partner and returned to Zurich. From there he was selected to be the global account team leader for Credit Swiss.

After several years in the team leader role, the auditor became the global co-ordinator for the financial services customer segment. The auditor was assessed in each assignment for audit performance and knowledge of the financial services industry as usual. But assessments were also made of teamwork, relationship with customers, ability to influence without authority, cross-cultural skills with customers, and cross-cultural skills and leadership on the cross-border team. Based on these experiences and training courses, the auditor was qualified to move into the global co-ordinator role. Thus the co-ordinator role adds to the lateral co-ordination but also increases the company's lateral co-ordination capability by building an infrastructure around the strategic dimension.

Global accounts matrix

To shift more power to the teams serving global customers, it is necessary to carve out units within countries and dedicate them to the global customers. The other country units will serve local customers. The global customer units report to the global accounts co-ordinator and to the local country manager. These country units place dedicated talent in the service of the global customer and form a matrix structure.

In some small countries, the country management may be reluctant to create a dedicated unit and share in its direction. They may have a surplus of profitable local business and prefer to avoid the multinationals. In these cases several professional services firms have created joint ventures between the headquarters and the local country management. Usually the dedicated unit is funded from headquarters and staffed initially with expatriates. Then after a couple of years, the local management notices that the unit is quite profitable. In addition they notice that the unit is a positive factor in recruiting. Many new hires are attracted by the opportunity to work with global firms. In this way the creation of a global customer joint venture changes the mindsets of local management. They eventually take over the staffing and share in the administration of the unit.

Customer profit centres

A final change is the creation of customers and customer segments as the line organization and profit centres. All of the global units report to the global industry units. The countries manage the local business and serve as geographic co-ordinators. The stepwise process described for Citibank is an example of this evolution. The structure is merely the last step in a development process that has built the customer profit-and-loss systems, the customer teams, the cross-cultural skills and the customer mindset. However, these capabilities do not just happen. Management must see its role as one of building the capability by capturing the learning and development that happens. Management should also evolve its own capabilities. It must manage a portfolio of customers now, rather than a portfolio of countries. But in addition it has a portfolio of multiple dimensions whose priorities change and are changing more quickly. Let us now turn to the decision process that guides the multidimensional multinational.

Setting strategic priorities

The ability to set and reset priorities is a key leadership capability in the implementation of lateral co-ordination. Citibank is an example of a company prioritizing four dimensions over 10 years. Many companies are now faced with more dimensions and shorter timeframes. These strategic decisions require a management process that includes more dimensions and their champions and a greater ability to manage and resolve conflicts in shorter periods of time.

Leadership teams have always been challenged to manage conflict; now they are being challenged to manage conflicts in a cross-cultural environment. Despite decades of recommendations from researchers who have identified conflict resolution to be a key organizational capability (Lawrence and Lorsch, 1967; Galbraith, 1978; Pascale, 1990; Eisenhardt, Kahwajy and Bourgeois, 1997), most managements fall short of being effective at managing natural conflict. How do companies cope with the complexity and speed of decision-making?

The pattern that appears to be emerging is that companies substitute a process for a plan, i.e. they quickly test and experiment rather than forecast, predict and plan. They get a concept in front of a customer, put a prototype in front of their suppliers and/or run a simulation. Then they modify the concept based on the data and test it again (Eisenhardt, 1989; Eisenhardt and Tabrizi, 1995). Eisenhardt's work shows that adaptive processes are more timely and superior than forecasts and plans in fast moving businesses. The process creates more data and more real-time data on which to base the resolution of conflicts. Predictions result in disagreements between regarding opinions of the future. So rather than argue, management should test the opinions. To be sure, the data that result are subject to interpretation; but these interpretations can be tested as well. Thus the leading companies appear to be using more facts and fewer opinions in resolving their differences.

The top performers also consider more alternatives simultaneously than the poor performers. The slower decision-makers work with one (usually the CEO's) or two alternatives sequentially. The quality of the debate around the boss's preferred alternative is questionable. One or two alternatives polarize the participants. Then, when one alternative proves to be inferior, there is a scramble for another one. Four or five alternatives, generated by the organization's many dimensions, give a wide range of options. Fall-back positions are readily available. Generating the alternatives can be a fun, creative exercise: integrative solutions are more likely to be discovered, and the participants can change alternatives without losing face. So superior strategic decisions result from more alternatives being considered and chosen with more real-time data.

Eidenhardt's work also confirms past research on conflict resolution. Conflicts are best resolved when groups can get agreement on a higher-level goal. Lou Gerstner at IBM tries to establish the customer's interest first, the company's interest second, and the business unit's third as the priorities for deciding on actions to be taken. The other feature of effective companies is that they decide by consensus. Consensus is not unanimity (Schein, 1988). It is the outcome of a process in which everyone has their say but if there is not unanimity, the CEO decides and everyone supports the decision. That is, the minority supports the consensus of the majority. This consensus contains a sense of urgency for deciding quickly. It also allows for everyone to be heard up to a point.

Many companies have stated values and beliefs to guide timely decisions. The belief at Sun Microsystems is that "The best decision is the right decision. The second best decision is the wrong decision. The worst decision is no decision." Implicit in this belief is that it is best to decide something while the window of opportunity is open. If the decision is wrong, follow up quickly and correct it. This process of "decide on a timely basis and quickly correct mistakes" is also followed by ABB (Taylor, 1990). So the effective practice appears to be one of giving everyone their say but having the leadership decide on a timely basis. Then there is an appeal to a higher-level goal to get support from the minority opinion holders. If the decision is incorrect, then quickly redecide and get on the proper course.

There are other decision tools that are evolving to support strategic decisions in an era of speed and uncertainty. Scenarios have been around for some time but are being used increasingly by companies (Schwartz, 1997). Whether the scenarios are right or wrong is less important than opening people's minds to possible futures. As events unfold managers, can see the possibilities in a new light. Similarly, options are being applied to strategic decisions not just to financial markets and financial decisions (Leslie and Michaels, 1997). Rather than predicting a future, real options confer flexibilities on the holder to respond to new information. Others see strategic planning as the creation of portfolios of options (Courtney, Kirkland and Viguerie, 1997). All of these tools increase the set of alternatives, base choice on real-time information, and open management's mindsets a range of options and probable change. These techniques are to create a capability with which management can resolve conflicts to establish priorities among the strategic dimensions and with which management can reprioritize on a timely basis. This process of prioritization and reprioritization is a key feature of the reconfigurable organization. Another reason for prioritizing is to match the level of effort of co-ordination with the strategic priority of the dimension.

SUMMARY

Lateral co-ordination capabilities are becoming essential to the focusing of organizational energy in the evolving multidimensional world. This chapter has described three steps toward the mastery of these capabilities. The first was matching the type of lateral co-ordination with the strategic priority of the dimension. The second was building the capability for any particular dimension by capturing the learning, and observing the leaders as more complex co-ordinating mechanisms were sequentially introduced. And finally, creating a leadership management process to set new priorities on a clear and timely basis.

BEST PRACTICE

There are three steps to mastering lateral co-ordination:

- Matching the type of lateral co-ordination with the strategic priority of the dimension.
- Building the capability for any particular dimension by capturing the learning as more complex co-ordinating mechanisms are introduced sequentially.
- Creating a leadership management process to set strategy (and resolve disputes on a clear and timely basis).

The aim is to match the types and amounts of lateral co-ordination in a bottom-up organization with the strategic priority of the dimension. The reason for the matching is that lateral co-ordination comes at a cost. The lateral co-ordination requires an investment of time in communicating, deciding and resolving conflicts. The matching is facilitated by the existence of different types of lateral co-ordination networks (shown in Figure 15.1). These are:

- voluntary
- formal team
- co-ordinator
- matrix
- line.

The further up the steps that the organization proceeds, the more difficult and expensive the forms of lateral co-ordination become. Therefore, the organization designer should proceed up the steps, adding more lateral co-ordination only to the point where the costs of co-ordination match the benefits of co-ordinating across units. That point will be determined by the strategic priority of the dimension being co-ordinated.

To execute the lateral forms and co-ordinate multiple dimensions, companies need to build the capabilities that support cross-border, cross-functional and cross business coordination. This capability consists of personal networks, teamwork across cultures, management of conflict, multidimensional accounting systems, and internationally experienced managers. Without networks and effective relationships across the organization, there will be no effective lateral co-ordination.

Setting (and resetting) strategy is key to matching the level of the co-ordination effort with the shifting strategic priority of different organizational dimensions. Research suggests that the leading companies appear to be using more facts and fewer opinions in deciding on strategic and organizational priorities. The top performers also consider more alternatives simultaneously than the poor performers.

References

Eisenhardt, K. (1989) Making Fast Strategic Decisions in High-Velocity Environments, *Academy of Management Journal*, **32**(3): 543–575.

Galbraith, J. (1978) *Organization Design*. Reading, USA: Addison-Wesley.

Galbraith, J. (1994) *Competing with Flexible, Lateral Organizations*. Reading, USA: Addison-Wesley.

Lawrence, P. and Lorsch, J. (1967) *Organization and Environment*. Boston: Harvard Business School Press.

Leslie, K. and Michaels, M. (1997) The Real Power of Real Options, *McKinsey Quarterly*, **3**: 4–23.

Malknight, T. and Yoshino, M. (1992) Citibank (A) and (B) – European Strategy, *Harvard Business School Case 9-392-021*.

Pascale, R. (1990) *Managing on the Edge*. London: Penguin Books.

Schein, E. (1988) *Process Consultation*, Vol. I., 2nd Edition. Reading, USA: Addison-Wesley.
Schwartz, P. (1997) *The Art of the Long View.* Chichester, UK: John Wiley & Sons.
Taylor, W. (1991) The Logic of Global Business, *Harvard Business Review*, March–April 1991: 91–105.

Further reading

Eisenhardt, K. and Tabrizi, B. (1995) Accelerating Adaptive Processes: Product Innovation in the Global Computer Industry, *Administrative Science Quarterly*, **40**: 84–110.
Eisenhardt et al. (1990) How Management Teams Can Have a Good Fight, *Harvard Business Review*, July–August, 1999: 77–84.

16

Personal Compacts

The bottom-up organization is built on relationships. To sustain and focus the energy, integration of individual and corporate objectives is key. In this chapter, **Paul Strebel** explains how to renew personal compacts in a way that promotes both personal learning and corporate value creation.

CASE STUDY: IMPROVEMENT AT GRANITE ROCK IN CALIFORNIA

Everyone in this quarrying and paving company has an individual professional devel-opment plan (IPDP) that gives them access to unlimited training, in-house advance-ment, and high-visibility recognition. In return, the CEO, Bruce Wolpert, expects his managers to flood the company with information, bring problems to the surface, con-sider all alternatives, and take responsibility for a full solution. (The example of Granite Rock is developed in more detail below.)

CASE STUDY: INNOVATION AT OTICON IN DENMARK

Shortly after Lars Kolind took over as CEO, he asked everyone in research and product development to resign, move to a new building without offices, and redesign their jobs from scratch with a focus on creativity, speed and productivity. A flexible network of project teams emerged, with people rotating between projects adapted to the innova-tion opportunity at hand. Every time they initiated, or agreed to serve on, a project team, people recommitted to the organization. Even though Oticon recently switched back to a more traditional organization, the Kolind years provide an excellent example of innovation. (The Oticon example is also developed in more detail below.)

Overview[1]

The ultimate focusing of a bottom-up organization comes with the renewal of rela-tionships between individuals and the organization. These relationships must support the overall corporate direction. Rather than cancelling each another out in mutually conflicting directions, they should direct individual energy towards a continually improving contribution to the company's value-creating objectives. The integration of individual commitments and aspirations with corporate objectives is vital.

Relationships with the organization are based on the individual's employment con-tract, performance agreement with superiors, and a psychological contract embody-ing the implicit expectations on both sides. To emphasize the specific individual nature of these relationships we denote them here as *personal*; to emphasize that they are agreements (pacts) between two parties based on trust, we call them *compacts*.

Managers and employees who learn to improve on what they are doing, or to inno-vate continually, have learning compacts. They are updating and changing their per-sonal compacts on their own initiative, not once, but repeatedly. They continually look for new and better ways of doing things, adapting to, anticipating, and possibly shaping their business environment; they prefer values and rules that promote con-tinuous individual and team change; they get satisfaction from the personal develop-ment in such learning.

We are not concerned here with one-time efficiency improvement, or a single inno-vation, but with ongoing, self-driven compact renewal that creates a stream of effi-ciency improvements and innovations on the frontline. To develop these, you have to

1. This chapter draws heavily on Chapter 15 of Strebel (1998).

put in place the right enabling processes, so people can build a process of ongoing learning about the business into their compacts. This chapter looks at:

- examples of learning compacts;
- enabling processes for the renewal of learning compacts; and
- enabling behaviour for learning compacts at the top.

Frontline learning compacts

There are two types of frontline learning compact:

- improvement-based
- innovation-based.

Improvement learning compacts require employees to explicitly commit to continually doing things better. Employees agree to learn how to continually look for better ways of doing things and change their working methods, while the company gives them the climate, training, logistical support, and recognition needed to make improvement attractive. Successful examples of ongoing widespread improvement exist, even in the most unlikely of industry settings, wherever management sees how to give frontline people attractive learning compacts.

Innovation compacts embody repeated innovation and ongoing learning about new business opportunities. Companies famous for their internal entrepreneurs and the number of their new products provide an environment that facilitates the discovery of new opportunities, with easy access to the necessary resources, and an incentive system that avoids punishing failure and rewards initiative. But they also co-ordinate their independent-minded entrepreneurs into a corporate learning network. (See Chapters 3 and 5.) Focusing the energy of internal entrepreneurs used to be a major challenge. However, the Internet has made this so much easier. The basic idea has been to create a network of self-forming, self-managing teams, held together by open information on the IT system and compacts that embody the commitments and focus the energy of the organization.

CASE STUDY: IMPROVEMENT COMPACTS AT GRANITE ROCK[2]

Granite Rock in California, profiled by John Case in Inc. *magazine, has a quarry, mixes paving material in 17 plants, runs a highway-paving operation, and sells building supplies. When Bruce Wolpert, the grandson of the founder, took over, he had an MBA plus eight years of experience with Hewlett Packard. Yet, he spent time talking to people throughout the company, in the quarry, the plants, and on the road, finding out what they liked and disliked about their jobs. He also asked them which companies they admired most because of excellent products and service. At the same time, Wolpert put together his own management team from both inside and outside the company. Together they began putting in the elements of a systematic approach to learning from top to bottom, based on collecting information about what is happening, analysing what it means, designing a new approach, and moving into action on an individual and team level.*

2. Based on Case (1992).

One of the most important jobs of a manager, according to Wolpert, "is to make sure there's a flood of information coming in to the company." Granite Rock gets its information from the usual sources, customers, internal operations, and external benchmarking. But Wolpert insists on creativity in finding the information. In addition to annual customer "report cards" rating Granite against competitors, periodic focus groups looking for new ideas, and longer, more detailed surveys every few years, the company hands out "quick response cards" for comment on products and service delivered today, and provides a 100% service guarantee – no charge for inadequate products or service. Inside the company, managers supplement the usual statistical control charts with data of their choice. In the logistics area, apart from on-time delivery, managers track customer loading time, the number of road service calls, driver attitudes etc. Outside, Granite Rock people benchmark competitors, take advantage of supplier seminars and training, and visit other best-in-class companies, such as Domino Pizza for on-time delivery.

Based on the rich supply of information, Wolpert expects the frontline managers and people leading the problem-solving teams to go wherever their solution takes them. The process begins with middle managers, who develop tools for systematic problem-solving and assemble multifunctional teams to assess, plan, and implement; for example, a product-service discrepancy report including a root-cause analysis that shows what must be done for the purchase of heavy equipment like bulldozers. (At the time the company was profiled, some 100 teams were in action among the 400 employees.) But the frontline leaders have to ensure thorough execution. Thus, when a team realized that customers often blamed Granite Rock when they ordered the wrong product, or used it incorrectly, they introduced customer training and education, plus a manager measurement reflecting the number of customer seminars they sponsor.

In return for getting information and acting on it, Granite Rock gives its people almost unlimited access to, and support for, their own training, opportunities for in-house advancement, and high-visibility recognition. In the words of a quarry supervisor: "I think Bruce wants us all to get a little smarter. We're allowed to learn anything we can." In addition to in-house courses on problem-solving skills, leadership etc, employees can attend customer-run industry training, and neighbouring college courses, all on company time and expense. Job rotation and internal mobility are hallmarks of the Granite Rock approach. When it comes to hiring, internal candidates get preference. Most of the managers have held positions in several of the divisions. And even hourly employees get training for several jobs.

Instead of relying on job descriptions and performance reviews, everyone maps out a personal accomplishment and development plan, an IPDP, with his or her supervisor once a year. Recognition does not come in the form of equity or large-scale monetary rewards. Rather, every year well over a hundred employees get bonuses of a few hundred to a few thousand dollars for specific achievements. The higher profile reward comes on Recognition Day, an annual event at every facility where the employees entertain top and other unit managers, showing them how much the facility has improved and learned, both individually and collectively, over the past year.

The net result is that Granite Rock has the lowest production costs in its region, with service and quality levels that allow it to charge a 6% price premium, while gaining market share.

The personal compact at Granite Rock can be summarized as follows, in terms of the answers available to some of the questions that shape a compact (Strebel, 1998):

1. *Economic dimension*:

- *What am I supposed to do?* Problem-solve, execute, follow through.
- *What help will I get?* Personal training, in-house advancement opportunities.
- *How will I be measured?* Based on IPDP.
- *What economic reward will I get?* Awards, the chance for job rotation, internal promotion.

2. *Social dimension*:

- *What vision will I share?* Make Granite Rock the high-quality, low-cost leader.
- *What values will I share?* Common sense, action orientation, mutual help.
- *What informal rules will apply?* Information-sharing, systematic problem-solving, internal mobility, commitment to personal goals.

3. *Psychological dimension*:

- *How good is it for me?* Show what I can do, dynamic work environment.
- *How risky is it for me?* Risk if I don't meet my development plan.
- *What personal satisfaction will I get?* Personal accomplishment, high-profile recognition.

The IPDP lie at the heart of these efficiency-based learning compacts. In effect, the IPDP are rolling frontline compacts, revised annually during the discussions between supervisors and employees. They are notable because they take learning all the way to the frontline – in the quarries, trucks, and so on. The ongoing compact renewal builds in the opportunity for progressive learning. As in most learning compacts, the rewards in these efficiency-based learning compacts are mainly on the psychological dimension – in this case, in the form of team accomplishment, personal development and recognition.

CASE STUDY: OTICON – AN EXAMPLE OF INNOVATION COMPACTS[3]

Oticon, the Danish hearing aid manufacturer, has received a lot of publicity for its innovation-oriented networking compacts. Oticon is a good example of the ongoing innovating arm of an energized organization.

The Oticon story started with the appointment of Lars Kolind as CEO in 1988. The company was losing money, so Kolind's first task was to turn it around. He did it in the standard way: cutting costs and loss-making activities. But there was a feeling that not much fundamental had changed: "Although I had cut costs and loss-making product lines and activities, I didn't believe that would significantly improve our competitive position in the long term." On New Year's Day, 1990, Kolind wrote a four-page

---

3. In addition to a first hand account, the Oticon story and all the quotes are from Gould, Stanford and Blackman (1994).

memo outlining his vision for the future. Kolind asked his people to "think the unthink-able": all paper, walls and jobs would go, to be replaced by dialogue and action to get creativity, speed and productivity. "We wanted to combine innovation with new records in productivity."

Kolind then asked his people to examine their jobs and identify what they did well, in effect to redesign their compacts. He wanted every employee to do several jobs, the one he or she did very well, and other tasks where new skills could be learned to pursue innovation. With multiskilling, Kolind believed people could better understand the jobs of others, reduce the need for time-wasting controls, and contribute to innovation.

To trigger the transformation, he proposed moving the head office to a remote pro-duction site in Jutland. The resistance to this move gradually turned into a revolt. Kolind relented. What he didn't expect, however, was the strong support for an innovation-based organization, unleashed by his change of mind: "I gave in on where Oticon is going to relocate, but I insisted on carrying through with the reorganization . . . From one week to the next there was a complete change." Kolind called in the media to cover the reorganization, and they came in droves to witness the preannounced Oticon inno-vation revolution. But he was not merely after publicity: "I made no secret of the fact that I was using the press as a tool, as a way of burning the bridges behind us."

Project leaders, most of whom had innovation compacts, were the centrepiece of the new organization. Project leaders might offer their services to, or be recruited by, the management committee. To assemble their teams, project leaders had access to avail-able employees and resources throughout the company, using the IT system to see who was free, plus persuasion and negotiation to bring them on board. Team members rotated from project to project, working on two or more at the same time. The infor-mation system listed current commitments. People soon developed reputations as good or bad colleagues to have on board. As one manager put it: "In the past, your im-portance was related to your position, now it comes from your contribution." Skill co-ordinators maintained basic competencies in each area through personal development reviews, additional training, and recruiting. Bonuses were given mainly for team per-formance.

After Oticon put the new organization and innovation compacts in place, they intro-duced two important new products in 18 months, half the time previously required. Moreover, over two years Oticon quadrupled its profits and increased its previously flat sales by 13% and 23%, respectively.

In terms of key employee questions, the innovation compact at Oticon can be sum-marized as follows:

1. *Economic dimension*:

- *What am I supposed to do?* Discover opportunities for innovation.
- *What help will I get?* Sponsorship, access to information and training.
- *How will I be measured?* Team performance, personal development reviews.
- *What economic reward will I get?* Salary increases and team bonuses.

2. *Social dimension*:

- *What vision will I share?* Make Oticon the leading niche player in hearing aids.
- *What values will I share?* Openness, low power distance, flexibility, team spirit.
- *What informal rules will apply?* Create one's own job, remove barriers, involve people.

3. *Psychological dimension*:

- *How good is it for me?* Opportunity to take initiative, develop personally.
- *How risky is it for me?* Innovation risky, but Oticon understands this.
- *What personal satisfaction will I get?* Scope to innovate, lead a highly motivated team.

In effect, the project leaders renewed their compacts each time they took on a new project, albeit within the context of the new organization. By the same token, individual employees renewed compacts when they agreed to join a new project team. The continual rotation between projects resulted in an ongoing renewal of compacts, always adapted to the innovation task at hand.

This type of innovation-based learning compact is most attractive on the psychological dimension. By contrast, it offers little in the way of economic reward. The flexibility, freedom and challenge appeal to independent, entrepreneurial types. It is less appropriate for the detailed, problem-solving work required for improvement-based compacts. Indeed, at Oticon, the spaghetti organization and innovation compacts were limited to the headquarters people in R&D and marketing.

Enabling processes for learning compacts

The organizational and information processes for supporting learning compacts in bottom-up organizations have to be installed and maintained. (See Chapter 13.) These processes can be broadly categorized as:

- collecting and sharing information;
- developing employee learning skills; and
- developing useful frameworks and routines.

In bottom-up organizations moving towards learning compacts, some combination of managers in information systems, human resources, and finance and control usually carry out these activities. A few companies, however, now appoint executives who are responsible explicitly for supporting learning compacts.

Collecting and sharing information

To encourage learning-based compacts, a bottom-up organization must have a corporatewide memory or database that incorporates internal information and experience, and external data on, and from, customers, competitors and other partners. This database provides the reference against which individuals can measure how much they have learned to make the company more competitive. Information systems have facilitated greatly the development and sharing of such corporatewide memories. Previously, most corporate information was in the form of accounting data, manuals and procedures, and in the heads of people, all of which were difficult to access; now middle managers increasingly have the task of ensuring that a user-friendly IT system captures the relevant data and experience for everyone to access. Databases listing individuals with their skills and experience are increasingly common, which makes it much easier for everyone to take advantage of everyone else's experience. Successful service and high-tech companies are the furthest ahead in this respect.

Developing employee learning skills

The information is of little use, however, unless people use it to solve problems and improve efficiency on the one hand, and innovate and create opportunities on the other hand. This requires decentralized, diverse and continual learning opportunities, such as on-the-job twinning to learn from others, job rotation, and involvement in teams. To focus the frontline energy on value creation, bottom-up organizations must have programs to provide the skills that matter and foster a learning mindset.

CASE STUDY: CANADIAN IMPERIAL BANK OF COMMERCE[4]

At the Canadian Imperial Bank of Commerce (CIBC), the person in charge of such programs is Hubert Saint-Onge, Vice President, Learning Organization and Leadership Development. CIBC has defined the objectives of employee education in terms of "what people must know to serve customers". Saint-Onge and his team have developed a series of about 50 competency models, which describe the different human talents that CIBC requires, for example selling skill, credit analysis expertise, and so on. To develop a particular talent, employees can use books and software at their local branch learning room, shadow colleagues to learn from them on the job, or take a course.

The key to the CIBC approach, however, is that employee learning is in the hands of employees. They are personally responsible for enhancing and adding to their own portfolio of skills. Employees are expected to develop the skills they need for their job, the range and depth required by a vice president being different from that of a branch manager, or customer service representative. There is no-one in Human Resources to tell them what they should take next. The training department is gone. In the words of Saint-Onge: "Most companies can't tell you how much they spend on training. It took

---

4. Based on Stewart (1994).

us six months to decipher $30 million a year! And one penny out of a hundred hits the mark." To correct this, CIBC training is now up to the employees, but it should be designed to perform their current job better, not prepare for the next one. Department heads track how fast their people are learning new skills and where they are apparently not doing enough.

The personal compacts at CIBC can be summarized as follows:
1. *Economic dimension*:

- *What am I going to do?* Enhance skills, continually change the way I work.
- *What help will I get?* Local learning room, colleagues, courses.
- *How will I be measured?* Competency models completed, competency lacking.
- *What's in it for me economically?* Learning progress, employability outside.

2. *Social dimension*:

- *What vision will I share?* Make CIBC number one.
- *What values will I share?* Responsibility for own learning and development.
- *What informal rules will apply?* Mutual commitment to share, learn from each other.

3. *Psychological dimension*:

- *How good is it for me?* Open-ended way of developing myself.
- *How risky is it for me?* May fall behind everyone else, without realizing it.
- *What personal satisfaction will I get?* Mastering skills, in charge of one's own destiny.

In contrast to the compacts that emerge from a one-time change process, this one incorporates a commitment to personal learning, in the form of a continual improvement in the way one works through the acquisition of new skills.

Developing useful frameworks and routines

The development and sharing of useful frameworks and routines for innovation and efficiency improvement is essential to support learning compacts in energized organizations. Recognizing this, some pioneering companies have appointed middle managers to identify, measure and manage the development of such corporate know-how. One of the leaders in this field is Skandia Assurance and Financial Services (Skandia AFS), the rapidly growing savings and investment products division of the Skandia Insurance Company in Sweden.

CASE STUDY: SKANDIA AFS[5]

Skandia AFS has appointed both a director and controller of intellectual capital. The task of the first intellectual capital director, Leif Edvinsson, was to identify, package, capitalize on, and further develop "intangible and non-material items".

Edvinsson and his team identified five focus areas of intellectual capital (or know-how), i.e. areas with distinct frameworks and routines: financial performance, customer-related, process efficiency, renewal projects, and human competencies. For each of these, they put together a set of measures of the quantity and quality of available frameworks and routines. Once the measures had been identified and tried out in pilot form, Skandia AFS appointed an intellectual capital controller to collect the corresponding data across the group. The combination of the five sets of measures was described as "Skandia's Business Navigator", a metaphor used for both internal and external communication of the state of Skandia's available frameworks and routines.

The next step was moving from measurement to management of know-how. A 1995 meeting of 25 controllers from around the group decided that all business units would begin using the indicators in the 1996 planning and reporting process. There was also discussion about how to set objectives for know-how development and the kind of bonus and incentive scheme that could be linked to it. In addition, the IT people began establishing an "international electronic knowledge networking and sharing system" to share knowledge and information with employees. The local area networks were connected into a global area network allowing all subsidiaries to access one another's data bases. For example:

- *Everyone could access the central libraries of Skandia AFS presentation materials.*
- *The IT function of smaller offices could be run from larger offices elsewhere.*
- *Product and fund information was distributed to thousands of brokers to demonstrate product features to customers and print out application forms for them on the spot in the local broker's office.*
- *The Business Navigator was made available on manager's desktops.*
- *A databank was developed on employees with information on their current job, competencies, experience, education and training.*

The employee information bank was important because it permitted employees to develop their own Personal Navigator describing the state of their individual know-how in the same terms as that of the company.

In May 1995, Bjorn Wolrath, the CEO of Skandia group called a corporate council meeting for the top 150 managers of the Skandia Group to discuss the next steps, as he put it, moving from "managing through instructions" to "managing through values". In "Qualification Accounts" employees listed what they had accomplished during the year, projects they had worked on, and development and training completed. These qualification accounts were linked to the Personal Navigators. Other frameworks available for enhancing one's own leadership behaviour included "work permits", introduced at an earlier 1992 Skandia AFS meeting, a statement expressing the freedom employees

---

5. Taken predominantly from Oliver, Marchand and Roos (1995).

had to collaborate, be curious and speak up. Other routines, such as job rotation and projects outside one's unit, were also discussed.

Most importantly, Wolrath closed the corporate council meeting by asking those present to send him a letter saying how they would contribute to the Skandia vision, develop the intellectual capital, and the trust needed for that in their business units. He wanted each manager to include in the letter three actions they would personally undertake to build a high-trust culture in Skandia. About a month later, Wolrath responded personally to each of the letters, outlining what he would do to help. The managers then repeated this process with their people.

The compacts at Skandia can be summarized as follows:
1. *Economic dimension*:

- *What am I supposed to do?* Improve performance, contribute to intellectual capital.
- *What help will I get?* Frameworks and routines, "work permits" to learn.
- *How will I be measured?* Business Navigator, plus my Qualification Account.
- *What economic reward will I get?* Bonus, incentives linked to learning and company know-how.

2. *Social dimension*:

- *What vision will I share?* Exploit intellectual capital for competitive advantage.
- *What values will I share?* Learning and trust needed to create intellectual capital.
- *What informal rules will apply?* Learning objectives, freedom to collaborate, curiosity.

3. *Psychological dimension*:

- *How good is it for me?* Extensive learning infrastructure linked to compensation.
- *How risky is it for me?* Bottom line may suffer, affecting us all.
- *What personal satisfaction will I get?* Control own destiny, contribute to intellectual capital.

In effect, with the letters he asked the top 150 to send him, Wolrath got his managers to design and sign learning compacts for themselves and their people. Those involved agreed on their part to the objective of a continually improving personal qualification account, as well as to developing corporate intellectual capital and trust. For its part, the company provided an implicit Work Permit that gave them the freedom and support to learn. These learning compacts, comprising a Personal Navigator, Qualification Account, and Work Permit, went well beyond those at CIBC by incorporating an explicit commitment to corporate learning, supported by an expanding infrastructure for capturing and sharing both information and know-how in the form of shared frameworks and routines.

The CIBC and Skandia examples show how bottom-up organizations can support learning compacts by helping employees develop the necessary skills by sharing information, and by making useful frameworks and routines available throughout the company. These supports are essential regardless of whether the learning contracts are efficiency- or innovation-based. However, if the focusing of energy is to be credible then it is essential that learning compacts extend all the way to the top.

Enabling behaviour for learning compacts at the top

Creating and renewing learning compacts at the top of an organization present a challenge. The CEO, in particular, is a special case. At the head of the organization, there is no-one but him/herself to provide the context for learning. Even the most enlightened of leaders have foundered on this issue. To learn yourself and, in particular, to look ahead for the next change over the horizon, you have to develop three habits:

- *Humility*: sensitivity to meaningful feedback.
- *Honesty*: objective self-evaluation.
- *Hunger*: psychological drive to succeed.

The difficulty of learning at the top is illustrated by what happened at Oticon, the Danish hearing aid company discussed earlier, after it successfully changed its organization into a new flexible network. The new organization led to the rapid introduction of new products, but it also resulted in losses at first. These losses were compounded by a product launch in the USA that failed completely. Yet Lars Kolind, the CEO, had difficulty updating his own compact to focus on cost control. As Kolind recalls, "Having just loosened everything a lot, it was difficult to tighten up again."

Without the necessary perspective, it is only natural to blame negative feedback on others. Even Jack Welch of GE fame fell into this trap. As GE's financial progress started to slow down in the mid-1980s, and some big automation investments went bad, Welch tried to find out why. When he started getting the same questions over and over at the GE Management Center, he couldn't believe it: "This is unbelievable! I'm getting the same questions I've gotten for five years! Doesn't anybody understand anything? I'm just not getting through to them." At this point, you need a call for humility, from inside or outside yourself.

Humility: sensitivity to meaningful feedback

To move towards learning and the continual renewal of your own compact, you must be sensitive to negative, but potentially meaningful, feedback. The challenge in adopting a learning compact at the top is that compact renewal has to be largely self-driven, with little facilitation from anyone else, apart from close members of the management team, or the board. At Oticon, Kolind had a board that sensed there was not enough control and pushed him to appoint a financial director. Kolind listened and, in early 1992, Niels Jacobsen arrived as executive vice president of Oticon.

At GE, Welch got help from Jim Baughmann, GE's head of management develop-ment, who played a big role in proposing and setting up the Workouts (question and answer meetings between employees and top-management designed to work out issues). In the firing line of the first Workouts, Welch got direct feedback from junior colleagues, not only about how GE was doing, but also, indirectly, about how he was doing. He began to realize that his commander style was no longer working. People were exhausted and demoralized. Something new was needed. Part of the problem was Jack Welch himself. The old social compact Welch had with his people for the purposes of the turn-around had unravelled. People were no longer willing to play by the same informal rules of the game that had developed for the turnaround. They were unwilling to talk about empowerment and accept top-down directives.

Honesty: objective self-evaluation

You have to be honest with yourself about what feedback on your behaviour and busi-ness performance means. The question is whether you have the right leadership style to energize and focus a bottom-up organization. Can a radical cost-cutter, for example, also inspire entrepreneurship? Would you want to? Do you have what it takes in new skills and energy to lead more change? To answer these questions, you need a good dose of honesty and self-knowledge.

At Oticon, Kolind saw his limitations. Instead of trying to manage control, he let Jacobsen do it. While Kolind took responsibility for R&D, sales and marketing, and overall strategy, Jacobsen focused on day-to-day operational issues. "He was a great help in managing the business more effectively, but it was not easy. . . . He was con-stantly reminding us about the bottom line . . . He had the determination and moti-vation to put everything together." The arrival of Jacobsen brought people into the organization whose main compact orientation was solving the problem of cost-control. By constantly "reminding everyone about the bottom line", Jacobsen pushed everyone else to revise their economic compacts to include a concern for costs. As a result, profits began to recover strongly and, in a very flat market, sales started going up by double digit percentages.

(To his great credit, Kolind recognized that the time had come to make way. Just 50 when he left in 1998, he observed: "I quit Oticon now because I feel that both the company and I will benefit from a change. There is a whole new generation of young people who are ready to run with the ball and why shouldn't I let them do it?" (Dearlove, 1998).)

At GE, it was not too difficult for Welch to figure out that if he wanted to keep the company on its earnings growth path, he had to unleash the talent of his people. The question is how he convinced himself that he could change his compact with his people. How could he shift from being the commander – he'd been called "Neutron Jack" during the turn-around – to being an inspirational leader capable of unleashing the potential of his people? Although he obviously had an ego commensurate with the job and was known to be very competitive, he was also credited with being honest with himself. In the words of one board member at the time he was appointed CEO: "He wanted you to know who he was. That was a very appealing quality for leader-ship. To be self-confident, to be honest with yourself."

Hunger: the psychological drive to succeed

Welch had one other quality that is central to spontaneously revising one's own compact. He had an insatiable appetite to grow personally. Welch knew he had to make some important changes to his leadership compact if the empowerment thing was to fly. He called for: ". . . redefining the relationship between boss and subordinate . . . In the new culture, the role of the leader is to express a vision, get buy-in, and implement it. That calls for open caring relationships with every employee, and face-to-face communication."

According to Larry Bossidy, the then vice president of GE: "He's a man obsessed with growth, personal growth. If you came back and interviewed him a year from now, he won't be the same guy you interviewed today."

To what extent did Welch really change his own behaviour? Quite a lot, according to Larry Bossidy, who had known Welch for a long time: "I do think there was change, vividly, from yelling and screaming for performance, to a much more motivational kind of approach. He became a lot more understanding, much more tolerant. Hey, if you get the job done even though your style is different from mine, that's fine. He wasn't that way in the beginning."

On the other hand, casual comments from GE managers reveal that fear is still an important part of Welch's style. At GE management meetings, Welch talks about how he had to "take out" various managers for not meeting their targets, or not living up to GE's espoused values.

The Oticon example, on the other hand, illustrates a learning compact at the top based not on trying to change oneself, but on changing the composition of the top team to reflect the shifting forces of change. Whereas frontline people can concentrate on a particular type of focused learning that suits their style, learning at the top either means adopting a management style that is not the manager's natural one, as in the case of Welch, or maintaining one's style and changing the team to deal with the shifting needs of the whole organization, as in Kolind's case. Neither approach is possible without a strong drive to succeed, to beat the odds against surviving major change at the top.

Ongoing willingness to learn at the top is vital if you are to develop learning compacts with your people, and then focus those compacts so your company can harness the energy in bottom-up organization.

 **SUMMARY**

Continuous integration of individual and organizational goals is the bedrock of the bottom-up organization. Learning compacts provide the framework for achieving harmony between corporate and individual objectives. Constantly renewed, they invigorate the organization at all levels, sustaining individual energy and focusing it on value-creation. Improvement compacts require employees to commit themselves explicitly to participate in ongoing compact renewal to improve continually the way things are done. Employees agree to learn how to continually look for better ways of doing things and change their working methods, while the company gives them the climate, training, logistical support, and recognition needed to make improvement attractive.

Innovation compacts embody repeated innovation and ongoing learning about new business opportunities. Companies famous for their internal entrepreneurs and the number of their new products provide an environment that facilitates the discovery of new opportunities, with easy access to the necessary resources, and an incentive system that avoids punishing failure but rewards initiative. But they also co-ordinate their independent-minded entrepreneurs into a corporate learning network. The ability and willingness of top management to develop habits that allow their own learning compacts to be refreshed and reinvented is critical to success.

BEST PRACTICE

To be effective, personal learning compacts require the willing and active participation of individuals.

Providing the opportunity to commit

Managers have to give their people the opportunity to commit to learning compacts. This means creating the space for, and/or developing, roles for people, as well as giving them the face-to-face opportunity to buy into the value-creating objectives of the organization.

However the organizational processes for supporting learning compacts have to be in place. These processes can be broadly categorized as:

- collecting and sharing information;
- developing employee learning skills; and
- developing useful frameworks and routines.

Much has been written about knowledge management in recent years. Creating effective knowledge management processes is a prerequisite for learning compacts. In bottom-up organizations moving towards learning compacts, some combination of managers in information systems, human resources, and finance and control usually carry out these activities. A better approach, and one now being introduced in some companies, is to appoint executives who are explicitly responsible for supporting learning compacts.

Collecting and sharing information

To encourage learning-based compacts, a company must have a corporatewide memory or database that incorporates internal information and experience, and external data on, and from, customers, competitors and other partners. This database provides the reference against which individuals can measure how much they have learned to make the company more competitive. Intranets have facilitated greatly the development and sharing of such corporatewide memories. Databases listing individuals with their skills and experience are increasingly common, which makes it much easier for everyone to take advantage of everyone else's experience.

Developing employee learning skills

The information is worthless, however, unless people apply it to improve efficiency (solving problems), or to innovate (creating new business opportunities). This requires continual learning opportunities, using a range of techniques such as on-the-job twinning to learn from others, job rotation, and involvement in teams. Employees also need to know what competencies or skills the organization wants them to develop.

Developing useful frameworks and routines

Frameworks and routines for innovation and efficiency improvement are also essential to support learning compacts. Some pioneering companies have appointed managers to identify, measure and manage the development of such corporate know-how. Skandia AFS, for example, has a director and controller of intellectual capital. The role includes codifying frameworks and routines.

References

Case, J. (1992) The Change Masters: Company Profile, *Inc.*, March, 1992: 59–70.

Dearlove, D. (1998) The Man Who Caused Chaos, *The Times* (London), May 7, 1998.

Gould, R.M., Stanford, M. and Blackmon, K. (1994) Revolution at Oticon A/S: The Spaghetti Organization, *IMD Case Study No. OB235*.

Oliver, D., Marchand, D.A. and Roos, J. (1995) Skandia Financial Services (A): Measuring Intellectual Capital, *IMD Case Study No. GM624*.

Oliver, D., Marchand, D.A. and Roos, J. (1995) Skandia Financial Services (B) Managing Intellectual Capital, *IMD Case Study No. GM625*.

Stewart, T.A. (1994) Your Company's Most Valuable Asset: Intellectual Capital, *Fortune*, 3.

Strebel, P. (1998) *The Change Pact: Building Commitment to Ongoing Change*. London: Financial Times Pitman.

CHAPTER 17

Turbo-kaizen

Providing a context for focusing the energy of employees in a bottom-up organization requires deep cultural commitment. The philosophy of continuous improvement through an empowered workforce provides a fertile environment for translating new employee ideas into action. In this chapter, **Tom Vollman** recommends an accelerated version of kaizen to support and drive the process.

Overview

We turn here to the vexing issue of how to integrate and execute all the good
employee ideas that bubble up in an energized organization. These come on top of
the bottom-up initiatives of entrepreneurial managers. In fact, the major problem
facing bottom-up organizations is not a shortage of good ideas, but the means to implement more of these good ideas. In recent times we have seen several companies trying
to increase significantly their ability to implement new employee ideas faster. None
of these efforts is the best, and most are somewhat ad hoc, but from our point of
view there is an emerging set of ideas. The underlying approach is to turbo-charge
the change processes we have come to call kaizen; to develop new forms of empowerment where the untapped energies of all employees are focused in new ways. This
also provides an integrating force to focus energy. In order to explain what is behind
turbo-kaizen, this chapter examines the following questions:

- What is turbo-kaizen, and how is it different from the traditional form of
  continuous improvement used by most companies today?
- What are the primary blockages to achieving turbo-kaizen in many companies?
- How does a company break out, and enable turbo-kaizen to develop and
  flourish?
- What are the underlying imperatives, or what factors must a company be sure
  that they are getting right?

The turbo-kaizen concept

Turbo-kaizen is much more than soliciting suggestions from workers on how to
improve their operating practices. Fundamentally, we need to develop a new engine
for change – one that runs faster than any previous approach.

The one-day-per-week imperative

In recent times at IMD, we have often asked a group of executives what they would
do if they had an extra day per week. The blank stares of incomprehension led to the

follow-on question: let us assume that you presently work five days per week (an unrealistic assumption perhaps), and that somehow this work could now be done in four days. What would you do with the extra day?

The first response to this question is usually some banter about playing golf, so we follow up with still another question: how many of you are bored with your job, and wish someone would call in at your office to talk to you because you have nothing to do? Now the discussion becomes lively and we quickly conclude that there is no shortage of good ideas. The constraining resource is the time of managers to implement the new ideas. Most of the emergent ideas in a bottom-up organization are very appropriate; the problem is how to implement more of them – more rapidly.

We conclude that managers of today must find their "one day per week". If you are not spending 20% of your time on the future, there may not be one. The ability to implement boundary-crossing networks, for example, depends largely on development of working relationships with executives in customer and supplier organizations. This takes time, and you must find the time.

Classic kaizen

Kaizen is a well-known process – a pillar of Japanese management approaches. The basic idea is that every person has a brain, and he or she must not park it at the door when arriving at work. Each employee is expected to continuously find ways to make improvements in the work methods, so that ever-better products are produced with ever-lower costs to make them. Shop floor workers can easily be taught the basic concepts of industrial engineering, and these can be applied to their work. The results can be quite spectacular. As an example, the times to set up or change equipment for making one item to another have been reduced in many companies by up to 95% simply by following a standard set of concepts for this problem. And it is the workers themselves who do this – not the managers who know far less about the details of the job than those who do it on a daily basis.

Kaizen embraces the concept of worker empowerment. Workers should be able to make changes in the ways they work based on their own initiatives. Moreover, workers can and should learn to do multiple tasks (cross-training/multiple skills) so that greater flexibility can be achieved both in work methods and in the variety of products and services provided to the customers.

Kaizen is supported by a management philosophy that recognizes the potential of the workers, and that explicitly does not require managerial review/approval of worker improvement initiatives. This is a critical ingredient of kaizen. The underlying (but unstated) assumption in far too many companies is that the workers are idiots and thieves, so we need many control mechanisms to ensure they do not steal things or make errors. But these add little value for customers; moreover, they keep managers from their day per week.

As the Toyota example at the start of this chapter indicates, kaizen embodies the essence of the bottom-up organization. It recognizes the contribution that those closest to the task or process can make to improving the business. An underlying objective of kaizen is to take a large number of small steps; collectively this will lead to a rate of continuous improvement that yields a competitive advantage. By harnessing the collective brainpower of all employees, a company can produce products of ever-better quality at lower costs. Does it work? Of course it does, and the results are seen on the roads of the world. It has taken time for Western companies to catch up to the Japanese application of kaizen, and each company has developed its own version, but fundamentally, the kaizen form of continuous improvement is well established in leading-edge manufacturing companies around the world.

Finally, there is one more aspect of kaizen that needs to be highlighted: it changes the work for the managers as well as for the workers. It is no longer the primary job of managers to find small improvements in the ways work is done, nor to be pushing constantly for higher levels of productivity. This is explicitly the domain of the workers, with the underlying assumption that working smarter beats working harder. Managers can focus on the major or big changes required – those that cannot be expected to be attacked by the detailed bottom-up approach of kaizen.

Turbo-charging kaizen

Although in principle kaizen works at all levels in a company, in practice it is mostly applied at the shop floor level. Moreover, the focus for application tends to be on doing things better rather than on doing better things. In order to turbo-charge kaizen, we need to go back to the major themes of this book. In essence, today's competitive environment requires winning companies to transform – to take on more initiatives, but to select them carefully, and then to execute them quickly. This implies some new kind of change engine to make this a reality on the frontline. We see turbo-kaizen as one of these engines.

Turbo-kaizen again requires a hands-on, empowered, multiskilled workforce, which operates with absolute minimal direction and approval mechanisms. But the problem application area needs to be greatly expanded. We need to develop empowered teams that can develop solutions to problems such as how to partner with suppliers and customers for mutual benefits. This implies new skills and training, new groupings of people on improvement teams (including people from different companies), new organizational forms, new reward mechanisms, and new thinking that concentrates on overall objectives – avoiding current suboptimal approaches.

The underlying driver for turbo-kaizen rests on the one-day-per-week imperative. The successful company simply must devote more time and people resources to out-of-the-box improvements. This in turn implies that the routine things in the company must be done even more routinely, with reduced managerial time spent. New teams need to be developed at the shop floor level, to take on an ever-increasing set of tasks that formerly were the province of managers in staff functions. We naturally start with quality control, scheduling and maintenance, but soon one needs to add routine working with suppliers and customers so that cumbersome up-over-and-down processes are replaced by simple communications between execution parts of separate companies.

This kind of empowerment/change implies major revisions in the ways sales and purchasing functions work, as well as most routine processes in the company. But a word of advice is in order here: be careful what you tell the accounting types about what you are doing. There will be great pressure to make short-term cost savings by downsizing the middle managers whose former work is now embedded in the basic infrastructure of the company operating processes. But if those middle managers are fired, there is no-one for the senior managers to offload to to gain the day per week.

We must understand that a fundamental objective in implementing turbo-kaizen is to create idle time – in fact to always maximize idle time. This time can then be spent on either new initiatives directly, or on offloading tasks from those who are most suited to take on the new initiatives. The creation of idle time should be an explicit goal, and the use of this time should be seen as being at least as important as any capital investment.

Networking

Best practice in turbo-kaizen will require an advanced stage of networking. Teams will need to be formed quickly, and they will need to get on with the work rapidly. This requires advanced levels of trust in the organizations involved, which in practice is best achieved by developing networks – both formal and informal – that allow a large number of people to come to know one another and to learn, through direct experience, that working together is not only possible but that it works well and is personally rewarding.

A further refinement on the minimal direction/approval concept is the encouragement of what we call "mafia networks". Informal networks of people who share common experiences and problems need to be encouraged. In many instances, these groups end up creating new ideas and initiatives that run counter to existing organizational forms and mechanisms. We believe the enlightened organization will encourage some of this kind of activity. It implies a certain willingness to tolerate those who are more inclined to ask forgiveness than permission. These groups can learn to circumvent blockages in fairly creative ways. Even when their efforts are not immediately successful, at times the learning for the future might well have justified the experience.

This form of working obviously must be subject to some limitations, and it will make many people very nervous. But the need for more rapid innovation favours the idea. Moreover, in virtually every company in which we have worked extensively, the sharing of practices is far too limited. We simply must find the ways to integrate the energy of individuals into networks of people interested in common problems.

Platform shifts

Turbo-kaizen differs from the more common version of kaizen in one other fundamental respect: rather than focusing on improvements to existing processes and ways of working, turbo-kaizen often needs to focus on changing the basic approaches to be used. For example, a consumer products company working with its suppliers implemented an e-business-to-business approach, which replaced its earlier ways of working with customers as well as the information systems that supported these practices. Turbo-kaizen in this case required the adoption of new processes, new systems, new exchanges of information, and new foci for improvement. Moreover, this turbo-kaizen required implementation of flawless execution now newly defined.

Blockages

Turbo-kaizen is not going to come about easily, and it should not be seen as a natural evolution from the more common forms of kaizen. In fact, there are some basic forces that tend to block implementation of the concept. Understanding the most important of these should help in minimizing their impact.

The country disease

This blockage arises because companies are divided organizationally into countries or other geographic divisions where profits are determined in each of the geographic units. The net result can often seriously retard implementation of major new initiatives. Examples abound, but we see many of them in consumer products companies that are now developing regional approaches. These typically call for closure of smaller factories, focusing of production so products are produced in fewer places with greater economies of scale, harmonization of designs and packages, regional procurement, cross-shipping, and integrated planning and logistics. The results can be dramatic, but the implementation is not easy. To the extent that these companies have country profitability measures, in far too many cases we see serious amounts of wasted time haggling over transfer prices, allocations of products to countries, and other activities that basically define sister companies as competitors.

In some cases, we see factories that in aggregate operate at 50% of capacity, while at the same time there are endless arguments against any closure of factories. Even worse is the situation where each country makes its own capital appropriation justifications, which result in these low-capacity utilization results. Most suggestions for co-operation tend to be viewed in terms of whose ox gets gored, instead of in terms of what is best of the overall corporation.

The most obvious solution to the country disease may be thought to be organizational centralization, but our experience does not support this conclusion. In fact, again the only real long-term solution appears to require a significant investment in trust building and informal networking. There simply does not seem to be any alternative to taking the time to eradicate the us versus them feelings that pervade many transnational companies. Changing the bonus schemes for country managers so that an increasing percentage of their compensation comes from overall results helps as well. But in the end, the people that work in each of the factories need to develop the spirit of searching for the overall best result. That spirit must be supported by open communication and transparent behaviour, proving that all are playing by the same rules.

Exclusive focus on costs

A second major blockage to implementing turbo-kaizen is an exclusive focus on cost-reduction. Reducing costs is always an objective of improvement efforts, and this is also true for turbo-kaizen. But we have yet to find a company that saved its way into prosperity. In order to transform or change the rules of the game, it is almost always necessary to focus on doing something new – which requires investments – particularly in new thinking and ways of working.

It is critical in this regard for a company to be completely clear on the issue of whether or not it can achieve its desired strategic objectives by cost-cutting alone. If there is consensus that cost-cutting will not be enough, the company must develop action programs that do not focus only on cost. In fact, our experience is often that it might be necessary to cut costs significantly in some areas to generate the funds necessary to invest in others. Similarly, we often see companies that must outsource some aspect of their present work in order to concentrate their attention on what is now a more important set of issues/activities.

There is always pressure on costs – and there needs to be. But in the spirit of turbo-kaizen, firms need to spend their one-day-per-week efforts on those activities that are going to create new competencies and new business opportunities. Some of these may result in significantly lower costs, but the key is significant. Firms need to resist the temptation to use the turbo-kaizen resource for squeezing more blood out of stones.

Lack of courage and leadership

Turbo-kaizen is not going to be easy to achieve, and the blockages are not easy to overcome. Experience has shown that at some point, one needs an executive who provides the necessary leadership. In one consumer products company we know, the purchasing personnel had been trying for years to harmonize the products and packaging. They produced lengthy analyses of the potential savings. They even held meetings where all the different variations were shown, in hopes of embarrassing people enough to change. All agreed on the problems and the wisdom of harmonization. But this agreement was followed up by each factory listing reasons why changes needed to be made by others – not by them. The problem was only solved when a very senior manager said: "I no longer want to hear the reasons why this cannot be done. I only want to hear what you are going to do to make it happen."

This case illustrates the turbo-kaizen concept as well. In order to achieve harmonization, cross-organizational teams had to be formed, and they had to work with many other parts of the company – as well as with suppliers, customers and distribution partners. The entire process was long and required the development of informal networks, alliances or "mafias". Implementing the harmonization required a great deal of detailed work in the factories, such as adapting packaging machines to run well with different materials. This process was costly and difficult for the individual factories to understand. They already had a local solution that worked very well, and asked: "If it ain't broke, why fix it?" Explaining the overall benefits as well as why they had to take on more work clearly required relief from the country disease.

Unwillingness to let go

The final blockage to achieving turbo-kaizen comes from the natural fear of turning loose a process over which the managers by definition will have much less control. The need to make rapid progress on many fronts simultaneously means that overall orchestration may be possible, but detailed knowledge of what is going on at all times is clearly not so. Even classic kaizen methods were difficult for many organizations to adopt. In these companies the managers managed – and the workers worked. We say "jump" and you ask "how high?" But in turbo-kaizen, the stakes are much higher. The empowered teams are free to work on projects that are not well understood at the outset. Organizational forms are much fuzzier. Most work is ad hoc and done in teams.

Job security is of a different character as well. Instead of working in some continuous progression, the best people are trying to constantly work themselves out of their present jobs, in order to free themselves up for the next challenging project. The managers of these people in turn need to be continually updating a prioritized list of next projects. Evaluation of personnel is more difficult as well. Many people will not like working in such an unstructured environment. But some *will* like it – and they may excel in it. This is the promise as well as a key challenge of implementing turbo-kaizen.

Breaking out

Turbo-kaizen is not going to be easy to implement. The concept sounds good, but how does a company create the enabling mechanisms? How does one get the right focus of attention? How can we get the shared awareness of the need, the belief that turbo-kaizen is the way to go, and thereafter the commitment to make it a reality? How do we chart our way, evaluate progress, learn from our successes and failures, and grow our people in the process? These questions are not easy to answer in an abstract sense. Instead, let us turn to some ways in which one might start on the journey. Perhaps thereafter it will be possible for a given company to capture the learning from specific experiences – and leverage them for subsequent projects. Or, as Jay Forrester used to recommend: "Start with specific cases then generalize as far as you dare."

Start from strategy

One way turbo-kaizen can be made to work is to apply it to some clearly articulated strategic objective. In particular, we have found that asking each business unit what they believe is needed in their business unit to secure the most important customers can be very interesting. The answers will usually be quite different, but there should be at least one business unit that sees a need to develop a very different set of working relationships with a specific customer. That is, their answer is "doing better things".

It is important that the right choice be made here. The company is about to invest significant resources (from its one-day-per-week reserve). The choice of business unit and customer needs to be made carefully. The business unit needs to be crystal clear on its objectives and underlying reasoning, and they need the determination to carry through on the project – having taken the time to realistically evaluate the required time commitments. The customer also needs to be studied carefully. Not only should you work with the best and smartest – they should also be trustworthy, and it would help if prior working relations have been positive. Overall, the company needs to be ready to support this business unit led project – wherever it might go.

Setting up an empowered team for this work is a good start. The team will almost surely need to work in many parts of both organizations. In fact, the team at some point may well become a cross-company team. The key point is that it will be difficult at the outset to know where this will end up. The work will become more detailed, and processes for working across the two companies will need to be established and continually improved. Routine operating linkages will have to be put in place. Measures of performance will have to be created, and the rewards for the joint work will need to be made explicitly clear.

Participation on the team might come from almost anywhere in the organization, but it clearly needs to have certain features. At least one key player has to be one of the managers from the business unit – with zeal and credentials in his or her organization as a person who delivers the goods. Another player needs to be someone who has overall credibility in the organization, a person who is trusted and respected so that his or her ideas will be supported by those who have to give up parts of their day per week in order to support this project. The other team members can come from various places, but those who interface with customers, such as order entry, logistics, and manufacturing scheduling, might be good candidates. It might also be useful to include someone who knows their way around all the information systems in the company, and who can command resources in this area.

The team needs to document what it is doing, and periodically make progress reports to a senior management group. The project is important in its own right, but it is doubly important as the flagship for achieving turbo-kaizen. The company needs to learn from its experiences – both the specific content and the process. The team should evaluate periodically what they might have done differently if they were to do it again.

Start from segmentation

A variation on the above journey might be to identify specific market segments that the company now wishes to dominate, and thereafter determine the right bundles of goods and services needed for each segment. Thus, a beer company we know identified a particular segment of end customers in the Chinese market. Thereafter it was possible to study this segment in some depth, understand what was different about the segment, and determine what needed to be provided on their part as well as by the downstream organizations serving the customer segment. The resultant bundle of goods and services needed to be developed by both the beer company and others in the chain. But since the beer company had the primary interest in the segment, they had to find ways for the other players to adopt the practices and processes to best serve the market segment.

Another example comes from a telecom manufacturer who developed specific customer segments based on whether the customer was more focused in their strategy on providing geographic coverage, on expanding coverage in existing market areas, on buying from several suppliers versus one-stop shopping, and one or two other criteria. The segmentation provided a good way to view the future in terms of the market growth in particular segments. Thereafter, some segments were of much greater inter-est than others – for what they offered on a long-term basis. This encouraged the telecom company to establish a highly focused team that concentrated on develop-ing the bundles of goods and services that would be most helpful to customers in that segment as they grew their business over time.

Learn by doing

Whatever way one starts to implement turbo-kaizen, it is imperative that the learning be captured. It is all too easy to concentrate only on a particular project and its imme-diate objectives. But the process of implementing turbo-kaizen is critical as well. One needs to find the ways to speed up the process, develop the organizational support mechanisms, and share the good and bad experiences so that others in the company can benefit. At the end of the day we wish to invest our days per week as wisely as possible.

Turbo-kaizen needs to be seen as distinctly different from regular kaizen, and we need to reflect the difference in the way it is evaluated. In turbo-kaizen, our objec-tive is always big change – the breakout or change in the rules of the game. It is not an incremental small-steps approach. Both regular kaizen and turbo-kaizen are required, but they should not be confused. One focuses everyone on the day-to-day improvement process. The other assigns our critical one-day-per-week resources to those strategic initiatives that will ensure the future competitiveness of the company.

The learning process for turbo-kaizen is so important that it must not be left to chance or treated in some ad hoc fashion. Each initiative needs to be evaluated on several dimensions, not just on whether we think the initiative was a success. Success is only one measure, and it can come in various degrees. Turbo-kaizen projects need to start with a clearly articulated set of objectives, timings, resource requirements, and desired measures of success. At the end of every project, a critical review is in order to share practices (both good and bad) and to sharpen our turbo-kaizen process.

Underlying imperatives

Turbo-kaizen will seem to some to be a great kind of organization – one where new ideas flow rapidly, and everyone is excited. While true to an extent, it is also critical to understand that turbo-kaizen does not operate in a vacuum, and the chaos it may create must be dealt with in other parts of the company. In short, generating great ideas that cannot be delivered routinely will not have a desirable result.

Flawless execution

We say that flawless execution is the ante to play in any game of significant change. That is, your company must be able to meet its delivery schedules, with perfect quality. It needs to do so with little or no inventory buffers, and achieve on-time per-formance against production schedules. It must have a planning horizon long enough so suppliers can co-ordinate readily. It has to establish information linkages to support flawless execution, and it must have recovery mechanisms for dealing with unforeseen events. Furthermore, your company needs to have its traditional kaizen engine running well so all these are done ever better at lower costs.

But flawless execution becomes more complex when we superimpose turbo-kaizen, since the result is almost always a new set of demands being placed on the organization to deliver enhanced bundles of goods and services. Each of these new bundles must be executed flawlessly while still providing the existing bundles. Initiatives such as business units working more closely with major customers or new segments will require more customized bundles of goods and services. All of them need to be executed flawlessly. Doing so often requires major new work in manufacturing, distribution, customer order servicing, and other parts of the company. When these initiatives are being rolled out, the resultant bundles may be provided as a special service, but at some point these enhanced bundles need to be provided routinely – without any heroic efforts.

This implies a continual change process in the factory and elsewhere in the company. The routine execution systems need to be updated continually to support the strategic initiatives. All this is hard work. Some, but not all, of it is supported by traditional kaizen. The critical point here is to not underestimate the magnitude of the requirements. We have seen several firms where great ideas were totally killed off by gaps in execution. If one cannot deliver the products as promised, there is little room for discussion with the customers. Flawless execution is the ante to play the game.

Lean manufacturing

Closely related to flawless execution is the need to improve continually the effectiveness of a manufacturing organization. Traditional kaizen is one part, but most companies have other improvement programs as well. Best practice clearly includes some sort of quality initiative, such as total productive maintenance (TPM); work on faster throughput, such as time-based competition; re-engineering of major processes, such as order fulfilment; information linkages across company boundaries, such as electronic data interchange (EDI) or Internet connections; and new systems for scheduling manufacturing.

A caveat is that some firms are suffering from initiative overload. Prioritization is important, but equally important is to resist adding the buzz word improvement of the month. One firm we know well limits the corporate-mandated initiatives to one per year. Thereafter, a clear tracking process is in place to see how these programs are proceeding. Results are shared – as well as best practices. We are a bit more dubious as to how well poor practices are shared, but the intent is good.

The key issue for us here is to understand the relationship between lean manufacturing, or other corporate initiatives, and those associated with turbo-kaizen. The former – or at least some subset of them – needs to be in place to ensure excellence in operations. But if these soak up all the one-day-per-week resources, then the ability to implement turbo-kaizen is severely limited. The key point is that continual excellence in operations is indeed an important objective – but it is one that needs to be supported primarily through traditional kaizen approaches. Turbo-kaizen needs to be focused on the breakout initiatives and must have the resources necessary to do so. Manufacturing excellence and turbo-kaizen should not be an either/or choice. One needs to be supported as part of the daily working, while the other is enabled through the one-day-per-week maxim.

Project management

The final imperative for turbo-kaizen is the need to work very hard on better project management. Each of the initiatives needs to be seen as a project in its own right, and it thereafter needs to be managed and delivered using the best project management approaches. The timing on turbo-kaizen projects must not be allowed to drift. The objectives need to be crisp. The activities required need to be planned and replanned on an ongoing basis. The resource requirements similarly need to be continually updated.

A real danger for turbo-kaizen projects will be that they use resources that are left over. That is, these efforts are worked on in the spare time of individuals. We must avoid this as much as possible. A turbo-kaizen project needs to be seen as a critical strategic initiative – one that ensures the future of the company. The resources need to be made available in creative ways.

One firm we know has a most interesting approach to projects. A project is developed and planned by a particular individual, the project owner. He or she specifies the timing, activities and resource needs for the project. Thereafter, the project owner takes a personal responsibility for delivering the project on time. This company has a policy that any project owner can have unlimited access to funding, as long as the project comes in on time. So if a project manager needs more resources, he or she is free to get them in whatever way seems most appropriate, such as by hiring a consulting firm. That is, the firm believes that cost is much less important than time and they do not wish to provide an easy excuse for underperformance. In fact, the senior managers of this company firmly believe that allowing unlimited funding saves them money. The costs of being late are much higher than any costs associated with expediting the project.

 # SUMMARY

The ideas here represent an amalgam of thinking and practices we have observed in many leading edge companies in the last several years. The ideas have also been tested with a large number of executives who have come through our programmes here at IMD. Several of them have taken the time to remark on the importance of some key ideas such as the day per week. We think that the turbo-kaizen concept is a good way to bring these ideas into a usable whole. At the end of the day, those companies that can harness the commitment of their frontline employees, as well as their entrepreneurial managers, will be the winners.

 **BEST PRACTICE**

Turbo-charged kaizen is a new concept, one for which there are no templates for implementing. It requires an advanced stage of networking. Teams will need to be formed quickly, and they will need to get on with the work rapidly. This requires advanced levels of trust in the organizations involved. In practice, this is likely to be best achieved by developing networks – both formal and informal – that allow a large number of people to come to know one another and to learn through direct experience. Only by doing this will they learn that working together is not only possible but works well – and is personally rewarding.

Turbo-kaizen focuses on rapid implementation of new concepts by frontline employees – not just improvements of existing approaches. Teams need to be formed that can break out of existing thinking – finding those new platforms or ways of working that are needed to implement new thinking. This implies an organizational culture that expects change and is never satisfied with the existing state. There is always another stair step to climb. Doing so often requires new thinking, new processes, new systems, and new ways of routine working across organizational boundaries.

An important element of turbo-kaizen is the development of networks that are able to subvert formal communications channels. The need for these "mafia" networks suggests that informal networks of persons who share common experiences and problems need to be encouraged. In many instances where they already exist, these groups end up creating new ideas and initiatives that run counter to existing organizational forms and mechanisms. Effective bottom-up organizations will encourage this kind of activity. These groups can learn to circumvent blockages in creative ways.

Turbo-kaizen should be expected to make people nervous. It requires a management style that accepts discomfort as the standard way of working. This approach must be subject to some limitations, and it will not be easy for those who like stability. But today's need for increasingly rapid innovation requires this approach to implementing change. Bottom-up organizations simply must find the ways to integrate the commitment of employees into networks that thrive in this kind of environment.

18

The Leadership Paradox

Leading a bottom-up organization is perhaps the greatest challenge that ever faced a CEO. The tension between sustaining and focusing energy creates a leadership role riven with paradoxes but rich in rewards. In this final chapter, **J.B. Kassarjian** reflects on the leadership style required for organizations of the future.

CASE STUDIES

At the time I took over this company 13 months ago, it did not take me long to figure out that the major problem was our management's mindset: they were like loyal soldiers. They had been selected and groomed in this old culture that was slow, hierarchical, and never-take-any-chances. So my top priority was to shake them up and change this culture; I wanted them to feel empowered! But it has not worked out that way.

Pierre, CEO of a Finnish Chemicals company

Lately we seem to be drowning in "initiatives from below", as the current hot button of our CEO is called. I have had to send some key people to go on a wild goose chase to do benchmarking on customer service in an unrelated industry. We have a taskforce to explore the Asian market opportunities – more special assignments; and all of us in senior management are taking part in a seminar on increasing shareholder value. So how am I supposed to deliver my targeted results?

Jan, division general manager of a Dutch bank

When we started this change effort, I explained the need for it and the direction we should take, and we agreed on the major steps involved. But now, some eight months into the process, we seem to have gone off track. My sales manager says head office doesn't understand the marketplace, the finance director is concerned that overhead costs are going up because of too many meetings, and HRD wants more training programs on change management. So where did we go wrong?

Jean-Luc, CEO of a French consumer electronics company

Overview

With minor variations, the dilemmas faced by the senior executives in the case studies above can be found in many firms across a range of industries (e.g. Pascale et al., 1997). Whether the goal is cutting costs, or shortening of process cycles, or enhancing customer service, attempts to lead such renewal efforts falter not because the intentions are flawed, but because the basic assumptions driving the actions may be false. For the leader who is trying to encourage bottom-up initiatives, while at the same time trying to moderate the centrifugal forces these could create, the effect of faulty assumptions could be specially unsettling – and often destructive.

We have argued in this book that the critical challenge for the new corporation is the simultaneous pursuit of two seemingly contradictory objectives:

- to encourage experiments and pioneering initiatives from below and across the organization; and
- to bring coherence to these often divergent efforts by focusing on overall value creation.

It would be tempting to conclude that the most important skill required of the leader in such a corporation is the ability to balance the two sets of forces. As in other areas of personal and organizational life, balancing is at best an ideal state, not a realistic guide to action. This distinction is more than semantic. Even in the case of a physical, balancing scale, the finer the measurement, the more likely you are to witness a difference between the two sides, rather than a real balancing (Bateson, 1972). Like a good thermostat, any effective self-correcting system is one that allows appropriate degrees of deviation on either side of the desired ideal, rather than a constant stream of corrections. Hence timing of interventions and choice of countervailing directives become pivotal leadership issues in bottom-up organizations.

We think leaders that are attuned to rapidly shifting contexts will come to recognize that to prevail in the new competitive arenas, they cannot afford to maintain a single tune for long. For example, the directive "Let's push decentralization so that we can release the creative potential of all our people" will have a limited half-life. What will be called for increasingly are leaders for more than one season. And a necessary corollary to this new orientation will be a discerning determination to strip away assumptions that originated with good intentions, that were in turn based on an ideology that is no longer (if it ever was) valid.

In this chapter, we will examine the most crucial of the false assumptions that appear to have guided the actions of organization leaders in the past two or three decades. We will try to make explicit the range of emerging challenges for leadership. And we will draw the paradoxes that we find at the core of leading energized organizations. There will always be elusive elements that each leader brings to a situation, that represent a unique blending of hard analysis with personal art and craft, but our task here is primarily to augment the former, while we acknowledge the latter. As Confucius is reputed to have prescribed: "While the advisers of a great leader should be as cold as ice, the leader himself should have fire, a spark of divine madness," (Gardner, 1995).

Perhaps the greatest challenge facing business leaders of the future is to recognize that, in the bottom-up organization, many of the old assumptions about the role are no longer valid. There are a wide array of situations in which a leader has to act. It is possible to trace the assumptions that underpin each of these actions, but to simplify the task we have clustered these under three broad categories:

1.   The role of the *leader*, and the critical choices that cannot be avoided.
2.   The role of the *followers*, and how the leader has to navigate through current fads that promise short-cuts to mobilizing management talent.
3.   The utility of *prescriptive models for leading change*.

All three represent good intentions that could pave the road to disaster.

What role should the leader play?

We start our examination of possibly false or misleading assumptions with the ones that revolve around the role to be played by the leader. The CEO of a Finnish chemicals company – let's call him Pierre – is absolutely clear about what his recently assigned job should entail: "The leader conceives the need, sets the direction, and drives the change." This may sound obvious, but it is wrong. The irony is that in some currently popular generalizations, Pierre has identified his problem: it is about mindset, it is driven by company culture, and there is a handy remedy. But when we ask what specific actions will result from his diagnosis, and how realistic is it to expect concrete benefits, the situation looks less promising.

Granted that mindsets are part of the cognitive baggage we all carry around, and they do affect how we organize our experience, but this raises at least three practical questions:

1. How do we change mindsets?
2. Will a different mindset necessarily result in change of behaviour in a desired direction?
3. How do we relate specific performance problems to actual elements of mindset?

The sad truth is that hard data about specific performance problems are less likely to be found at the head office, or to be high on the agenda of staff groups. What your company needs to do in order to meet, anticipate, or exceed customer expectations, for example, is more likely to be found out at the periphery with your front-line managers who are in constant touch with the market. Your engineers who attended the latest trade show and came back alarmed or excited, or your after-sales-service managers who get a daily diet of genuine customer complaints and priorities, are your sources of realistic diagnosis. The CEO's declarations, whether about changing mindsets, or the need to be market-oriented and customer-focused pale in comparison to the concrete realism that these other sources of corrective action can provide.

Just as in the case of Pierre, when executives are asked to identify the most serious challenge facing their company's ability to compete, a significant number respond: "Our company culture!" I have used a variation of this question at the start of numerous executive programs in both company and institutional settings, and some reference to "company culture" never fails to be cited, even when the question is phrased to include "most serious competitive threat". Given this widely-held view, all too often setting the direction turns out to be an aspiration about changing mindsets, or the company culture, or both. Changed mindsets and modified company culture may turn out to be highly desirable by-products of learning to compete effectively in novel circumstances, but both are complex phenomena, and neither is amenable to a priori modification.

Three years ago, in a Western European country known for its technological prowess, a large, highly profitable government-owned monopoly was privatized. The new CEO was given a broad mandate for change – significant shifts in product-offering, new commitment to customer and service orientation, and so on, all designed to transform this comfortable giant to competitive agility and shareholder value-creation. The CEO met with his mostly hand-picked senior management team over a period of some months, and they eventually distilled the core values that would characterize the new culture of the transformed firm. "Our New Credo", as the final list was labelled, included:

1. Empower all our people – they represent our biggest investment.
2. Customers – they are our most important partners.
3. Sense of ownership – we control our own destiny.
4. Innovation is the path to performance.

With expensive help from consultants specializing in culture change, a training program was designed that would expose the entire management group (some 3000 plus) to these core values. Some senior managers volunteered to participate in the teaching, and the CEO tried to attend as many of the closing sessions as he could to answer questions. On completion of the Core Values Program, participants went home with certificates and elegant copies of the new values rendered on parchment paper. More than a year after these programs were started, senior line management came to the sad conclusion that the body count of those who had completed the Care Values Program was not noticeably matched by changes in actual behaviour at work. Apparently, managers and engineers were not able to connect the substance of these new core values to their everyday world of work. In fact serious resentments were voiced loudly enough to reach the CEO's office, when new organizational arrangements meant the break-up of long-established groups, or the change of work assignments. An anonymous survey of Core Values Program graduates (conducted by another consulting firm) revealed a range of reactions:

●   It was great fun to have these discussions with senior level people, many of whom we had not met before – very interesting ideas.
●   We discussed competitive forces and serving the customer, but it was never made clear what I was supposed to do differently in my department; besides my boss does not buy many of these new ideas.
●   I work in a team, and we are very proud of our record in technical innovations, but this Program had no impact on our team.
●   The joke in our department is that Our New Credo is what they preach, but you would be a fool to practice it if you want to survive all the changes around here.

Culture change against the grain of a company's long-established heritage usually follows concrete and multiple changes in the performance of particular units, which produce readily visible results. Unless the company is in the midst of a widely shared sense of crisis, culture change, no matter how frequently advocated, cannot lead the change process. And even then, a real change in company culture starts with the hard struggle to change specific performance outcomes; when these produce results, gradually new hero stories begin to circulate, and eventually these become the occasions for celebration. As has been wisely observed, what a company celebrates gives a good reading of its culture (Quirke, 1996).

Returning to Pierre, given the way he had initially identified the priorities ("shake them up and change this culture") and set the direction of corrective action ("make them feel empowered"), he was most likely to be the overall driver of his agenda. In fact he did discuss his diagnosis with his management team, but received lukewarm response. With the exception of his HR director, and a younger member of the strategy staff group, his senior line managers generally agreed that some aspects of the old culture needed polishing up, but they were not too enthusiastic about any of the actions he proposed. So an ad hoc steering committee was formed. The strategy staff person was given the task of preparing a specific set of competitive goals and the mindset these required. The HR director was given the mandate of designing a program that could best achieve these goals. And Pierre himself would become the advocate and champion of the overall change program.

Stop for a moment and ask, of these three – the CEO, the HR director, and the strategy staff person – who is best qualified to orchestrate this renewal process in a way that can produce tangible results? The unfortunate answer, probably, is none of the above, but for somewhat different reasons.

HR directors, unless they have significant experience in line positions with widely recognized track records, usually possess neither the business credibility nor the skills required to spearhead a process that requires some tough power-plays. A high-potential young staff person assuming the role of change architect could well be the kiss of death – to the accumulated past resentments left behind during rapid rotations through company departments, will now be added every frustration that the change process itself creates. Pierre may feel comfortable working with his two strongly supportive allies, but neither is in a position to bring compelling frontline realism to the efforts being planned, and nor does either one of them have high credibility with senior line managers. By acting as the heroic leader, Pierre had actually painted himself into a corner.

Hence the first element of the leadership paradox: tempting as it may be for a forceful leader to set the direction and drive the change, the energized organization will require multiple and often contrasting goals to be pursued, and leaders can ill afford to narrow their options. While CEOs may shape a goal, personally leading the charge could limit their effectiveness, it could interfere with their peripheral vision (de Geus, 1997). They may have to provide hard analysis or passionate persuasion as the company situation demands, but when they take on a heroic leadership role they reduce their capacity to observe from a distance and take corrective action. Taking on such a role also narrows their perspective on the choice of talent needed at specific turning points in the competitive evolution of a company.

Mobilizing followers

The second set of doubtful assumptions relates to how a leader mobilizes management talent, either to pursue new goals or to adopt new performance capabilities. The hard evidence from real organizational experience suggests that some of the most widely held ideas about promoting needed change do not work out in practice. Pierre (the CEO cited above) had to abandon his attempts to change mindsets and company culture when lower-cost imports began invading some key markets in Europe. He did so reluctantly, under pressure from the two most senior directors on his team; he may have also considered the effect of lower returns on his incentive pay package. A year later he still finds ample evidence of what he calls "loyal soldiering", and wonders how he should tackle such entrenched attitudes. The division general manager of the

Dutch bank cited in the case study at the start of the chapter – let's call him Jan – expresses deep frustration and some anger about what he considers mixed signals from above. Ironically, both are victims of admirable intentions; Pierre truly wanted to empower his people, as did the new CEO of the recently privatized company, and Jan's CEO was championing bottom-up initiatives.

Embedded in the good intentions of all three CEOs are at least two sets of assumptions. Assumptions about the role of the leader, and the corollary assumptions about the motivation and behaviour of followers. At both organizations, the leader was trying to mobilize management talent, to revitalize the business, and to encourage creative initiative. We could phrase this set of assumptions as "involvement and participation are critical to getting buy-in for important company initiatives, and the key is empowering your people." There seems to be a large overlap between advocates of empowerment and those who make frequent and facile use of the phrase "paradigm shift". The former appears to be as ill-informed about organizational realities, as the latter are about Thomas Kuhn's seminal ideas. This would be an accurate rendition of currently popular writing on management, but it has also proven to be grossly misleading.

All too often, empowerment programs, or bottom-up initiatives – unless linked directly to specific and measurable targets related to prevailing business realities – tend to produce cynicism and confusion. The optimism of a single dynamic (be it empowerment or bottom-up initiatives) to overcome employee apathy, release creative potential, and mobilize human talent to ease the road to renewal, is in fact a hollow promise. Empowerment confuses the sources of responsibility and blunts the possibility of realistic action. Bottom-up initiatives could dissipate company focus, often create false expectations, and, as in the case of Jan at the Dutch bank, tend to drive the best talent toward cynicism.

People have hopes, fears, aspirations, the potential for intense commitment as well as obstinate resistance, but no leader can give them a sense of empowerment – to be real it has to be earned, it cannot be bestowed. But what are the minimal conditions required to spur achievement that could earn genuine confidence? The truth is that more often than not management talent, like water, finds its level of least discomfort – unless it is tapped, channelled or challenged. It is in this sense that the challenge posed by a demanding boss can take many forms, but it should always entail raising the bar, or tilting it to unfamiliar angles. The effect on the subordinate should be to stretch beyond past achievements, outside the arc of past competence.

Some years ago when he was still head of the Power Transmission Division at ABB, Goran Lindahl (who is now CEO of ABB) was describing how he had been utterly dismayed earlier in his career when his boss assigned him to a sales position in the worst performing region when he was expecting to be rewarded for his work in engineering. "I thought I had failed, that I should look for another job; but thinking it over, I realized that my boss had a gleam in his eye when he made the offer; he was not being punitive but actually testing me. So I started – naively at first – to apply an engineering approach to how a major sale is closed. It was the toughest challenge I had faced in my life, but it became a turning point in my career." The route to a genuine sense of confidence has always started with some form of challenge given and taken.

Another example of a determined stretch to overcome the unanticipated is provided by the Latin America regional director of a multinational personal care products company. Having built an enviable record as country manager in successively larger markets, for the first time in his career he had to face failure. "I took this regional job with great hopes, but we failed to make budget *two years running*. I guess I had no experience to prepare for this. My boss gave me the choice of accepting head office help, or going on my own, which of course meant my head would be on the block. We had no time to lick our wounds, we took every product in every market, tore them down to essentials and put them back together one by one . . . you could say we all learned a thing or two, but not everyone survived," (modified from Kassarjian, 1991). By whatever terms designated, there are no shortcuts to mobilizing human talent.

Which brings us to the second element in the paradox of leading the new corporation: when a variety of initiatives needs to be triggered, often simultaneously, the task of leadership demands the agility to change modes of mobilizing human talent. To truly mobilize management talent either to overcome unfamiliar barriers or to tackle the familiar with innovation or novel determination, it takes greater courage for the leader to create the conditions and to pose the challenges for others to prevail, than for him to empower the people.

Is a change model essential?

We now turn to the third, and possibly the most pernicious, set of assumptions that could bedevil the bottom-up organization, precisely because multiple goals have to pursued, often at the same time. Whether trying to move the pendulum toward greater bottom-up initiatives or toward top-down attempts to focus organizational effort, leading the organization will necessarily require orchestrating a variety of changes and different magnitudes.

As it is, in most large organizations today (and quite a few smaller ones), managers are experiencing and complaining about too many changes being imposed on them. They feel that they don't get the chance to fully grasp why a change is needed, and before they have had a chance to master one, another initiative is launched, *ad infinitum*. As the division manager of the Dutch bank says, "We seem to be drowning in initiatives from below." The natural response to such confusion is the search for reassurance, for a proven model that could be followed with some confidence.

Not surprisingly, in this climate of growing demand for clear handles on how to manage a change process, books offering such programmed certainty proliferate. In almost a vicious circle, the frustrations experienced in the example of the Dutch bank lead to the adoption of a popular and ostensibly complete change model, and the organization ends up in a situation similar to the French consumer electronics company cited earlier as the third example in the case study. In a sense, all three examples in the case study have an embedded change model, but only the third has a model that has been adopted explicitly. So we could phrase the core of this assumption as "the way to implement major change is to choose a proven change management model, and make sure that everyone understands the total process, and that all will follow the sequence of steps prescribed."

This may be true as a description of what most management programs either teach explicitly, or suggest implicitly, about effecting organization change, but examining these theories and prescriptive models exposes some basic premises that are simply false, and we begin to suspect that these authors have not lived through a wrenching change themselves.

Apart from assuming that the direction and the destination of the change effort were clear to the leader at the outset, there is a fundamental error in using an *explanatory* model for *prescribing* what will work in *your particular company at a point in time*. These change models are typically based on identifying the apparent bottlenecks that caused the failure of otherwise great change programmes, and converting these to general principles of what should have been done, in terms and constructs that are exhaustive enough to cover almost any situation. For example:

- Apparently, there has been rampant confusion about the goals of many change initiatives. Prescription: develop and communicate a clear vision.
- Some critical units did not support the change effort at important junctions. Prescription: create a guiding coalition of sponsors.
- At the operating level, where the abiding concern has been how to meet specific output goals that had been targeted with rewards and penalties, the new change was ignored as another quick fix. Prescription: empower all employees and get buy-in.

This way you end up with an eight- or ten-step change model that, in hindsight, covers all the bases. It's like reviewing the loss of an important basketball game, and explaining that the team needed a better game plan, more effective passing, and faster court action. What was lacking, in fact, was effective improvisation in the face of a well-practised new offensive by the opposing team. Just as a masterful jazz band cannot be controlled by a detailed musical score, carrying through a major change effort cannot be controlled with prescriptive steps. It requires improvisation by many players, and at many points. Living through a major change is an intensely personal affair, one that has little resemblance to the logical sequence of reasonable actions prescribed by most change models (see, for example, Kotter, 1996; O'Toole, 1995).

The experience of companies that have gone through wrenching shifts in performance level suggests that even the most cardinal (and the most frequently cited) of prescriptive mandates – "develop a clear vision" – has to be violated at times. When Louis Gerstner took over the tottering giant IBM in the early 1990s, he is reported to have declared: "The last thing IBM needs now is a vision: it needs lower costs and better market focus in all divisions," (Gardner, 1995).

Looking back over the three examples, it is interesting to note that at Pierre's Finnish chemical company, tough business realities forced the misguided attempt to change mindsets and company culture to be abandoned. At Jan's Dutch bank, senior line management frustrations are rising, and may come to a head – all that is needed would be a noticeable shift in profitability figures. And at the French electronics company, the sense of confusion and growing dismay is experienced all the way to the CEO's office. In all three companies, the attempt to implement change was not related directly to clear business performance realities, be these reflections of customer demands, competitive moves, or innovation attempts. As Jan recognized, nothing shoots the credibility of a goal espoused by top management so rapidly as a measurement system that violates it.

In reality, those who have lived through a significant organization change know that the process is messy and unpredictable, with extraordinary tenacity by some to stonewall all attempts at change, and equally amazing courage by a few others to take wide-open risks – and sometimes to prevail. What produces change is more often the jolt of recognition, the risky commitment, the new sense of conviction that the steep wall can be scaled. Hence the third element of the paradox of leading the new corporation is that, no matter how daunting the expressed need for ordered coherence in the change efforts, the leader would be wise to avoid adopting a prescribed model or a set of predetermined steps. The true leadership challenge may appear less dramatic, but it is certainly more demanding of insight and subtlety.

As positions of advantage get increasingly less time on the competitive stage, it is only natural that leading the bottom-up organization will primarily entail the prudent orchestration of change initiatives. To prevail over shorter cycles of calm growth alternating with frequent periods of turmoil, the leader has to demonstrate keen sensitivity to often muted signals from the front lines. And the leader has to attend to the choice of champions who could be challenged to shape the response to unforeseen developments. Having examined some of the more critical false assumptions about organizational leadership, and having sketched some of the particular paradoxes these present, we now turn to explore this terrain with some simpler tools, more modest in scope and promise but with possibly greater realism.

Starting points, maps and destinations

In recent years I have sampled more than a few books on change management and organizational leadership, and there seems to be a remarkable degree of similarity in the basic cast of these tomes – they focus primarily on maps and destinations. That is, more often than not they describe worthwhile destinations and the steps needed to get there, in the spirit of "Twelve steps to customer service and market orientation". This may partly explain the wide popularity of the old adage: "If you don't know where you are going, any road will take you there."

Turning this clever phrase on its head exposes another dimension, curiously lacking in most prescriptions for competitive vitality: "If you don't know where you are starting, no road can take you *from* there." Ask yourself this question: when change initiatives have failed to produce the promise, how often have the reasons revolved around the poor fit between the current realities of the company and the process adopted, or the mismatch between the prescriptions and the leader's own pattern of preferred behaviour?

Reviewing the three examples in the case study, the absence of clear linkage between starting points and intended destinations puts the outcomes in a different perspective. Pierre, as the new CEO at the Finnish chemicals company, seems to have arrived at his diagnosis of the need to change mindsets before digging into specific operational or competitive shortcomings. His goal to change the company culture was apparently not anchored in concrete signals from the frontlines.

At the Dutch bank, division manager Jan is angered because his CEO's penchant for encouraging bottom-up initiatives is not related to specific performance goals, or to financial targets on which he is being measured. And at the French consumer electronics company, the CEO – let's call him Jean-Luc – has launched a major change effort almost on a separate track from the company's current business challenges. I know that all three CEOs would argue for their accurate assessment of what needed to be done, and at some abstract level they may be correct. But in all three cases, although their goals may be justified, their actions did not engage the most pressing current business dilemmas each company was facing.

Including clarity about starting points as a critical part of the leader's change agenda modifies initial priorities in a number of specific ways. Let's examine some dimensions of starting points:

1. Your company's history and legacy of past success and how this may contrast with changing customer needs, evolving market structures, challenges by competitors, and opportunities for innovation.
2. Your own leadership pattern, and the skills and approaches that best fit your hand.
3. The range and disposition of talent you have available.

The answers for your company, the change model for your unit, will have to be woven out of these strands.

Where are we now, and how did we get here?

Historically, most companies have gone through stages characterized by long periods of relatively calm growth, followed by short periods of turbulence when some form of a more radical change was needed to refocus effort (see Figure 18.1). These periods of turbulence were usually the result of a growing mismatch between the firm's capabilities, and the evolving needs and expectations in the marketplace.

Whatever the source of the challenge for an altered relationship between perceived value and delivered cost, to survive the challenge required some major reconfiguration of company performance. All too often, the solution that resolved the crisis at T-3 became the bottleneck at T-4 because it was being carried beyond its limited period of utility. For example, having restructured successfully into autonomous product divisions to gain focus and accountability (at T-3), the increased cost of multiple plants, or separate sales forces, or divisional R&D centres created the next bottleneck at T-4. If the pattern of past success had been dramatic and long-lived, such as IBM's dominance with its System-360, or Xerox's overwhelming market share in copiers, the required change approached the revolutionary.

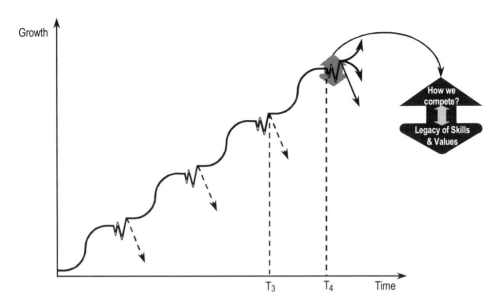

Figure 18.1: *The natural cycles of evolutionary growth, followed by turbulence that may require revolutionary change, occur in all organizations and most managers' careers*
Adapted from Greiner, 1972.

These points of turmoil or crisis, such as at T-3 or T-4, could produce three outcomes:

1. The company could be unable to adapt rapidly enough to changed conditions, and cease to exist or be acquired (examples abound).
2. The company could start on a slow decline, shedding units or contracting operations to cut costs, until it is finally rescued from its misery by a more adaptive competitor, as happened tragically to Digital Equipment Company (DEC), previously a proud innovator and market leader.
3. The company, usually with a new leader brought from outside, is able to change radically enough and rapidly enough to prevail in the new conditions, as happened at IBM with Gerstner.

But in almost all cases, the turbulence or crisis is driven by the escalating tension between the changing competitive imperatives, and the entrenched set of skills, values and attitudes that form the legacy of the company.

When Dr Franco Mariotti, the late Chairman of Hewlett-Packard (HP) for Europe and the Middle East, was asked how HP seemed to avoid having the sharp upheavals, the crises-laden redirections or painful revolutions that some of its major competitors in the computer industry have experienced, his reply was stunning in its simplicity: "I don't think our decisions have been necessarily smarter, but I think we have managed to ask questions and identified problems *earlier*."

There is a dynamic to the vicious cycle that spirals success into failure, where past achievements produce the complacency that leads to disaster. While IBM, DEC and Apple Computer have undergone, and are still undergoing, profound changes to their earlier dominance of certain market segments, HP seems to manage with some anticipation and some early corrections. When asked whether the change initiatives at HP were produced top-down or bottom-up, Dr Mariotti made his second provocative point: "It's neither top-down nor bottom-up; I suppose you could call it 'management across', but it usually starts with people who are most in touch with what's going on in the marketplace or with the technology."

With the shortening of all cycle times, this pattern of longer periods of calm growth followed by shorter ones of turbulence is being reversed. What Dr Mariotti seems to be suggesting may provide a way to avoid these alternating modes of apparent calm and mounting crisis that can only be resolved through wrenching change. By encouraging managers and engineers to raise tough questions from the frontline, HP seems to trigger smaller, intentional disruptions that anticipate necessary change and initiate corrections *before* the need for change is magnified into a major crisis (see Figure 18.2).

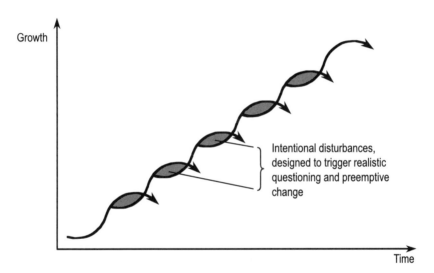

Figure 18.2: *Anticipatory questioning and pre-emptive change require triggering disruptions*
The idea of using a pair of sigmoid curves as a metaphor for company performance was offered by Charles Handy (1994).

The smooth sequence of timely corrections portrayed in Figure 18.2 is at best a conceptual ideal. (Even HP today is having difficulty moving to a solutions-based organization, one that can integrate across its lines of business.) But before even contemplating such moves, the first essential task is to paint an accurate picture of your company's starting point, asking questions such as:

- In what specific ways have our past successes affected our ability to focus on current demands of the marketplace?
- What particular internal practices seem to get in the way of faster response to changing conditions?
- What are the most serious specific barriers to risk taking or innovation?

- How would our smartest competitor describe our greatest strength, and our most serious vulnerabilities?
- What could be the two or three most useful sources of intelligence – about markets and about technologies – that we are not tapping yet?

This first task is basically analytical; it requires asking good questions and listening with care. It requires physically and mentally wandering around – from company hallways to customer sites, from customer service centres to industry shows – to gather unfiltered information and unfettered impressions. And, lastly, it requires putting these together into a credible picture of your company's current situation.

The second task is much more personal, it requires the courage to gain realistic insight into your own pattern of leadership.

What is my personal leadership pattern?

Possibly the most common source of failed change initiatives is to be found in the poor fit between the talents of the leader and the requirements of the particular changes in the company at a point in time. Even CEOs who have been recruited carefully for their demonstrated skills as change agents have been known to falter in novel circumstances. Recent research by Farkas and Wetlaufer (1996) suggests that CEOs and business leaders possess very distinct patterns of talents and skills, and that the more realistic path to effectiveness starts with acknowledging one's own pattern, and either consciously modifying it (some experts consider this a futile approach (Drucker, 1999)) or finding the truly complementary talent to share the evolving demands of the situation.

Three of the more common leadership patterns that can throw a change program off course (if not moderated or supplanted) are the strategist, the orchestrater of management talent, and the change agent. For the strategist, the obvious danger is the tendency to impose a well-formulated analysis of the value chain and leverage points as starting premises for the change program. Such a fixed road map could frustrate and turn off the very sources of realistic market assessment or competitive intelligence. It could also misdirect effort into nonproductive avenues. If being viewed as a keen strategist has been your abiding source of pride, your biggest challenge may be to learn to listen hard to those at the frontline – or consult closely with someone who can.

For the leader who has fine-tuned the ability to identify and nurture management talent, the danger is somewhat more subtle. Those you may have identified as possessing high potential are often attuned acutely to your style, priorities and biases – that is probably how they got on your short-list in the first place. Just as teachers have a tendency to identify smarts by the student's ability to show discriminating agreement, CEOs or line leaders have a tendency to pick and promote those who are the quickest to grasp the leader's vision. If you think you are particularly good at picking talent, it is time to focus on those who challenge you directly – but with well-reasoned evidence. You may also check your judgement of specific talent by asking for the candid appraisal of other seasoned executives.

The personal pattern that is probably the hardest to acknowledge, and even harder to moderate, is that of the proven change agent. Having been the successful champion of change in one or more other contexts, such a leader often arrives fully convinced about the universality of the carefully designed pace and process to drive change effectively. The problem is, of course, that process is only part of the equation; there are also very specific industry dynamics, market realities, and technology imperatives, and those who possess these insights typically resent externally imposed change processes. If you are an experienced change agent in a novel setting, your hardest task may be to moderate your initiatives, to challenge sceptical frontliners to take charge – and then to get out of their way.

In at least two of the three company examples cited in the case study, the CEO defined the problem on his own, charted the vision, and drove the change – with less than desirable results. For a contrasting example, we can look at the major strategic and organizational change undertaken at Sony Europa starting in 1994 (Kashani and Kassarjian, 1996).

Jack Schmuckli, then chairman and CEO of Sony Europa, who probably would consider himself as a nurturer and judge of talent, speaks about bringing Ron Sommer (now CEO of Deutsche Telekom) from Sony's US operations specifically to be the change agent for Sony Europa's reorganization. When Sommer left Sony to head Deutsche Telekom, Schmuckli this time chose Shin Takagi, a respected country manager and veteran of many European operations, to introduce greater certainty to operating decisions. Reading the case and watching the accompanying videotapes, it is clear that Schmuckli is aware of his own abilities and skills, and that he consciously tries to find talent complementary to his.

Where is the best talent located?

Even though the leader has to define reality to trigger those actions that can best create new value, the question of who possesses the best information that can channel effort becomes pivotal to any change process. It also leads to a series of very specific questions:

- Who has the best antenna to receive early signals about a new breed of competitor?
- Who are the frontline managers who are most likely to have their hand on the pulse of the market?
- Where are the technical mavericks who keep track of technology shifts?
- Which of the typically more cynical managers, who keep their distance from the head office, may have the latest customer, product, or after-sales service intelligence?

These and similar questions can be answered realistically only within a specific company context with a given history and culture and a particular range of talent. But a few factors may be common to most situations. First, the more current data is usually found at the periphery with those who are in daily contact with customers and competitor moves. Second, there are certain natural databanks that are often rich in insight, such as design engineers who track technological developments, or after-sales-service managers who have a penchant for identifying pattern in seemingly random events. And third, there are always some mavericks and revolutionaries who are secretly waiting to be flushed out – some of them *will* rise to a tough challenge when confronted directly. This third group requires active courting; they are often more skilled at presenting unwelcome news in an abrasive tone, and they are not ready joiners in any head office bandwagon.

Recent research sheds new light on the potential of individuals who make up a part of this third group. Howard Gardner (1995), a cognitive psychologist at Harvard who has been studying twentieth century leaders in many walks of life, makes this suggestive observation: "Among the early markers of a leader's personality, the most telling indication is a willingness to confront individuals in authority." Apparently, such individuals have the capacity to disagree with superiors but, always well fortified with facts, they challenge the prevailing norms with revealing aspects of reality.

Examples abound of missed opportunities to use such hidden talent, as well as cases where relevant insight was uncovered and effectively leveraged. When Xerox first encountered a new breed of Japanese competitor tackling the Western US market with comparable copiers at considerably lower prices and more prompt service, they seemed unable to grasp the significance of the new challenge until they had lost more than a score of percentage points of market share. During the painful turn-around some years later, when challenged why it had taken the West Coast sales and marketing organizations so long to wake up to the new competitor moves, a service manager spoke forcefully enough to make an impression: "I remember vividly, for the third time in one week I saw some new brochures at customer sites during service calls, and they were asking new types of questions, but when I tried to speak about these to the senior sales people, they said they had noticed no change in the monthly numbers – can you believe that?"

A very different outcome is provided when news from the periphery is used to sharpen the customer service focus. When Jaguar cars was trying to change its image of very poor maintenance track record, on a visit to the USA the new English CEO, in response to a sarcastic remark after his speech to New York area dealers, challenged the sceptical dealer to produce hard evidence. It turned out that this dealer had made an audio cassette recording of a very angry and equally articulate customer complaining in great detail about the maintenance problems of his new Jaguar. Apparently, this dealer had kept the recording, possibly hoping someone would challenge him at some point. The CEO, in a move that surprised the dealer, thanked him, asked him to get permission from the customer to use the recording, made copies for all the dealers in the area, and made all the dealers listen to the tape every morning on their way to work! (For other examples of ways to jolt the organization, see Killing (1997).)

Going back to the case studies, we find no evidence that the well-intentioned changes launched in those three companies had any specific connection to what I have called starting points in the three business contexts. For the sake of brevity, I did not cite much about the personal dispositions of the three leaders involved, or the range of talent each had available in-house. The continuing irony, and sometimes the tragedy, is that in most organizations the required talent is present. At a minimum, there are some reluctant rebels who are aware of the critical needs, but are waiting to see if anyone takes notice. At the frontline, there are always people, whether on the sales side or the technical, who are waiting for an opportunity to provide disturbing news.

There are also political in-fighters, finely attuned to the subtle shifts of power, especially at times of change – be it a reorganization, a new CEO, or an acquisition – who specialize in aligning themselves with sources of emerging clout. Given both elements of these organizational facts, leading the new corporation will require, first, a skilful blending of the starting points into a workable definition of the company's reality at a point in time, and second, the talent to compose these inputs into a compelling story that can move people to action.

The leader defines reality

Max de Pree (1989), former CEO of Herman Miller, the singularly successful office furniture company, sums up the progress of an artful leader: "The first responsibility of a leader is to define reality. The last is to say thank you. In between the two, the leader must become a servant . . ." Whether this definition is simplistic would most likely depend on two conditions: how seriously we take the task of defining reality, and what we mean by "the leader as servant". In practice, defining the reality of a company's challenges, pitfalls and promises at a point in time is neither as passive nor as easy as it sounds. And it may prove to be more realistic than charting a new vision.

For the leader, the task of defining reality can wait for neither the eruption of a crisis nor the annual Christmas party speech. At times of relative calm and evolutionary growth, when the company seems to be winning, the role of the leader is to discover and define reality in ways that can stimulate anticipation, encourage experimentation, trigger a sharper scanning for opportunities, or the targeting of new segments.

Johan van der Werf, the recently appointed managing director of Spaarbeleg, the wholly owned financial services subsidiary of Aegon (the second largest insurance company in Holland), was frustrated with sales results (Kassarjian, 1994). He gathered his sales people: "I chose a small room intentionally and closed the door. My opening line was: 'I don't believe the identical stories I am hearing – this is BS!' "After much heated debate, he asked in exasperation: "What do you need to be successful?" After some silence, one of the sales people looked around the room nervously, and responded, "What we need is a new product, a product based on stocks." A challenge was given *and* taken; the boss had taken a risk which had been reciprocated, and both had made public commitments to test the new definition of reality. Inadvertently, the new managing director had also made a critical selection of possibly the next sales manager for the division.

In a very different context, during one of the darkest periods in Intel's history, Andy Grove describes the agonizing process that he and (the then chairman) Gordon Moore were going through to decide if they should exit their memory chips business, the mainstay of their company up to that time. "Our mood was downbeat . . . Then I turned to Gordon and I asked, 'If we got kicked out and the board brought in a new CEO, what do you think he would do?' Gordon answered without hesitation, 'He would get us out of memories.' I stared at him, numb, then said, 'Why shouldn't you and I walk out the door, come back and do it ourselves?' " (Grove, 1996.)

At times of growing turbulence, when staff are feeling confused about how to succeed, or are demoralized about their ability to prevail, the role of the leader is to define reality in a way that can clarify choices, focus the direction, and show the path. In both instances, the leader has to define reality to provide a counterpoint to the existing company momentum, to jolt the conventional wisdom.

In either instance, the great temptation is to give a rousing speech, counting on emotional inspiration to carry the day. In almost all instances that would be a mistake. As Katzenbach's study (1995) concludes: "Change may well be a game of feelings, and emotions, but you need a way to keep score." This distinction is not simply about contrasting emotion with logic, but about realizing that although either may seem more necessary at a certain point, neither is sufficient alone. Whatever the change goal or specific objectives, reality has to be defined in a way that can make both business sense and engage personal commitment. (For a good discussion on how individual contracts are negotiated during a change process, see Strebel (1997).)

Defining reality can take many forms, and can be stimulated in a variety of ways. But however it is arrived at, the resulting clarity sheds a practical light on the path to be taken. For the leader, the task of defining reality requires blending a set of diverse skills, the honing of a personal craft. You have to combine listening astutely with challenging forcefully, stepping in to provide a spur or a corrective push, and stepping out to give space enough for others to take the initiative. The true master of this craft brings the self-awareness necessary to turn being a servant into the highest form of leadership.

There is an old mainframe-computer era joke that has been recycled recently as a central theme in learning theory, in discussions of both individual and organizational learning, and in debates about artificial intelligence. The simple exchange of the old joke remains intact in the current, more serious telling. The computer is asked: "Can you think like a human being?"

After an appropriate number of flashing blips and magnetic tape skips, the computer answers: "That reminds me of a story!"

I have used this story with many groups of executives for some years to stimulate a discussion about why Johan van der West, the managing director of Spaarbeleg, insists on calling his product matrix chart "The House", instead of what every good MBA knows should be called a "strategic competitive positioning map". In the same case, this managing director concludes his description of a very tough sales group meeting with: "I guess this is when I learned that you build a company story by taking pieces of individual stories and putting them together in a way that it becomes *their* story." (Kassarjian, 1992.)

As Figure 18.3 suggests, for a full portrayal of a company at a point in time, two sets of realities need to be accommodated. The upper triangle, which can be defined more crisply, shows the competitive thrust of the enterprise; it specifies the organization form that is prescribed to augment the competitive strategy, and the operating systems designed to support the way the firm competes.

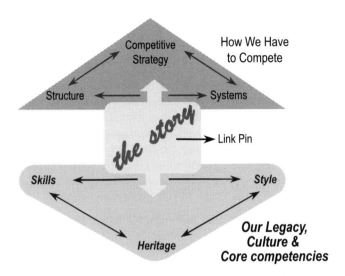

Figure 18.3: *At times of major change - strategic or organizational - the role of the story is pivotal to move from intention to implementation*
Adapted from Waterman et al.

The lower triangle is considerably more amorphous but, despite its lack of crisp boundaries, it often demonstrates extraordinary resilience and tenacity. The heritage of a firm shapes some of the most critical, but unexamined, choices that are made. Harder to pin down, but more sustained than a strategy, heritage is likely to be expressed in rituals and celebrations, hero stories and cautionary tales. Often, the clearest manifestation of it appears when violated. It is the repository of unwritten rules about appropriate style, skills particularly respected, and attitudes valued and shunned.

At a time of major change, whether strategic, organizational, or both, the task in the upper triangle is relatively straightforward. It is to clarify the new strategic focus, to conceive the new organization form that will be essential to make the new strategy workable, and to design the systems that can encourage the newly required behaviours. This part of charting a change is essentially analytical; it requires a grasp of emerging competitive forces, a candid examination of internal capabilities, and fitting the form and the systems that can drive the new way you need to compete. The approximate timeframe to achieve all of this is a matter of a few months.

The typical timeframe for modifying a firm's heritage, or its company culture, in any significant way probably should be counted in years. When a radical departure from past - and often successful - practice is being introduced, explaining the need for the new strategy, no matter how described and defended, is perceived and internalized only through the heavy filter of the firm's heritage. "The story", as I have designated it, carries the pivotal burden of linking and relating the competitive imperatives to the heritage and the widely accepted traditions of the firm.

When Ron Sommer was brought back to Europe to spearhead the major organization change at Sony Europa that was designed to support a pan-European strategy, many of the old country managers referred to the change as the "Big Bang". But Sommer always made a point to underscore how the change was exactly in the proud traditions of Sony. He emphasized the pioneering spirit that had guided the company from its early days. He repeatedly talked about how Sony had always been the leader with new approaches that violated old industry rules. He demonstrated forcefully an intuitive knack for composing his "story" in the historical Sony idiom and Sony spirit.

Howard Gardner (1995), coming from the academic discipline of cognitive psychology and looking far beyond business organizations, identifies the central role that stories seem to play. In his book *Leading Minds,* he chooses the capacity to compose and tell compelling stories as the single most crucial common thread in the lives of 11 twentieth century leaders in all walks of life, ranging from Alfred P. Sloan, Jr, to Mahatma Gandhi, to Pope John XXIII. In Gardner's own words:

It is important for leaders to know their stories, to get them straight, to communicate them effectively, particularly to those who are partial to rival stories, and, above all, to embody in their lives the stories that they tell.

Furthermore, according to Gardner, "Stories speak to both parts of the human mind: its reason and its emotion."

Although not aimed at business leaders specifically, Gardner's conclusions pose a worthy challenge to those who have to lead the new corporation. The irreducible core of the task will remain the composing and telling of stories that have a human scale, that can combine alarming news with abiding talent to achieve unexpected goals.

SUMMARY

Going back to the senior executives in the case study, and the dilemmas they had created by the way they tried to revitalize their companies, we can see that all three were applying remedies that simply did not work. The remedies these well-meaning executives applied neither responded to the specific conditions each was facing, nor engaged the experience and capability of frontline managers.

It would be tempting to conclude that each CEO missed one or more crucial steps in a good change model. But in reality their approaches were seriously undermined by more fundamental problems that no general model could correct. The CEOs' actions seemed driven by a desire to scale new heights, but using maps and destinations that were informed by neither their starting points nor the disposition of available talent.

As the leader of the bottom-up organization tries to orchestrate the dual themes of multiple initiatives from below and a sharper focus on value-creation, the need to define reality at more frequent intervals will increase, as will the need to compose compelling stories that can engage and challenge the managers who will drive the changes. Effective leadership that can produce tangible change will neither come from attempts at creating charismatic mandates based on the CEO's personal vision, nor will it be led by a prescribed set of generalized steps. To transcend the paradox of leading effective change – indeed the challenge of leading the new corporation – will depend more on the ability to recognize that what may appear less heroic in fact will require more astute listening to signals from the frontline.

In a sense, the leader will become the reality tester who stimulates frontline managers to search for viable options and measurable targets. Then the leader will compose this accumulated intelligence into a story powerful enough to overcome other older and competing stories. The leader may have to come in at a few critical junctures to open up a bottleneck, and the leader will certainly lead the cheering section when concrete results begin to emerge. But the real work of specific change that can sharpen the competitive edge will be conceived and carried out by frontline managers. Increasingly, they will become the indispensable agents of leading change in energized organizations.

BEST PRACTICE

Below we offer some pointers, drawn from this chapter, to help meet the challenge of leadership in the bottom-up organization. This book argues that the critical challenge for the bottom-up organization is the simultaneous pursuit of two seemingly contradictory objectives:

- to encourage experiments and pioneering initiatives from below and across the organization; and
- to bring coherence to these often divergent efforts by focusing on overall value-creation.

This has important implications for the role of the leader. In particular, it gives rise to three elements of the new leadership challenge.

First, tempting as it may be for a forceful leader to set the direction and drive the change, the new corporation will require multiple goals to be pursued. While CEOs may shape a goal, personally leading the charge restricts their peripheral vision, when they take on a heroic leadership role they reduce their capacity to observe from a distance and take corrective action. It also narrows their perspective on the choice of talent needed.

Second, the task of leadership demands the agility to change modes of mobilizing human talent. It takes greater courage for the leader to create the conditions and to pose the challenges for others to prevail, than it does simply to empower the people.

The third element of the paradox of leading the new corporation is that it requires the orchestration of efforts to create a unique solution. No matter how daunting the challenge, adopting a prescribed model – a set of predetermined steps – is ultimately unwise. This also means that change agents need to be identified according to the organizational context.

The question of who possesses the best information that can channel effort becomes pivotal to any change process. This leads to a series of very specific questions:

- Who has the best antenna to receive early signals about a new breed of competitor?
- Who are the frontline managers who are most likely to have their hand on the pulse of the market?
- Where are the technical mavericks who keep track of technology shifts?
- Which of the typically more cynical managers, who keep their distance from the head office, may have the latest customer, product, or after-sales-service intelligence?

These and similar questions can be answered realistically only for a specific company context with a given history and culture and a particular range of talent. But a few factors may be common to most situations:

- The more current data is usually found at the periphery, with those who are in daily contact with customers and competitor moves.
- There are certain natural databanks that are often rich in insight, such as design engineers who track technological developments, or after-sales-service managers who have a penchant for identifying pattern in seemingly random events.
- There are always some mavericks and revolutionaries who are secretly waiting to be flushed out, and some of them *will* rise to a tough challenge when confronted directly.

This third group requires active courting; they are often more skilled at presenting unwelcome news in an abrasive tone, and they are not ready joiners in any head office bandwagon.

These factors mean that the key role of the leader in the bottom-up organization is that of defining reality. Defining reality can take many forms, and it can be stimulated in a variety of ways. Many of the best examples involve developing the art of story telling. The art of story telling does not lend itself to neat prescriptions. But, however reality is articulated, the resulting clarity should shed a practical light on the path to be taken.

For the leader, the task of defining reality requires blending a set of diverse skills, the honing of a personal craft. You have to combine listening astutely with challenging forcefully, stepping in to provide a spur or a corrective push, and stepping out to give space enough for others to take initiative. The true master of this craft brings the self-awareness necessary to turn being a servant into the highest form of leadership. This, then, is a challenge worthy of the leaders of the twenty-first century.

References

Bateson, G. (1972) *Steps to an Ecology of Mind*, pp. 494–505. New York: Ballantine.

Drucker, P.F. (1999) Managing Oneself, *Harvard Business Review*, March/April, 1999.

Farkas, C.M. and Wetlaufer, S. (1996) The Ways Chief Executive Officers Lead, *Harvard Business Review*, May/June, 1996.

Gardner, H. (1995) *Leading Minds*. Basic Books.

de Geus, A. (1997) *The Living Company*. Boston: Harvard Business School Press.

Greiner, L. (1972) Evolution and Revolution As Organizations Grow, *Harvard Business Review*, July/August, 1972.

Grove, A.S. (1996) *Only the Paranoid Survive*. Currency-Doubleday.

Hardy, C. (1994) *The Empty Raincoat*. London: Hutchinson.

Kashani, K. and Kassarjian, J.B. (1996) IMD, M-488, 489 and 490, 1996.

Kassarjian, J.B.M. (1991) Jolt Your Managers . . . , *IMD Perspectives for Managers*, November 4, 1991.

Kassarjian, J.B. (1992) Shaping Spaarbeleg: Real and Unreal, IMD case No. GM 537, revised February, 1994.

Kassarjian, J.B. (1994) Shaping Spaarbeleg: Real and Unreal, IMD case No. GM 537, revised February 1994.

Katzenbach, J.R. (1995) *Real Change Leaders*. New York: Random House.

Killing, P. (1997) Managing Change: The Urgency Factor, *IMD Perspectives for Managers*, February, 1997.

Kotter, J.P. (1996) The Eight-Stage Process, in *Leading Change*. Boston: Harvard Business School Press.

Pascale, R. et al. (1997) Changing the Way We Change, *Harvard Business Review*, November/December, 1997.

de Pree, M. (1989) *Leadership Is an Art*. Dell Trade Paperback.

Quirke, B. (1996) *Communicating Corporate Change*. Maidenhead, UK: McGraw-Hill.

Strebel, P. (1997) The Politics of Change, *IMD Perspectives for Managers*, February, 1997.

O'Toole, J. (1995) Creating Order through Design, Composition, Tension, Balance and Harmony, in *Leading Change*. California: Jossey-Bass.

Contributors

PAUL STREBEL
Professor of Strategic Change Management
E-mail: strebel@imd.ch

Paul Strebel is Professor of Strategic Change Management and Director of the Breakthrough Program for Senior Executives at IMD.

Paul's main area of activity is high speed strategy, especially the anticipation of industry break-points and the design and implementation of change processes, including new compacts (commitments) to support on going change.

He has directed a variety of in-company programs for IMD's business partners and associates and has worked privately, both as a keynote speaker, seminar leader, and consultant for numerous multinationals and several large financial service firms. He is also a board member of several companies.

Prior to his current position, he was director of research at Imede, one of the founding institutions of IMD. Professor Strebel is Swiss, of South African origin, received his B.Sc. from the University of Cape Town, his MBA from Columbia University in New York, and his PhD from Princeton University.

Professor Strebel's most recent books are *The Change Pact: Building Commitment to Ongoing Change* (Financial Times Pitman) and *Breakpoints: How Managers Exploit Radical Business Change* (Harvard Business School Press). His publications have appeared in *Harvard Business Review, California Management Review, Strategic Management Journal, Handbook of Business Strategy*, plus many others, including numerous articles in the business press. He is on the editorial board of several change management journals.

ANDREW BOYNTON
Professor of Management
E-mail: boynton@imd.ch

Andy Boynton is a Professor of Management and the Director of IMD's new Executive MBA Program. He has previously held faculty positions at IMD, the Darden School at the University of Virginia, and the Kenan-Flagler Business School at the University of North Carolina Chapel Hill.

Professor Boynton has written numerous articles on strategy organization transformation, and the competitive use of information for leading journals such as *Harvard Business Review*, *Sloan Management Review*, and the *California Management Review*.

He is the co-author *of Invented Here: Maximizing Your Organization's Internal Growth and Profitability. A Practical Guide to Transforming Work*, which was published by the Harvard Business School Press in the spring of 1998. He is actively conducting research and consulting with firms in North America, Europe, Asia and Australia.

JEAN-PHILIPPE DESCHAMPS
Professor of Technology and Innovation Management
E-mail: deschamps@imd.ch

Jean-Philippe Deschamps is Professor of Technology and Innovation Management at IMD.

Prior to joining IMD in November 1996, he was based in Brussels as a Corporate Vice-President with Arthur D. Little, and Chairman of the firm's Technology and Innovation Management practice, which he created in 1981. He has thirty years of international management consulting experience throughout Europe, North America, Asia and the Middle East. He has lectured in several business schools throughout Europe and is a frequent speaker at Management Center Europe. He has been invited twice as a speaker to the World Economic Forum.

He is the co-author of a book, *Product Juggernauts – How Companies Mobilize to generate a Stream of Market Winners*, (Harvard Business School Press, 1995) which has been translated into several languages and features on the list of Harvard Business School best-selling teaching materials.

He focuses his research, teaching and consulting activities on product-based competition, with a particular interest in product creation and the management of innovation as a seamless cross-functional process.

JAY R. GALBRAITH
Professor of Management
E-mail: galbraith@imd.ch

Jay R. Galbraith is Professor of Management at IMD. He was previously at the University of Southern California, where he was Professor of Management and Organization and a Senior Research Scientist at the Center for Effective Organizations. Prior to joining the faculty at USC, he directed his own management consulting firm. He has previously been on the faculty of the Wharton School at the University of Pennsylvania and the Sloan School of Management at MIT.

His principal areas of research are in organizational design, change and development; strategy and organization at the corporate, business unit, and international levels of analysis; and international partnership arrangements including joint ventures and network-type organizations. He recently worked on a joint research project with Institut Pendidikan dan Pembinaan Manajemen in Jakarta, Indonesia. The focus of this study was the formation and development of joint ventures between Indonesian firms, other Asian firms and Western firms. Professor Galbraith has had considerable consulting experience in the United States, Europe, Asia and South America.

Professor Galbraith has written numerous articles for professional journals, handbooks, and research collections.

XAVIER GILBERT
Professor of Industry Analysis and Strategy
E-mail: gilbert@imd.ch

Xavier Gilbert is Professor of Industry Analysis and Strategy and holds the LEGO Chair in International Business Dynamics. He was Acting Director General of IMD from early 1992 until June 1993. His areas of special interest are competitive analysis, strategy implementations with specific attention to management development implications.

He has considerable experience in executive education having been Professor of Business Administration at IMEDE – one of the two founding Institutes of IMD – from 1971. During that time he directed several programs including the Program for Executive Development and the one-year MBA program.

Professor Gilbert is a consultant, chiefly on strategy formulation and implementation, to several leading companies in the fields of consumer and industrial manufacturing, and retailing.

JACQUES HOROVITZ
Professor of Service Marketing and Management
E-mail: horovitz@imd.ch

Jacques Horovitz is Professor of Service Marketing and Management. He focuses on how to compete through service and improve customer satisfaction with heavy emphasis on service as a strategy for differentiation, customer loyalty programs and creating a service culture.

He has a wide range of experience. He has practised service marketing and management as Executive Vice President marketing and sales for Club Med North America as well as Managing Director, Marketing and International of the GrandVision group, a retail speciality store chain; and as coach to the Executive Committee of Disneyland Paris. Second, he has advised the CEOs of over 100 companies throughout Europe on service, having founded, developed and managed a pan-European Consulting company with offices in seven countries and 50 consultants. Finally, he has extensively researched and published in the areas of service strategies and service quality, relationship marketing, customer bonding.

His book, *Quality of Service*, published by InterEditions in 1987 became a worldwide success: translated into ten languages. He is currently finishing a new book called *The Seven Secrets of Service Strategy* to be published by FT/Pitman.

J.B. KASSARJIAN
Professor of Strategy and Organization
E-mail: kassarjian@imd.ch

J.B. Kassarjian is Professor of Strategy and Organization at IMD (from 1989), and he holds a joint appointment at Babson College as Professor of Management (from 1980). He has also been Chairman of the Management Division at Babson (1981–1987).

Prior to joining IMD and Babson, he was on the faculty of the Harvard Business School, where he taught in the Organizational Behavior area, and he was involved in establishing Harvard-related graduate institutes in Iran and the Philippines. He has served as consultant to private and public organizations in the Americas, Asia, Europe, and the Middle East, in such areas as leading change, strategic restructuring, and senior management team building.

He has published a book, numerous articles, and a large number of cases in a variety of industrial and geographical settings. More recent writings aimed at a practitioner audience include: "Jolt your managers out of their comfortable groove – they may learn to lead change", IMD Perspectives 1991; and "The Paradox of Leading Change", IMD Perspectives, 1997. Most recently published case is a 3-part series, Sony Europa (A), (B), and (C), 1998.

Professor Kassarjian's career reflects an abiding interest in management education at the senior level in diverse cultural settings.

PETER KILLING
Professor of Strategy
E-mail: killing@imd.ch

Peter Killing is Professor of Strategy. His areas of particular interest are strategy creation and execution, the management of change, and the design and management of alliances.

He has worked with major companies in many industries, including European aerospace, oil and gas, aluminium, chemicals, food, and financial services. At IMD, he is founding director of the Senior Executive Forum, Director of Leading Corporate Renewal, and the Pechiney in-company program.

Prior to joining IMD in 1995 Professor Killing taught at the Ivey School of Business in Canada for 20 years, and was Associate Dean of Executive Education at the time he came to IMD.

With Professor Nick Fry, Professor Killing has published four editions of a strategy textbook. He is also an author of an International Management text which has been adopted by more than 100 business schools. Professor Killing has also published a book and numerous articles on the design and management of alliances.

PETER LORANGE
President of IMD and Nestlé Professor of Strategy
E-mail: lorange@imd.ch

Dr. Peter Lorange has been the President of IMD since July 1, 1993. He is Professor of Strategy and holds the Nestlé Chair.

He was formerly President of the Norwegian School of Management in Oslo. His areas of special interest are global strategic management, strategic planning and entrepreneurship for growth. In management education, Dr. Lorange was affiliated with the Wharton School, University of Pennsylvania, for more than a decade, in various assignments, including director for the Joseph H. Lauder Institute of Management and International Studies, and The William H. Wurster Center for International Management Studies, as well as The William H. Wurster Professor of Multinational Management. He has also taught at the Sloan School of Management (M.I.T.).

Dr. Lorange is Norwegian. He received his undergraduate education from the Norwegian School of Economics and Business, was awarded an MA degree in Operations Management from Yale University, and his Doctor of Business Administration degree from Harvard University.

Dr. Lorange has written or edited 13 books and some ninety articles. He has taught at the undergraduate, Master and Doctoral levels, and worked extensively within his areas of expertise with U.S., European and Asian corporations, both in a consulting capacity and in executive education. He serves on the board of directors of several corporations.

DONALD A. MARCHAND
Professor of Information Management and Strategy
E-mail: marchand@imd.ch

Donald A. Marchand is Professor of Information Management and Strategy at IMD.

Professor Marchand is currently Director for the IMD/Andersen Consulting Partnership Research Project entitled **Navigating Business Success.** This two-year study examines the perspectives of senior executives on the management of information, people, and information technology in achieving superior business performance. The study includes surveys of over 1300 senior managers representing 103 international companies in 22 countries and 25 industries as well as over 25 case studies. The Project will be completed in December 1999.

Professor Marchand is a well-known speaker and advisor to senior executives of leading service and manufacturing companies in Europe, North America and the Asia Pacific.

Professor Marchand is the author/co-author of six books and over 140 articles, book chapters, cases, and reports. He is the co-editor of a *Mastering Information Management* published by Financial Times Pearson Group Publishing, London, 1999. He is also the co-author of *Information Orientation: The Link to Business Performance*, a forthcoming book published by Oxford University Press, 2000.

From July 1987 to June 1994, Prof. Marchand was Dean and professor of information management at the School of Information Studies at Syracuse University.

He received his PhD and MA at UCLA and his BA at the University of California at Berkeley. He has also served as Vice President of Worldwide Chapter and Alliance Development for the Society for Information Management – SIM International.

PIERO MOROSINI
Professor of Strategy and Execution
E-mail: morosini@imd.ch

Piero Morosini is Professor of Strategy and Execution at IMD. He has, since 1988, besides his academic interests in mergers, acquisitions and alliances, pursued an international career in strategy consulting, as well as change management in the financial/banking industries.

Prior to joining IMD, he was a Managing Consultant at Andersen Consulting Strategic Services Group in Milan Italy, having formerly worked at McKinsey & Company (1989-92), JP Morgan (1992-94), Robert Fleming (1994-95) and the Andean Community (1984-86), in several locations across Europe, the US and Latin America.

He is a Thought Leadership award winner worldwide at Andersen Consulting Strategic Services Group (1997-98), and has been a Research Fellow at the Wharton Risk Management Center, Philadelphia (1995-98), as well as at the Strategy Department of the Bocconi University, Milan (1993-94).

He has recently authored a book, *Managing Cultural Differences: Effective Strategy and Execution Across Cultures in Global Corporate Alliances* (Pergamon, Oxford, U.K., 1998)

THOMAS VOLLMANN
Professor of Manufacturing Management
E-mail: vollmann@imd.ch

Thomas Vollmann is Professor of Manufacturing Management at IMD. His areas of special interest are manufacturing planning and control, performance measurement, supply chain management and enterprise transformation. He is a consultant to numerous companies in manufacturing, benchmarking and supply/demand chain management and lecturer in executive development programs throughout the world.

He has been actively involved in executive education, notably as Professor of Business Administration at Indiana University, as Professor at INSEAD, as Professor of Operations Management at Boston University, and as Professor at the University of Rhode Island and Dartmouth College.

Several of Professor Vollmann's recent cases have won awards, including: *Nokia Mobile Phones: Supply Line Management Multi Media*, with Prof. Carlos Cordon and Jussi Heikkila. This case is the winner of the 1998 European Foundation for Management Case Writing Competition in the category of "Multi Media", and *Thomas Medical Systems Outsourcing Policy A, B, & C* with Carlos Cordon and Denyse Julien, which won the same competition in 1999, in the category of "Supply Chain Management."

He is the author of numerous books and articles, most recently: *Manufacturing Planning and Control Systems*, Fourth Edition, with W.L. Berry and D.C. Whybark, McGraw-Hill Companies, 1997. *Building Successful Customer-Supplier Alliances*, with Prof. Carlos Cordon, Long Range Planning, October, 1998. *Thinking Clearly about Outsourcing*, with Prof. Carlos Cordon and Jussi Heikkilä, Financial Times Mastering Global Business, February 1998, and *Building a Smarter Demand Chain Partnership*, with Carlos Cordon, Financial Times Mastering Information Management, February 1999.

Index